A TOLERANT NATION?

A TOLERANT NATION?

Exploring Ethnic Diversity in Wales

Edited by

Charlotte Williams, Neil Evans and Paul O'Leary

UNIVERSITY OF WALES PRESS • CARDIFF • 2003

British Library Cataloguing-in-Publication Data.
A catalogue record for this book is available from the British Library.

ISBN 0–7083–1759–6

Published with the financial assistance of the Commission for Racial Equality Wales/Cymru

Typeset by Bryan Turnbull
Printed in Great Britain by Dinefwr Press, Llandybïe

Contents

Foreword

We in the Commission for Racial Equality are delighted to have the opportunity to introduce *A Tolerant Nation?* for a number of reasons. Such a book is long overdue. Part of our brief in promoting racial equality is to ensure that sound research is undertaken and disseminated to a wide range of organizations and individuals. This is the first book of its kind in Wales and it provides an important overview of both historical and contemporary research in the field. From a historical base, it documents the important contribution black and ethnic minorities have made in the development of the Welsh nation and details the association of Wales with the processes of imperialism, colonialism and, more latterly, globalization.

The book is also very timely. In post-devolution Wales the Welsh Assembly Government has committed itself to a programme of activities aimed at promoting racial equality. The book tracks these developments and provides baseline information and data from which it will be possible to evaluate progress and change. It is clearly a book that will be of interest to politicians, policy-makers and practitioners, as well as students and academics, and it should be made widely available in key institutions in Wales. It also provides a point of reference for comparative study across the nations of the UK and Europe.

Racial equality and the full social inclusion and participation of minorities represent a fundamental challenge to our new and developing political nation. Racism in all its forms – at street level, at an institutional level and at an ideological and cultural level – must be eliminated if we are to grow and prosper. As Race Commissioner for Wales, I welcome this book as it presents factual information and research vital to our critical understanding of race relations in Wales and opens a number of important and necessary debates.

Cherry Short
Commission for Racial Equality, Commissioner for Wales

Contributors

Professor Jane Aaron teaches English and Welsh studies at the University of Glamorgan. She is the author of numerous articles in Welsh and English on nineteenth- and twentieth-century Welsh women writers. Her latest book, *Pur fel y Dur: Y Gymraes yn Llên Menywod y Bedwaredd Ganrif ar Bymtheg*, a Welsh-language study of images of Welsh women in the nineteenth century, won the Ellis Griffith prize for the best scholarly contribution to Celtic studies in 1999. She also co-edits a series of reprints of 'classic' Welsh women's writing for the feminist press, Honno, including her edited collection *A View Across the Valley: Short Stories by Women from Wales 1850–1950* (1999).

Dr Kirsti Bohata is currently lecturing at the University of Wales Swansea. Her thesis explores Welsh literature in English in terms of the paradigms of postcolonial theory. Her publications include 'Beyond authenticity? Hybridity and assimilation in Welsh writing in English', in Tony Brown and Russell Stephens (eds), *Nations and Relations: Writing Across the British Isles* (2000), and 'The Black Venus: atavistic sexualities', in Meic Stephens (ed.), *Rhys Davies: Decoding the Hare* (2001).

Dr Paul Chambers is a lecturer and researcher at the University of Glamorgan. A sociologist of religion, his research interests include all aspects of religion in Wales and he is currently writing a book on 'Religion, Secularization and Social Change in Wales' (forthcoming). Previous publications include work on education in Wales, religious decline and social change in Wales, religion and identity and neo-Pentecostalism. He is also currently working on a research project examining contemporary religious institutions and civil society in Wales.

Dr Paul Chaney is a lecturer in the Department of International Politics, University of Wales, Aberystwyth. He has worked on a number of research projects examining aspects of devolution in Wales and he has recently completed a study commissioned by the statutory equality commissions and the Institute of Welsh Affairs that examined the equality policies of the Assembly government between July 1999 and March 2002. He is currently working on an ESRC-funded project 'Social Capital and the Participation of Marginalized Groups in Government'. In 2001 he co-edited (with Tom Hall and Andy Pithouse) *New Governance: New Democracy? Post Devolution Wales*.

Dr Neil Evans is joint editor of *Llafur: The Journal of Welsh People's History*, and has published extensively in many areas of Welsh history, especially on racial and ethnic issues. He is writing a book on Cardiff's multi-ethnic community, 'Darker Cardiff: The Underside of the City, 1840–1960'. He teaches part-time in the University of Wales.

Professor Aled Jones is the Sir John Williams Professor of Welsh History at the University of Wales, Aberystwyth. His publications include *Press, Politics and Society: A History of Journalism in Wales* (1993), and *Powers of the Press: Newspapers, Power and the Public in Nineteenth-century England* (1996). He is Literary Director (Modern) of the Royal Historical Society. He is currently researching and publishing in a number of related areas, including the history of satire, the writing of Welsh missionaries and travellers in the British Empire, and the connections between British and North American journalism.

Ivor Wynne Jones is a local historian and the international authority on the Congo Institute and its founder. He is the author of numerous books, including the pioneering *Shipwrecks of North Wales* (1973, 1978, 1986), *Llandudno, Queen of the Welsh Resorts* (1976); *Colwyn Bay: A Brief History* (1995), *Gold, Frankenstein and Manure* (1997); *Money for All* (1969) and many smaller but seminal booklets. He has just completed a history of broadcasting in the Middle East and has a major topographical study due for publication. He is a member of the Welsh Academy/Yr Academi Gymreig.

Dr Vaughan Robinson is Reader in Geography at University of Wales Swansea. He has authored or co-authored a number of titles including *Transients, Settlers and Refugees* (1986) and *Exploring Contemporary Migration* (1998). He has also edited or co-edited *Ethnic Segregation in Cities* (1981), *The International Refugee Crisis* (1992), *Geography and Refugees* (1993), *Geography and Migration* (1996) and *Migration and Public Policy* (1999).

Dr Paul O'Leary is a Senior Lecturer in the Department of History and Welsh History at the University of Wales, Aberystwyth. He is author of the first book-length study of the Irish in Wales, *Immigration and Integration: The Irish in Wales, 1798–1922* (2000) and co-author of *Wales of One Hundred Years Ago* (1999). He is currently researching the relationship between political languages and identities in Victorian Wales.

Charlotte Williams is a Lecturer in Social Policy at the University of Wales, Bangor. She has undertaken research and written widely on issues of racial discrimination and equal opportunity including co-editing the book *Social Work and Minorities: European Perspectives* (1998). She is proactive in community organizations aimed at protecting the rights of minority ethnic groups at national and international levels. She was lead researcher on the National Assembly 'Equal Opportunities Study for Inclusion in the Structural Fund Programming 2000–2006' and most recently co-researcher on the ESRC-funded project 'Social Capital and the Participation of Marginalised Groups in Government'.

Abbreviations

AM	Assembly Member (i.e. Member of the National Assembly for Wales)
AWEMA	All Wales Ethnic Minority Association
BNP	British National Party
CIACS	Cardiff International Athletic Club
CMS	Christian Missionary Society
CRE	Commission for Racial Equality
NAW	National Assembly for Wales
NGO	Non-Governmental Organization
NHS	National Health Service
NLW	National Library of Wales
NWREN	North Wales Race Equality Network
PRIAE	Policy Research Institute on Ageing and Ethnicity
REC	Race Equality Council
RSL	Registered Social Landlord
UNHCR	United Nations High Commissioner for Refugees
VSPC	Voluntary Sector Partnership Council
WCVA	Welsh Council for Voluntary Action
WRC	Welsh Refugee Council

Introduction: Race, Nation and Globalization

NEIL EVANS, PAUL O'LEARY AND CHARLOTTE WILLIAMS

At the opening of the twenty-first century, Wales is changing rapidly: a new government, an expanding capital city, economic regeneration, a revitalized language and sense of nationhood and the development of Wales as a nation of Europe. Evidence of this dramatic change is all around us, with many symbols and images signalling the new-found confidence – the Millennium Stadium, the Manic Street Preachers, and the redevelopment of Cardiff Bay. The picture of a black hurdler at the Olympic games sporting the Welsh flag on the podium beckons a new imagery of the country. There is plenty to celebrate in contemporary Wales. Wales has become 'sexy' – the National Assembly *Plan for Wales* speaks of *Cŵl Cymru*. But what prospects does the new nation offer to its ethnic minority population? How does it speak to their sense of belonging, involvement and identity?

The Parekh Report[1] on the future of multicultural Britain poses some testing questions in the light of rapid social change, arguing that there is a need to 'rethink the national story' and for nations to review their understanding of themselves and to 're-imagine themselves'. In this endeavour nations will need to explore the cultural fabric of the society and consider 'what should be jettisoned, what revised, what reworked?' And they will need to review how everyone can have a recognized place within the larger picture. The historian Gwyn A. Williams famously stated 'Wales is impossible. A country called Wales exists only because the Welsh invented it. The Welsh exist only because they invented themselves . . . they survived by making and re-making themselves and their Wales over and over again.'[2]

Wales has long demonstrated its ability to adapt, accommodate and shift in the face of wider social change and yet retain its essential values. It has always been – and will always be – a multicultural, multi-ethnic society. Multiculturalism is one element of historical continuity, an enduring quality of this small but ancient nation. Nevertheless, recognition of the fact of multiculturalism and any systematic response to it has been patchy and contradictory. What has become identifiable in contemporary Wales is a patterning of neglect of the issues of 'race' and ethnicity and a consequent failure to address issues raised by a multicultural society. In the new Wales there is evidence of a turnaround in this state of affairs and the emergence of the issue of minorities as a focus of public policy. Yet therein lies an immediate paradox. On the one hand, there is renewed interest at policy level, research and in the media, while a plethora of policy statements carry the statement 'and ethnic minorities'. On the other hand, there is growing awareness of disenfranchisement, compounded by marginalization, widening inequalities and widespread racism. Unemployment among some African groups in our capital city runs at 90 per cent. Increased awareness reveals a legacy of neglect.

The notion of minorities/majorities is a complex one and provides an altogether inadequate terminology for exploring the issues of central concern to this book. It is not simply that the terms imply some kind of fixed, unchanging and quantifiable entities but that they impute rather simplistic positionalities of superiority/inferiority, domination and subordination that are not borne out by the lived experiences of individuals. In reality, people may experience a number of minoritized positionings that are contextually given. Similarly the term 'ethnicity' is not without contention, notably because it is all too often used exclusively to denote people of colour with little acknowledgement of the fact that we all have an ethnic background. Terminology frequently undergoes change, and necessarily so. Transitions in our understanding of 'race', from its crude biological connotation to meanings that reflect social constructions, will be apparent in this text. Further terms frequently in use in policy circles such as 'black', 'black and ethnic minorities', 'minority ethnic people', 'Asian people', have all been found wanting both in terms of their political connotations and their inadequacy in describing the subjective experiences of individuals. This is particularly apparent in Wales, where identifications of skin colour are not the only 'ethnic' marker for the many individuals of mixed descent, a category only now officially recognized in the 2001 census.

This book focuses primarily on issues affecting visible ethnic minorities. This is not to deny the importance of the Irish, the Poles, the Greeks, Gypsy peoples, Eastern Europeans and others; nor does it seek to downplay religious minorities such as Jewish and Muslim communities or, indeed, linguistic minorities such as Welsh speakers. Their concerns and experience are central to any understanding of the key issues of nationhood, identity and difference. A text of this kind could easily and justifiably have discussed different minority groups and their experiences chapter by chapter. However, while references to many of these groups appear in the contributions, we have concentrated broadly on the notion of the 'racialized' other and on the *processes* that produce that positioning of inferiority. Hence themes such as 'race thinking' are pursued through a consideration of historical and contemporary references, and attention is given to the *institutionalization* of processes of discrimination. It is, however, necessary to acknowledge a two-way process, and one strong ambition of this text is to mark up the significant contribution of the minority population to the development and profile of Wales as a nation both domestically and internationally, both historically and in a contemporary sense.

With the coming of devolution interest has grown in questions of national identity, both in popular and academic quarters. This interest is shared by the other devolved nations as the notion of black Britishness comes to the fore. We are witnessing the emergence of new ethnicities at home and, indeed, across Europe. Nations can no longer ignore the issues and demands of multiculturalism. This book is therefore extremely timely. World events, the impact of globalization, migratory movements and the European Union's strategic attention to issues of racism, xenophobia, religious diversity and institutional racism following the 1997 Amsterdam Treaty all imply the need for deliberation, debate and action.

Given the range of issues discussed and the timescale covered (some 150 years) the book is necessarily multidisciplinary. It draws on the work of historians, literary critics, political scientists, social geographers, sociologists and social policy specialists. Producing a single text from this combination of different academic traditions and requirements, different theoretical and philosophical positions, different terminology and style of presentation of the material, was no easy task. Even agreeing on a standard referencing system proved difficult! The book is, nevertheless, richer for this diversity and we would suggest that it has broad appeal to individuals and groups in minority communities, to policy-makers and policy-shapers, as well as to the academic community. It initiates debates and establishes a bedrock of information which we hope will act as a basis for further research and writing.

The studies gathered together here cluster around two major themes. One is the nature and identity of the Welsh nation. The other is globalization. They point towards a future in which we explore the intersections of these ideas, in the past and present, by analysing what is particular to the Welsh experience in the light of global influences and developments.

In Wales positive images of the nation frequently draw upon ideas of tolerance of difference and a welcoming approach to outsiders. This is frequently – if sometimes implicitly – contrasted with the attitudes of the English, who are perceived to be imperialist and domineering. In the first chapter, Neil Evans confronts this issue with the abundant historical evidence of conflicts and intolerance in Wales. But there are also instances of open-mindedness and tolerance. Even so, it is not sufficient to end with an approach that says: 'on the one hand . . . on the other'. The point, he argues, is to address the underlying circumstances which produce racism and xenophobia and those which act against it.[3] Identifying what is specific about Wales in this context means that more rigorous comparisons with other places have to be pursued, instead of simply adopting a broad-brush and impressionistic contrast with England. Locating the experience of Wales against those of Merseyside, Scotland and Northern Ireland helps him to do this. Elsewhere he has shown that another problem with generalized and loaded comparisons is that they can be found in virtually all European nations and are frequently used to pass the responsibility for xenophobia from one country to another.[4] From the beginning, then, the idea of the nation carries us outside its bounds and into the realm of comparison.

The second theme, globalization, is often seen as a purely contemporary phenomenon. Most historians would reject this perspective.[5] While there have been major recent developments in instant communications and the collapse of distance, it is important to remember that the different parts of the globe have been connected for at least 500 years. It is essential to appreciate this in order to understand the importance of ethnic minorities within nations. To provide a specific and graphic Welsh illustration of this point we need to look no further than the multiracial community of Butetown (once known as 'Tiger Bay') in Cardiff, which dates from before the First World War. It is a clear and tangible indication of an earlier phase of globalization.

Even before the European voyages of 'exploration' of the late fifteenth century, which inaugurated the era of proto-globalization, there was significant movement around the Eurasian landmass by overland routes. The Jewish diaspora that was enacted on this stage clearly touched Wales; there are Jewish names to be found among the inhabitants of medieval Welsh boroughs and at least one anti-Semitic poem exists in medieval Welsh. They came into a medieval Welsh society that was ethnically diverse, comprising the native Welsh, Norman and English conquerors, and Flemish colonists. Gypsies probably arrived in Wales at the end of this era – which has been called 'archaic globalization' – around the time that European voyages outwards were beginning in earnest and the era of proto-globalization was starting.[6] This flow illustrates an interconnectedness between Wales and the wider world even in the remote past. Nor was there an ethnically homogeneous Wales with a simple and defined border with its English neighbour.

The era of proto-globalization made relatively little impact on Wales. A few minor colonial ventures issued from Wales – such as the 'Welsh Tract' in Pennsylvania – and quickly failed. It is in the era of modern globalization, coinciding with industrialization and the rise of the nation-state, that Wales was transformed and came to occupy a less marginal place in the world of the enlarged European empires. After the loss of the north American colonies in 1783 the centre of gravity of the British Empire shifted eastwards. It was in this context that more Welsh people came to have experience of the colonial encounter.

In her analysis of the impact of missionaries on Welsh attitudes to the outside world, Jane Aaron demonstrates that many children and adults had their ideas about other peoples shaped by the stories that came back in person and in print from these outposts of Western values and religious conversion. The major Welsh contribution to imperialism, she argues, was through missionary activity, which often ranged the missionary against the more material and military imperial interests. She finds at least a coincidence in the final demise of this activity in the 1960s and the growth of a nationalist movement in Wales. Aled Jones provides a parallel study by examining the work of the largest single Welsh missionary activity, the Calvinistic Methodist outpost in Khasia, and the way that this was refracted in Wales through the medium of the press. Like Aaron, he finds that the attitudes engendered by such work simultaneously helped foster enthusiasm for empire and celebrated the role of Wales in it. Yet they also led to discussions of racial and social justice. An unintended consequence of it was an internationalism which rivalled the more vaunted one of the labour movement and introduced discussions of colonialism to Welsh-speaking Nonconformist culture.

A crucial element of European expansionism in the period from the sixteenth century onwards was the slave trade which linked Europe with Africa and the Americas, imposing a triangular network across the Atlantic. This system had a protracted death in the modern era, though it hung on in Brazil and Cuba until nearly the end of the nineteenth century. The peoples of the African diaspora came to retrace their roots via the movement known as Pan-Africanism. This reversed the triangular relationships of the slave trade by bringing back to Africa what Africans had learned in the New World. Religious leaders and politicians aimed at ending the imperial control of Africa and creating some degree of unity across the continent.[7] Ivor Wynne Jones's chapter shows the relationship that was forged between Wales and this movement. The missionary William Hughes feared that his African aides would not develop the full panoply of Western and Christian values if they were trained in Africa, where they would be open to local values. He found his solution to this problem by bringing the Africans to Wales for training. He chose Colwyn Bay because of his perception of Welsh religiosity, in effect because of his view of the nature of the Welsh nation. Colwyn Bay had the added advantage of being close to Liverpool, one of the major ports of the African trade. Some Welsh people regarded the Africans as interesting exotica, while others saw them as threats to the Nonconformist values which now held Wales in their thrall. When a local woman was made pregnant by one of the African students it provided an opportunity for stereotypes of African sexual prowess and physical endowments to be paraded. This fascinating episode provides another window into racial attitudes in Wales.

Kirsti Bohata's essay provides us with a means of assessing how much the ideas generated by imperialism entered the minds of people in Wales. Her close reading of three representative literary texts reveals how deeply racial stereotypes had entered the consciousness – and perhaps more so the unconscious. She also stresses the interconnections between different forms of social exclusion: racial discrimination overlapped in major ways with anxieties relating to gender, sexual orientation and class. Her essay is a reminder that these categories of analysis are relevant to an understanding of the experiences of ethnic minorities and complicate our understanding of race.

These essays provide the context for a group of three studies which focus on the changing nature of Welsh society and link the era of modern globalization with the post-colonial era. Neil Evans provides an overview of ethnic riots in the nineteenth and twentieth centuries, set against a background of wider communal violence. This provides a context for examining the upsurge in racial attacks in Wales in the past decade. He finds cause for both optimism and pessimism in the current situation: optimism, because ethnic antagonisms can no longer mobilize large and representative portions of the population as they did in the nineteenth and early twentieth centuries; pessimism, because contemporary racial attacks are more murderous for being marginalized and lacking the constraints of wider community values. Communal violence in the past was more restrained and at some levels more symbolic than at present, where it is carried out by socially marginal groups and fuelled by the ideas of the far right.

Neil Evans and Paul O'Leary find a different way of examining the experience of ethnic minorities in Wales. Sport, like communal violence, is a central concern of historians in Wales and it provides a different insight into the nature of society. This preliminary examination of the experience of ethnic minority sportspeople in Wales reveals both layers of discrimination and very positive achievements which have done much to enhance the self-esteem of minority communities. The achievements of Jim Driscoll, Gus Risman, Billy Boston, Clive Sullivan and Nigel Walker can be set alongside those of other entertainers like Shirley Bassey and Victor Spinetti. Equally the prominence of broadcasters like Linda Mitchell and Jason Mohamed provides role models. Yet it needs to be remembered that many of these made their careers outside Wales, sometimes because they felt that their opportunities were blocked in their native land. And in the contemporary world sport remains an ambiguous arena of achievement for ethnic minorities. Without in any way detracting from what has been achieved by many people in this field, there is a danger that the black sportsperson has become an ethnic stereotype. But for many Welsh people of Asian backgrounds this remains a field in which it would be good to see some progress.

Paul Chambers's wide-ranging essay elegantly provides an overview of the role of religion in Welsh identity and of its role in constructing ethnic Others. He stresses the dominance of Nonconformity in nineteenth-century Wales, which allowed it to react to the Irish Catholic immigration from a position of strength. Integration was aided by the common causes of temperance and Liberal politics.[8] Nonconformity has long lost its dominance, and it has reacted to this decline by embracing ecumenicalism. This has often gone beyond Christian unity and edged towards a united front of faiths. This is particularly important at a time when a 'clash of civilizations' (which are rooted in religious cultures) is alleged to be the dynamic of the world order. In this context, the potential for culturally based racism is significant, but Paul Chambers shows that the impetus for it does not come from organized Christianity.

These last three essays straddle the divide between the modern and post-colonial eras of globalization. The remainder of the book explores vital and interconnecting aspects of our time. Vaughan Robinson identifies the 1980s as a turning point, as it was then that refugees became a central issue in ethnic relations in Wales. While Wales had gained a precocious black community in the modern era it did not benefit to a very marked degree from the general influx of New Commonwealth immigration in the early post-war period. It was under-represented in this movement, as it was with the settlement of 'displaced persons' from Eastern Europe in the immediate post-war period, though significant bodies of Poles and Ukranians did make their homes in Wales.[9] The refugee crisis which has grown out of the collapse of European empires and the international uncertainty of the post-cold war era has renewed the ethnic minority population of Wales. In the case of the Somalis, whose newcomers are grafted on an old-established group, they are the biggest community in Britain. Modern communications allow them to retain close links with their countries of origin, a phenomenon that is sometimes referred to as transnationalism.[10] Of course, it was often possible to retain such links in the past but there is little doubt that they are more intense now. For example, after the recent earthquake in Gujarat, the Indian community in south Wales raised a good deal of money for their country of origin. This issue provides another intersection of our themes of nationalism and globalization.

Our images of nations are often rural in nature, involving an implied or an explicit contrast with the alleged rootlessness of urban society. In popular comment it has sometimes been argued that ethnic violence in Wales has come exclusively from the anglicized industrial areas, implying the freedom of a more settled rural society from such demons. Vaughan Robinson, in his second essay, confronts this romanticized perception by addressing the experience of the small ethnic minority population of Powys. He finds much evidence of hostility and an ethnic minority population which lacks the protective shelter that an ethnic enclave often provides.

One of the first questions raised in this book is the way in which the treatment of ethnic minorities reflects the nature of the nation. Charlotte Williams returns to this theme in her chapter on social inclusion and racial equality. She finds a lack of substantial research, and a scattering of what there is, a situation that mirrors the diverse ethnic groups in Wales. She finds too many simple contrasts being made and insufficient efforts to track the complex reality. But certain themes are clear, whatever the limitations of the research. Ethnic minorities overall consistently fare worse in health, education, housing, employment and other key social indicators than their counterparts in the majority population. Williams concludes that strategies of social inclusion may be found wanting in terms of achieving racial equality. Paul Chaney and Charlotte Williams extend this theme by looking at the experience of ethnic minorities in political participation. They find that a rhetoric of inclusiveness, especially surrounding the National Assembly for Wales, has not been matched by achievements. There are low levels of minority representation at all levels of the political process and in some ways the Assembly has been a retrograde experience because it has led to the raising of expectations that have been frustrated. There is a striking contrast between the determination of the Labour Party (the dominant political institution in Wales for over half a century) to deal decisively with the lack of women's representation in the political process and its unwillingness to tackle the issue of ethnic diversity in Welsh society.

Once again, the diversity of the minority populations in Wales has been a key issue. It is difficult to establish the unity which is necessary for effective political action. In the past, Butetown provided an example of united action across a range of groups. Robinson's chapter on rural racism raises the question of the isolation and division of ethnic minorities and the debilitating effects of these on action and resistance.

The final chapter, by Charlotte Williams, returns us to our point of departure, the nation. It is a common perception that there are two racial issues in Wales, she argues. On the one hand, there is the experience of the ethnic minorities who are concentrated in south Wales, and especially South Glamorgan, while on the other, there is the conflict between Welsh and English in Gwynedd. Welsh people in Gwynedd accuse the English of colonial attitudes, while the English in the region accuse the Welsh of racial discrimination. In fact, the multicultural nature of Wales cuts across these divisions. Certainly, this is a sharp contrast with the situation a hundred years ago when English incomers were concentrated in south Wales, as were minorities from outside Britain. In the intersection of these issues at present, Charlotte Williams finds a prevalence of the idea that to be Welsh is to be white, and in north-west Wales to be Welsh-speaking. While the modernizing leadership of Plaid Cymru adopts a multicultural perspective, it is constantly challenged by its core membership in the north-west, which is less reconstructed. Debates over English incomers tend to reinforce the idea of an unchanging and united Welsh community. This is an important argument but Gwynedd is not the whole of Wales. Stark opposition between English incomers and Welsh speakers in rural Wales is not inevitable. In Ceredigion members of those two communities have formed a political alliance that is the basis for Plaid Cymru winning the parliamentary seat. One way forward from the problems revealed in this chapter may be to develop such alliances and to use them as the basis for a redefinition of the nation. On such a basis, the concept of nationhood could be made inclusive. Secondly, the territorial divisions of language and culture in Wales are likely to be reduced in the long run. Welsh speakers are more likely to form a scattered community than a geographically concentrated one. This is already the case to a large extent, with most Welsh speakers living outside what were once regarded as the heartlands of the language. But, in the shorter term, as the majority Welsh-language communities decline there is likely to be increased conflict of this kind.

How do we assess the position of contemporary Wales in terms of our interacting themes? Perhaps we can specify what is distinctive about Welsh identity and its connections with the wider world by means of some comparisons with the other nations in the British Isles. In England there is now a substantial ethnic minority population that is quite widespread geographically. This – along with the recognition of England's centrality in the British Empire – has forced issues of multiculturalism onto the political agenda and led to racial equality becoming a prominent issue, and one which has well-established institutional linkages. By contrast, in Scotland, where the role in the empire is well acknowledged and a source of pride and identity, there is only a small and concentrated ethnic minority population. Ireland has had even fewer representatives of ethnic minorities, until very recently, but it has a broad awareness of its international connections. Some of these came from the role that Irish administrators, politicians and soldiers played in the British Empire. More come from the massive and sustained emigration from Ireland for well over a hundred years after the Great Famine of the 1840s. Modern Irish identity is much shaped by these links.

The situation in Wales is a distinctive blend of these elements. Unlike Ireland, emigration was never of massive proportions.[11] By contrast, the role of Welsh people in the British Empire is little explored. Although Welsh people were under-represented among the servants of the empire, and some people would want to see the Welsh as the colonized rather than the colonizer, the military victories of imperial Britain were celebrated here and some Welsh politicians had well-developed imperial attitudes.[12] In addition, the place of ethnic minorities in Wales is much more limited than in England, though it is more prominent than in Scotland, which has no equivalent of Butetown's multiracial community. Both Scotland and Wales have largely avoided the racialized politics of England, partly because the Scots–English and Welsh–English ethnic issues have forced race further down the agenda than in England.

This distinctive position has slowed down the development of a concern for multiculturalism in Wales. Only in the 1990s did the issue begin to make a serious impact on the political agenda, when the rise in racial attacks confronted the myth of tolerance, while TV documentaries, newspaper articles, and the Oscar-nominated film *Solomon a Gaenor* examined aspects of cultural diversity in the past and the present. At the same time the institutional structures to promote racial equality were being more firmly established. In this context, Ron Davies's concern that the new National Assembly should be inclusive was bound to raise expectations of further progress.

Yet, as Charlotte Williams notes, these issues have not entered fully into the sense of Welsh identity. Certain avenues are available through which they might travel. Gwyn A. Williams undermined the idea of an unchanging, fixed Welsh identity,[13] while Dai Smith has stressed the pluralism of Welsh experiences in his much-quoted phrase: 'Wales is a singular noun but a plural experience'.[14] He had in mind mainly the plurality of English- and Welsh-language cultures, though the cosmopolitanism of south Wales was part of the remit. We hope these essays will develop this approach to identity, and link it with the way that Wales is connected with the outside world. In a radio debate a few years ago, Betty Campbell, the inspirational black headteacher of a school in Butetown, wondered whether the idea of Welshness embraced her.[15] If it does not, it will not be worth having. Perhaps we need inspiration to imagine our futures. A number of contemporary novelists have demonstrated that they are well in advance of many people in public life.[16]

The problems we face in reconciling nationality with a globalizing world are not unique to Wales, nor are they unprecedented. We will have resources to draw on from other countries and from our own past. Particular places everywhere are coming to be seen as distinct blends of elements from diverse origins rather than as hermetically sealed units.[17] The new, more fluid criteria for selecting sportspeople to represent a country is related to this changing reality. We need to broaden this understanding and approach. An important contribution to this task will be research and analysis such as that which is contained in this book. Creating links between our developing understanding of the past and our explorations of the present in a number of disciplinary fields provides a basis for thinking about the Welsh nation in new ways. That task will be difficult and contested, and it is about citizenship as much as scholarship. But we ought to have some confidence that we have resources available to prepare us for the task. Raymond Williams, the greatest Welsh intellectual of the twentieth century, referred to 'resources of hope'.[18] This is what we offer here. But intellectual resources need to be applied and debated. These essays, we believe, make important contributions both to the way we understand the past and to the way we build our futures.

Notes

[1] B. Parekh, *The Future of Multi-ethnic Britain: The Parekh Report* (London, 2000).

[2] Gwyn A. Williams, *When was Wales?* (London, 1991 edn), 13, 15.

[3] This approach has been developed further in his 'Comparing immigrant histories: the Irish and others in modern Wales', in Paul O'Leary (ed.), *The Irish in Wales* (Liverpool, forthcoming).

[4] Neil Evans, 'Can we compare racisms? Regions, nations and Europe', in Eberhard Bort and Neil Evans (eds), *Networking Europe: Essays in Regionalism and Social Democracy* (Liverpool, 2000).

[5] A. G. Hopkins (ed.), *Globalization in World History* (London, 2001) is an excellent recent collection addressing these themes.

[6] These variants of globalization are derived from Hopkins, *Globalization in World History*.

[7] Imanuel Geiss, 'Pan-Africanism', *Journal of Contemporary History*, 4, 1 (January 1969); George Shepperson, 'Notes on Negro American influences on the emergence of African nationalism', *Journal of African History*, 1/2 (1960); Shepperson, 'Pan-Africanism and "Pan-Africanism": Some Historical Notes', *Phylon*, 23/6 (1962).

[8] Paul O'Leary, *Immigration and Integration: The Irish in Wales, 1798–1922* (Cardiff, 2000).

[9] For Poles in Wales see Evans, 'Comparing immigrant histories'.

[10] See Nancy Foner, *From Ellis Island to JFK: New York's Two Great Waves of Immigration* (New Haven, London and New York, 2000), ch. 6, which is rightly sceptical of the novelty of this.

[11] But it has made a deep impact on Welsh consciousness, see W. D. Jones, *Wales and America: Scranton and the Welsh* (Cardiff, 1993); and his continuing work on the Welsh in Australia.

[12] Neville Masterman, *The Forerunner: The Dilemmas of Tom Ellis, 1859–1899* (Llandybïe, 1972); John Grigg, *Lloyd George: The Last Best Hope of the British Empire* (Caernarfon, 1999).

[13] Williams, *When was Wales?*

[14] Dai Smith, *Wales: A Question for History* (Bridgend, 1999), 36.

[15] Debate on 'The Millennium History of Wales' series, BBC Radio Wales, January 2000.

[16] Patrick Corcoran, *Last Light Breaking* (Bridgend, 1998); Trezza Azzopardi, *The Hiding Place* (London, 2000); John Williams, *Cardiff Dead* (London, 2000); Charlotte Williams, *Sugar and Slate* (Aberystwyth, 2002).

[17] Doreen Massey, 'A global sense of place?', *Marxism Today* (June 1991).

[18] Raymond Williams, *Resources of Hope* (London, 1989).

1 Immigrants and Minorities in Wales, 1840–1990: A Comparative Perspective[1]

NEIL EVANS

Vaclav Havel believes that a nation can be judged by the way it treats minorities.[2] Wales has often measured itself favourably by this standard and outsiders have also applied the same rule. It is an encapsulation of one of the subthemes of the Welsh idea of the *gwerin* – the Welsh people were the most upright, God-fearing, radical, moral, philosophical, cultured and tolerant in the world. The principled internationalism of the *gwerin* receives some academic support from one of the major studies in modern Welsh social history, Hywel Francis and David Smith's *The Fed: A History of the South Wales Miners in the Twentieth Century*.[3] Here the proletarian solidarity of the miners – most marked in their support for Irish independence in the 1920s and the Spanish Republic in the 1930s – is seen as being rooted in the plural experience of the coalfield: minorities are so well integrated that they contribute more than their mite to the radical tradition.

More recently, a dissenting tradition has arisen from the work of historians who have excavated the tangled history of ethnic conflict in Wales. For instance, Paul O'Leary has unearthed twenty major violent incidents against the Irish between 1826 and 1882.[4] Geoffrey Alderman and Colin Holmes have atomized the Tredegar anti-Jewish riots of 1911 and Jon Parry has examined the anti-Irish disturbances of 1882. He eloquently understates the conclusion of the new line: 'The Welsh have never been immune to prejudice.'[5]

I

Riots were not weekly or even annual events in modern Welsh history. However, there is evidence that an ethnic ordering of society was apparent in everyday situations. Migrants to south Wales in the nineteenth century moved along ethnically laid tracks. Until the 1890s, English incomers went predominantly to the ports, while the Welsh headed for the Valleys. Similar segregation was discernible within Swansea. The English and the Irish tended to settle in the town itself, and to form separate communities. The Welsh went for the northern industrial fringe in communities such as Landore and Morriston. Such a distribution implied differences in occupations as well as in residence, for the jobs of the commercial core would be quite different from those of the industrial villages. In the south Wales ports similar hierarchies existed; the best seafaring jobs were the weekly ships to London which allowed the maintenance of family life, and these were dominated by the native-born. Diverse ethnic groups filled the bulk of Cardiff's tramp trade. This also applied in the coalfield, where those English people who arrived in the Valleys found that the best jobs – coal cutting – went to the native Welsh while they were left with haulage and surface work. The influx of English into nineteenth-century Wales also caused occasional friction, especially in the north Wales coalfield where this was one of the ways in which class solidarity was mobilized.[6] There was a tradition of running English managers out of town, culminating in the incident which gave rise to the tragic Mold Riots of 1869. Accusations of favouritism shown to English colliers had formed the background to the conflict. Less evidence of this has come to light in south Wales, but there were occasional suggestions of conflict and hostility. In 1874 Welsh workers backed locally based trade unions in preference to those from across the border in the 'Red Dragon' revolt, and later the Miners' Federation of Great Britain was often referred to as 'the English union'.[7]

The 1911 census showed that quite substantial foreign minorities were located in Wales. As south Wales in the previous decade had attracted incomers at a rate only surpassed within the Western world by the United States, this is not surprising. As far as the male population is concerned, areas of south Wales had high proportions of foreign-born. Cardiff was second only to London, while Swansea came fourth and Newport sixth. Merthyr trailed behind at 34th and Glamorgan at 43rd. The figures for women were quite different, with Cardiff coming 17th, Swansea 21st and Merthyr 28th. No figures were given for Newport and Glamorgan, which had insignificant proportions of foreign-born women. This implies that relatively few incomers emigrated as families, and meant that the potential for conflicts based upon sexual jealousy was always present. In marked contrast with this relative cosmopolitanism within Britain came rural Wales, the counties of which formed a solid phalanx from no. 6 to no. 11 in the table of counties with the highest proportion of native-born in Britain.

While some places in south Wales came to be quite cosmopolitan, they also had distinct cultural hierarchies. The Irish were often perceived as being less inclined to work than the native-born. Nor was the situation much different amongst the younger generation in the inter-war period. A survey of schoolchildren in different parts of Wales found a prevalence of stereotyped views of foreigners, often based on books and the cinema and which the authors thought offered little hope of fostering international understanding unless educational institutions intervened more directly.

Abercraf, at the head of the Swansea Valley, had diversity thrust suddenly upon it just before the First World War. In the space of a few years about 250 foreign migrants, mainly Spaniards, arrived. They were seen by many of the local populace as part of a devious ploy by coalowners to subvert the Minimum Wage Act of 1912 with cheap foreign labour. Their huts were said to be highly overcrowded, and the people themselves a moral threat. In July 1914 there were protest meetings which called for their expulsion from local pits, and an incident when native miners refused to work if they were allowed underground. M. Esteban defended his compatriots by claiming that the Spaniards were proportionately more unionized than the local miners and appealed to the international solidarity of the Welsh. The 'moral panic' in the agitation gives the lie to the claim by the chairman of a protest meeting (and the socialist newspaper *Llais Llafur*) that there was no hostility to foreigners as such in the campaign. In the end the issue seems to have been swallowed by the outbreak of war, and the growing prosperity which it brought.

Naturally, the bulk of such reactions came in industrial south Wales, but they were not confined to that area. One intriguing case of ethnic conflict occurred in mid-Cardiganshire at the turn of the century. The local lead industry had almost slipped into oblivion by then, but in 1899 a Belgian company bought the Frongoch mine near Ponterwyd. Some of the workers they engaged were Italians, who were placed in specially constructed barracks, and an old English Wesleyan chapel was converted as a Catholic place of worship. The employers sought to foster good feeling between the two sections of the workforce by providing a free tea, after which both communities sang their favourite songs. Yet the reputation of both countries as lands of song did not prove strong enough to overcome animosities which developed in the course of work. The whole enterprise was a marginal one, and the economic pressures exerted by management were intense. Resistance was conducted along ethnic lines with the Italians going out on strike on one occasion, followed by the Welsh on another. Once the Welsh bodily prevented the Italians from entering the mine. In one dispute dynamite was placed near the barracks of the Italians, and near the home of the mine captain. No one was injured, and care was taken that this was the case, yet it is a scene more reminiscent of the American hard-rock mining frontier and the dynamiters of the Western Federation of Miners than of 'tranquil' rural Wales.

Not all settlements of ethnic minorities gave rise to pathological reactions, however. Jews, for instance, settled into Cardiff and formed a distinct but non-ghettoized community which seems to have suffered little overt hostility and to have been typical of the smaller Jewish settlements in British cities. The earliest Jewish settlements in Wales stretch back into the eighteenth century, and Swansea was probably the first town with a Hebrew community. In the late nineteenth century the influx of Jews fleeing East European pogroms pushed small numbers of them into scattered settlements in the valleys. The chief rabbi visited south Wales and stressed that Jews were a community which had developed in parallel with the general development of Cardiff (and, by implication, of south Wales). A few worked underground but the strictly orthodox would not work the Saturday shift and were sometimes dismissed for this.[8]

The development of Italian settlement was similar. They came from a concentrated area of the country, Bardi in the Ceno Valley in Emilia-Romagna, escaping rural poverty to find a niche in the development of temperance bars in south Wales. Expanding prosperity drew them from Cardiff and other cities into the Valleys, and they became less clustered than the Italians who settled in England. They offered something new, even exotic, a welcome alternative to the pub. Many challenged the Sunday trading laws to provide a service and a profit – it was one of the more lucrative days of the week for takings. They recruited their labour from home along the *padrone* system and survived in a marginal trade by self and family exploitation. By 1938 they ran more than 300 cafés in south Wales. Because every café needed its catchment area, they never formed a concentrated community, and had few communal institutions. This meant that they were well integrated and formed only a loosely knit community.[9]

Less edifying were the reactions to Gypsies. An encampment at Barmouth in 1901 drew the wrath of a local newspaper which demanded that it be cleared away, and in 1914 the *Welsh Outlook* published an interview with a Gypsy named Eli Burton who stressed that real Gypsies were not thieves, murderers or rapists and stressed the need for education. He argued that every town ought to have a field with proper conveniences and affordable camping fees. A hundred years on many of his descendants are still waiting.

Both world wars provide evidence of conflict and cooperation between ethnic groups in Wales. There was a rapturous early reception for Belgian refugees at the outbreak of the First World War, with crowds turning out on the streets in welcome, and hints that no society hostess was complete without at least one Belgian family to display. Large numbers were dispersed from Cardiff throughout south Wales, and offers of places exceeded the number of refugees. Many went to Swansea, where an existing community of metal-workers from Belgium provided the focus for settlement. Members of the Welsh intelligentsia foresaw a great cultural bonus for Wales because of the presence of so many distinguished writers and artists. Their talents were rapidly drawn upon in order to launch concerts which would finance the refugees' stay. However, when it became evident that the war would not be over by Christmas, tensions began to emerge. It was felt that Belgians could be either working or, better still, fighting. Yet trade unions were sometimes suspicious of their claims to work. The South Wales Miners' Federation was cool, but not hostile, when its opinions were sought. It did not oppose the claim of Belgians to jobs, but stressed that unemployment still existed in some areas of south Wales.[10]

A more sinister aspect of the wartime experience is a generalized hostility to aliens, encouraged by the governmental policies enshrined in the Aliens' Act of 1914. The press emphasized the alien presence in south Wales, particularly in reporting court cases. For enemy aliens the situation could be frightening. At Aberystwyth a crowd set upon the septuagenarian Professor Ethé, who had given forty years of service to the University College of Wales. Much of the college and enlightened Welsh opinion was appalled, but this did not prevent him from being forced away from his chair (with a pension) in 1915. There was also an attack on German immigrants in Rhyl.[11] The intolerant side of the heritage did not disappear at the end of hostilities. The dislocations of the war and a generalized hostility to 'foreigners' provided the backdrop to the anti-black riots in the ports of south-east Wales in 1919.

In the Second World War, evacuees from England played the part that the Belgians played in the First World War. There was an early welcome, and there are many stories of lifelong attachments being formed, which cannot be discounted. In the coalfield, in particular, this seems to have been a fairly smooth process. Yet there were also tensions, as East-Enders and Carmarthenshire farmers experienced culture shock in encounters that they both felt were too close. In north Wales the problems arose from the unsympathetic billeting of Catholic Irish from Liverpool on a highly Protestant Nonconformist population: 'Bohemian Ideals versus the Puritan Ethic', as one newspaper headline had it; Catholics were disturbed to find that the Protestant Sunday denied them both their church *and* the pub! Friction arose mainly out of the attempts by Catholic priests to enter homes to look after the spiritual welfare of evacuees, and the decision of many locals to take children to chapel services rather than to leave them unsupervised or with long walks to Mass. Plaid Cymru was concerned that the whole process was a threat to the Welsh language and culture, an issue which foreshadowed the issue of in-migration of the 1980s. Yet it failed to rally any significant support. Perhaps the friction was exaggerated by the shortage of solid news in the 'phoney' war, yet there certainly was some localized concern as the multicultural nature of Britain was forcibly displayed.[12]

During the war, it was chiefly the Italians who were on the receiving end. In Swansea, on the night that Italy entered the conflict, large crowds roamed the streets and damaged the property of Italian café owners. A café owner living at Aberdare later remembered having had a window broken during the war and there were also some incidents at Tonypandy. This hostility does not seem to have been long-lasting or even especially widespread. Perhaps Italians were too well established in south Wales for the feelings to be really intense. In Swansea, a suspicion that Italians had been involved in fascist movements and were sympathetic to Mussolini's regime may have contributed to the outbreak. The deaths of many Italians from south Wales on the liner *Arandora Star*, which was taking them to wartime exile in Canada when it was sunk by a German U-boat, may have turned public feelings around. Italian and German prisoners of war were put to work in some parts of south Wales, particularly around Bridgend.[13]

After the war Italian workers were recruited to fill gaps in the workforce, along with other displaced persons from Europe. The census of 1951 showed a quite substantial rise in the numbers of foreign-born in Glamorgan and Monmouthshire as compared with the last pre-war census of 1931. At Llanelli there was some resentment at the Italian presence. Yet a clear legacy of the war was a general sentiment of hostility to fascism. In Cardiff, Butetown suddenly became respectable and a symbol of tolerance to the world, though actual behaviour towards blacks changed less than did the rhetoric. In the South Wales Coalfield there was a debate about the recruitment of black labour in 1948, though much of the comment was against the colour bar.

II

The momentous social changes of the nineteenth and early twentieth centuries were frequently punctuated by anti-immigrant riots, ranging from the first serious attack on the Irish in 1826 to anti-Jewish and anti-Chinese riots in 1911 and the assault on black newcomers in 1919. This ended a tradition of communal violence against outsiders, though this did not mean the end of ethnic violence.[14] Does this mean that the troubles of the mid-nineteenth century and early twentieth century were simply problems of adjustment – once the Welsh came to understand their guests they learned to live peaceably with them? There is certainly some mileage in this argument. It seems to fit the Irish best of all. A string of riots over almost sixty years gave way to growing cooperation over Home Rule and labour politics in the 1880s. Wales and Ireland increasingly marched together in political terms from 1868 to 1922. In Cardiff an Irish 'ghetto' broke down and at least some of its former inhabitants experienced increasing prosperity. In the 1890s Cardiff had an Irish Catholic mayor. Indeed the Irish were integrated enough to be among the major assailants of blacks and Arabs in 1919, though perhaps this also shows the precariousness of the improved position of the community. An Arab or black invasion of 'their' quarter of the city threatened to place them back at the bottom of the pile. A West Indian with whom I discussed this issue once told me that Newtown was 'Irishmen's quarters' and 'this [Butetown] was our quarters'. When Jim Callaghan was selected as Labour candidate for Cardiff South, he (correctly) informed Protestants that he was a Protestant, but apparently omitted to do so in Catholic areas (where presumably his name made him seem like a Catholic). This suggests some ill ease over the issue, but there is no evidence of serious conflict either.[15] This integration presumably applies to the Spanish community by the 1930s, given the size of the Spanish Aid movement in south Wales, though some evidence from the 1920s suggests that if this is true it must have been a fairly recent change.

Other evidence suggests that for European immigrants the processes of adjustment were not too severe and that there was considerable integration. Some groups with immigrant origins found it difficult to maintain their identity in the post-war world. Italians complained that they were 'Bloody Italians' in Wales, and 'Bloody Inglesi' (*sic*) in Italy. Newcomers faced less fracturing choices: Greeks in Cardiff, for instance, could largely impose their home-country values on their children. But the most poignant story is that of the Jews. The numbers of the Orthodox declined throughout the post-war period, and already by the 1930s they were funnelling back from the Valleys to Cardiff and the other coastal towns. Contrary to popular belief, the pawnshop trade in which they were concentrated was devastated by the Depression and the Valleys communities never recovered. Politically it took Jews a long time to arrive, with Cardiff getting its first Jewish councillor in 1928 and its first Jewish lord mayor in 1987, though there were several Jewish deputy lord mayors in the mean time. They gained a collective voice for the first time since the turn of the century with the publication from 1951 onwards of *CAJEX* – the Journal of the Cardiff Jewish Ex-Servicemen and Women. It became the mouthpiece of all south Wales Jewry and an important repository of historical articles on their experience. Yet it tended to slip into nostalgia for departed Jewish communities and personalities, along with fears for the future as the birth rate fell, employment prospects took young people out of south Wales and they were not replaced by incomers.[16]

The problem was acutely felt by the Cathedral Road Synagogue in Cardiff, a symbol of the Victorian expansion of the faith. Yet their spokespeople stressed constantly the way in which they were integrated into Welsh society, and the lack of anti-Semitism. Recorded instances of grave desecration in Brynmawr in the early 1970s do not seriously challenge this picture. Jews were so well integrated that they shared the central experiences of the majority population – the movement to the coast, an ageing population and secularization. Perhaps many felt less need for an all-embracing faith and culture in these circumstances.

The argument for integration over time carries us a little of the way forward, but it does not have a great deal of stamina. It falls at two major hurdles. Most importantly, there were, of course, few incomers in Welsh society in the 1920s and 1930s. The history of that period is one of devastating emigration, with somewhere between a fifth and a quarter of the Welsh population leaving Wales. We should hardly expect to find massive conflict between incomers and natives in these circumstances. Immigrant communities were not being created or, generally speaking, even 'topped up'; the Depression was too big to be explained by anyone as being the product of the fairly small minority groups that there were in Wales. In short, the *circumstances* for conflict did not exist to any great extent.

The second reason is in some ways the exception which proves the first rule. There probably were black newcomers to Cardiff in the 1920s and they faced unrelenting hostility from the local authorities and the trade unions. The absence of overt riot is misleading here, for there were far more effective ways of continuing the process that had begun on the streets in 1919 into the post-war period. Inverting Clausewitz we might describe it as the continuation of war by other means. After the publication of a hostile report by the chief constable on the 'coloured' population of Cardiff in 1929, Swansea did its own investigation, but decided it had nothing to fear. A Colonial Office investigator during the Second World War found the Barry black community to be less depressing than Cardiff and more united than South Shields. Yet he was not complacent and pointed out that people remembered the events of 1919 and they feared that they would not retain equality of opportunity at the end of the war. They were right to be concerned about the way that blacks were treated in south Wales. Colin Holmes, the most knowledgeable historian of the experience of immigrants and minorities in modern British history, after discussing the registration of black British seamen under the Aliens Order of 1925, concludes: 'Viewed in a sober historical perspective there are few clearer cases of the institutional oppression of minorities in early twentieth-century Britain.'[17] This points towards the need for comparison if the picture in Wales is to be understood. Belfast, Liverpool and Glasgow provide measures which allow us to find a scale for ethnic conflict in Wales.

III

Belfast could lull us into a false sense of security. Its ethnic conflict is so deep-rooted and persistent that no other city in the Western world compares with it. There was little in its situation which really compared with south Wales – a pre-existing pattern of segregation, rooted in the plantations of the seventeenth century was disturbed by the rapid urbanization of Catholics in the earlier part of the nineteenth century. By mid-century Catholics accounted for a third of the population. The violence which followed from the 1850s onwards seems to have been a more-or-less conscious effort to force them out of Belfast – and Ulster – and one which was overwhelmingly 'successful'. By 1900, Catholics had been reduced to a quarter of the population of the city, and confined to a tight ghetto within it. Economic competition played a vital part in this whole process, but the occasion (rather than the reason) for the decisive political realignment (one which Ulster still lives – and dies – with) was the Home Rule split of the 1880s. Where politics had once been an alliance of Presbyterians and Catholics against the dominant Church of Ireland, it was now a Protestant common front against Catholics. At the risk of sounding antique, the superstructure some-what tardily followed the base. The peak of violence came in the years of rebellion and civil war, between 1920 and 1922, but sectarianism remained a constant thread throughout the inter-war period, expressing itself most forcibly in the riots of 1935. There was also a strand of Protestant extremism which saw its own community as riddled with traitors, while Catholicism was united, aggressive and bent on domination. Since the 1960s these conflicts have been renewed; old conflicts have been reproduced in new settings, and the peace process seems to be a fragile instrument for breaking the vicious circle.[18]

Liverpool is different, but not by a great deal. Its sectarianism is also deep-rooted, and predates the Irish Famine. It has been constantly renewed by being one of the key centres of Irish immigration into Britain. Not only did this result in massive bloodletting on the streets, but it also infected social institutions and politics. Liverpool has Orange and Green divisions – and a Catholic community which returned an Irish Nationalist MP throughout the period 1885–1929. The issue took enough votes from the left to stop Labour from winning control of the city council until 1955; Tories needed the Orange card to win power. Liverpool had much closer connections with Ireland than did south Wales, but unlike Glasgow, it has few links with Ulster – apart perhaps from economic ones in the shipbuilding industry. Its fierce Protestantism seems to have been a native growth rather than an import. Lancashire was an area where the Reformation had not taken very deep root and fear of recusancy fuelled Protestant visions. Tories found that defence of church and state also made a good electoral rallying cry in the era of industrialization. The city's international trade drew in a diverse group of migrants from the British Empire as well. It became not just an Orange and Green city, but what Merfyn Jones has described as a rainbow city. Between 1909 and 1919 there were five major outbreaks of ethnic violence, not all of which have yet found their chronicler.[19]

Glasgow was not quite like either Liverpool or Belfast. There, in the other major reception area of Irish migration to Britain, Orange and Green rivalries became set into social institutions, notoriously into its two football teams. Celtic, founded in 1887, gathered up existing Catholic support over the wider industrial area and its success in a society in which Catholics had few advantages was a symbol of achievement. Rangers was founded to counter this, and because it had a much larger pool of potential players could remain far more exclusively sectarian than Celtic could be without sacrificing success on the field. The teams were both champions and surrogates for wider Scottish/Irish, Protestant/Catholic divisions and helped channel bitter conflicts. The flow of people ensured that such institutions of civil society had a high longevity. Like Liverpool, it was part of an 'industrial triangle' which bound it to Belfast, but here there was also substantial contact with Protestant Ulster as well as with the Catholic majority of Ireland. Yet sectarianism did not dominate politics in Scotland in the way that it did in Lancashire. The redeeming factor was Scottish (and Glasgow's) Liberalism. It wavered in the 1880s with a swing to Liberal Unionism, but there was nothing like the Lancashire Tory tradition for sectarianism to feed upon. Indeed, in Glasgow it was probably the Tories who were the victims of sectarian division; Liberalism partly rested on the division of its opponents. Scotland's lurch to sectarian politics came in the period between the wars. It was a rapid rise and fall, originating in exaggerated fears of an Irish influx during the disturbances of 1920–2 and dying as the exponents of Protestant fundamentalism drifted too close to the flame of fascism and burned their wings. They plummeted into oblivion.[20]

How did south Wales differ from this experience? In the nineteenth century, it was never one of the major centres of Irish migration, even though it had a significant Irish presence. Only in a few communities were the Irish a central presence in the 1850s. In 1861 they were about a third of the population of Cardiff, and local opinion considered with alarm the prospects of a town which was fairly evenly divided between Welsh, Irish and English. These Irish were overwhelmingly from Munster, and therefore Catholics; unlike Glasgow there was no link with Ulster Protestantism and, unlike Lancashire, no pre-existing Catholic–Protestant tensions to draw upon. Anyway, the Irish soon lost much of their visibility in Wales. In Cardiff the Irish-born remained more or less constant in numbers for the rest of the century, while the city's size mushroomed until they became dwarfed by its growth. Outside the major south Wales ports the largest concentrations of Irish by the late nineteenth century were within a ten-mile radius of Tredegar, in the old iron-making district. In the Rhondda there were very few and the Sunday mass at Tonypandy needed to draw on all parts of the two valleys to sustain itself. For most of south Wales Joseph Keating's description of his native Mountain Ash as a colony would apply admirably. Adding the second and third generation to this picture would, of course, enlarge the Irish population, but not change the basic argument. The minority became integrated into Liberal and Labour politics, and into trade unions. They caused none of the enthusiasm for Liberal Unionism which was a Scottish reaction to their presence.

In south Wales the Irish become increasingly 'invisible' from the 1880s, as they did in most parts of Britain, apart from London, Central Scotland, Lancashire and the West Midlands, where their communities continued to grow significantly into the twentieth century. They ceased to be serious competitors to the Welsh in the expanding areas of the economy after 1850. This was partly the result of riots which prevented them from obtaining anything more than toeholds in the burgeoning steam coal areas. A series of riots in the early 1850s, the culmination of a very tense period throughout south Wales, bodily expelled them from the Rhondda; there was more than a shade of Belfast in this process. They seem to have been acceptable in established areas like Cardiff and Merthyr, where they were confined to a fairly narrow range of occupations. Merthyr probably had a more settled Irish population than did Cardiff but it was mostly confined to jobs in the more poorly paid sections of iron-working. In Merthyr Vale and Aberfan, however, the Irish did become more integrated into the coalmining workforce. Tellingly, the riot in Tredegar in 1882 came when that community was undergoing the shift from iron-making to steel-making and coalmining. Again, the Irish were not welcome in an expanding sector. Occasionally, there were tensions at a later period, as in Pembrokeshire in the late 1930s, where a series of fights with locals took place. In Cardiff the ethnic conflicts did not intertwine in the way that they did in Liverpool. The tensions of the Irish were mid-Victorian and slowly faded away. European sailors were seen as competitors for jobs, holding the centre of the stage until the turn of the century, when they were displaced by people of diverse skin colours. There was a succession of issues rather than an entanglement of them. None of these issues became central to politics and society; religious and national freedom – and later class dignity – were much more compelling.[21]

IV

The story so far has taken us up to, and slightly beyond, the Second World War. What has happened in Wales in the period when Britain has become recognized as a multi-ethnic society? Have the Welsh been immune to prejudice? There were no riots in 1958 when Notting Hill and Nottingham experienced scaled-down versions of the disturbances of 1919. Nor were there major riots in the 1980s when the population of inner cities rebelled (rather in the manner of the American ghetto rebellions of the 1960s) against the way in which they were policed and their economic position.

Wales, in the post-war period, was not a major centre of black immigration. It took until 1961 for the overall population of Wales to regain the level it had been in 1921. Compared with many areas of

Britain it had a persistent problem of unemployment. Black immigrants headed instead for the 'industrial coffin' – the south-east, Midlands and north of England. West Indians largely bypassed Wales. Some tried to come to Butetown, but on the whole they were not well received. It is not unusual for an urbanized minority to see a further rural influx as a challenge to whatever social position it has won for itself. Yet the relative lack of jobs was surely more important. The established black population began to make the transition from shipping to shore-based work in this period. Black newcomers went either for rapidly expanding areas like the south-east of England, where there was low unemployment, or for areas like the Midlands where the population was fairly stable, but where whites were abandoning certain jobs and areas of housing. Most of the later comers in Wales were from the Indian subcontinent. They came in a rush before the first Act to restrict Commonwealth immigration was passed in 1962 and overwhelmed the existing Asian communities. The result was more widespread dispersal than had been characteristic of West Indians. Only in Cardiff have they formed a very significant community, in terms of numbers.

Philip Jones's study of the dispersal of black immigrants in the decade 1961–71 does not consider any community with a black population of less than 1,500. Cardiff is the only place in Wales that he had to locate on his map. At the beginning of the 1980s there were 11,485 Commonwealth-born people in Wales, though the black population would have been considerably bigger, with an estimated 20,000 in the Cardiff travel-to-work area alone by 1989. Generally speaking, these people did not head for Butetown, but for the other inner-city areas of Cardiff, and Grangetown in particular. They formed clusters of different nationalities, each with its own place of worship, and largely apart from the city in their social and cultural life. One group which has been particularly studied – the Bhuttra Sikhs – have displayed this tendency to an unusual extent. Few of its 300 or so members in the 1970s could speak English comfortably. Since then there has been some further dispersal. Butetown and the Valleys both have some shopkeepers from the Indian subcontinent, but there are no large concentrations. In the 1980s the South Glamorgan Community Relations Executive found a good deal of discontent among the black population who were in touch with larger communities elsewhere in Britain, and were well aware of the lack of progress in south Wales in areas like multicultural education.

It had taken ten years to persuade the police to appoint a liaison officer, and longer to gain a social worker with knowledge of Asian languages. It is no surprise that a survey in the late 1980s found blacks to be overwhelmingly concentrated in the unskilled, semi-skilled and basic clerical categories of employment, or that in Cardiff in 1987 only 3 per cent of black school leavers found jobs, compared with 11 per cent of their white contemporaries.[22]

The lack of any major concentration of blacks probably influences the degree of expressed racial prejudice in Wales. Studies of Britain generally show that propinquity to black immigrants increases hostility to them – or at least it did so in the 1960s – in the short run. On the other hand, casual contacts (as opposed to living close together) tended to reduce feelings of hostility. In the same period Liberal and Labour voters – the bulk of the Welsh electorate at that time – were less inclined to be racially prejudiced than were Conservative supporters. Two surveys of Welsh opinion, in 1966 and 1984, support this conclusion. The evidence shows that the Welsh came into the lowest segments of racial hostility in both the studies. This may not mean a great deal – it is after all just attitudes rather than behaviour – and in the case of most people, attitudes that are formed without there being much experience to root them in. Possibly the very idea of Welsh tolerance has helped to produce these results. There is less scope for optimism in a study of attitudes conducted in Swansea in 1983–4, where 44 per cent of the population showed no overt prejudice, but 56 per cent did so; among the young there was little middle ground with a clear split between tolerance and extreme prejudice as compared with older age groups.

Race has not entered Welsh politics to any large degree in the post-war period. Nor have there been any major disturbances. This may be the result of Cardiff's having a low percentage of its population in the most deprived categories, certainly as compared with Manchester and Liverpool. Butetown is also rather cut off from the rest of the inner city and this may have made a difference. When an incident did start there in July 1981, a media blackout was operated. The police were fearful of being drawn into an ambush and allowed the destruction of thousands of pounds' worth of property in Bute Terrace as a result. As riots were generally spread by word of mouth rather than television, local geography may have played a part. Anyway, in Butetown it appears that the established leadership has largely maintained its position and authority, whereas a key feature of riots which broke out elsewhere was the mounting of a challenge to leaders who were seen as too accommodating to the local authorities. Also, in a long-settled community there would not have been the rift between the experiences of first and second generation, which was crucial in many English cities. In 1981 the energies of Cardiff's Rastafarians were absorbed on a project to convert the old slipper baths into workshops and a centre for the unemployed. When they failed to gain government aid for the project, they wondered whether rioting would have been a more productive use of their time![23]

The Welsh context is illuminated by studies of race in Scottish politics conducted by Robert Miles and his associates at the University of Glasgow. Like Wales, Scotland parades the idea that it is exceptionally tolerant and thinks the English could learn a thing or two from them in this respect, as in others. In the surveys for which Welsh evidence was quoted above, Scotland's position is contradictory – high in one, low in the other. Miles, however, demonstrates that while racism is not absent in Scotland, and was fostered by a history which included participation in the slave trade and missionary activity, Scottish politics have not become racialized as English politics have become. The reasons for this are not tolerance but because of the nature of Scottish society and politics. Nationalism has been a major concern of the post-war period, with the result that many blame the decline of the Scottish economy on central control rather than upon immigrants, as can be the case in England. As there are relatively few immigrants they are not very conspicuous and tend not to come to the forefront in politics. Scottish civil society is also deeply divided into Orange and Green components, so that it is more difficult to see just what identity and culture black newcomers could be seen as threatening. Finally, there has been no strong tradition of fascism in Scottish society, and fascist groups have played a key part in putting race onto the political agenda in England. Most of this can be simply lifted from Scotland and applied to Wales. The main difference is the absence of Orange and Green divisions in Wales, but perhaps the growing divisions over language as this became a central political issue from the 1960s onwards have filled this particular gap. Language came onto the political agenda in Wales just as race was coming to prominence in England. The landmark BBC lecture *Tynged Yr Iaith* (The Fate of the Language) was delivered in the very year that the Commonwealth Immigration Act of 1962 was passed.

In the 1980s both Scotland and Wales encountered the issue of different kinds of incomers – English in-migrants who seemed to challenge important aspects of local life and culture. They were instances of what have been called 'dominant minorities'. In Scotland the dispute was chiefly over the 'Englishing' of key institutions – education, art galleries, museums – and, though this has not been mentioned, one might add Rangers. Cultural imperialists running such institutions, it is charged, have failed to make distinctively Scottish aspects of their charges flourish. In Wales the issue is different, despite some attempts to link them. The domination of institutions by incomers is less apparent, if only because the requirement of speaking Welsh for many jobs reduces their impact. It is most marked in the University of Wales, outside its distinctively Welsh enclaves. The more serious issue in Wales is that of the impact of incomers on the heartland of the Welsh language. This is causing an anguish which is visible among many Welsh speakers. While it would be rash to make any real or sustained comparison with Loyalist and Republican terrorism in Northern Ireland, this was the only other sustained political campaign using violence in these islands in the 1980s. A recent opinion poll shows considerable support for the cause, if not for the methods. A dominant minority is, by its nature, a different thing from the poor and frequently despised immigrants who have figured more often in modern Welsh history. At least it forms a convenient place at which to conclude this survey. [24]

V

How do we conclude? In the past 150 years Wales has been the host to substantial numbers of immigrants in the period before the First World War, and relatively few thereafter. If there has been relatively little conflict with them – at least compared with Belfast, Glasgow and Liverpool – this must be the reason, rather than some inherent tolerance in the Welsh psyche. When there have been conflicts, they have been among the most vicious within Britain. It is only the peculiar historical circumstances of Wales that have ensured that these have not become ingrained as a tradition. The mechanisms which have sustained and escalated conflicts in other parts of the islands, have – mercifully – been missing. There would seem to be little scope for self-congratulation in this. Breast-beating – or its converse, remorse – are not the most important things in the study of the history of minority groups and immigrants. The point is not to praise tolerance, but to uncover the causes of antagonism. Understanding is the thing we need most desperately. While Marx rightly stressed that understanding the world and changing it were different things, there is no need for him, or us, to conclude that the two are not closely related to each other.

Notes

[1] This is an abridged and slightly revised version of an article which first appeared in *Llafur*, 5/4 (1991), 5–26.

[2] The best general study of this topic for Britain as a whole is Colin Holmes, *John Bull's Island: Immigration in British Society, 1871–1971* (London, 1988), which has much Welsh material.

[3] Hywel Francis and David Smith, *The Fed: The South Wales Miners in the Twentieth Century* (London, 1980; new edn in paperback, Cardiff, 1998), ch. 1.

[4] Paul O'Leary, *Immigration and Integration: The Irish in Wales, 1798–1922* (Cardiff, 2000); O'Leary, 'Anti-Irish riots in Wales, 1826–1882', *Llafur*, 5/4 (1991).

[5] Geoffrey Alderman, 'The anti-Jewish riots of August 1911 in south Wales', *Welsh History Review*, 6/2 (1972); Colin Holmes, 'The Tredegar riots of 1911: anti-Jewish disturbances in south Wales', *Welsh History Review*, 11/2 (1982); Jon Parry, 'The Tredegar anti-Irish riots of 1882', *Llafur*, 3/4 (1983).

[6] Philip N. Jones, 'Some aspects of immigration into the Glamorganshire coalfield between 1881 and 1911', *Trans. of the Honourable Society of Cymmrodorion* (1969), part I; J. Ronald Williams, 'The influence of foreign nationalities upon the social life of the people of Merthyr Tydfil', *Sociological Review*, 18/2 (1926); Hywel Francis, 'The secret world of the south Wales miner: the relevance of oral history', in David Smith (ed.), *A People and a Proletariat: Essays in Welsh History, 1780–1980* (London, 1980); Ieuan Gwynedd Jones, 'The making of an industrial community', in Glanmor Williams (ed.), *Swansea: An Illustrated History* (Swansea, 1990).

[7] Emlyn Rogers, 'The history of trade unionism in the coalmining industry of north Wales', *Trans. of the Denbighshire Historical Society*, 16–18 (1967–9); Alun Burge, 'The Mold riots of 1869', *Llafur*, 3/2 (1982); Aled Jones, 'The Red Dragon revolt', *Welsh History Review*, 12/2 (1984); L. J. Williams, 'New unionism in south Wales, 1889–1892', *Welsh History Review*, 1/4 (1963).

[8] Ursula Henriques, *The Jews of South Wales: Historical Studies* (Cardiff, 1992); Bernard Goldblum, 'Swansea' (Papers presented to the Jewish Historical Society Conference, 1975); N. H. Saunders, *The Swansea Hebrew Congregation, 1730–1980* (Swansea, 1980).

[9] Lucio Sponza, *Italian Immigrants in Nineteenth-Century Britain: Realities and*

Images (Leicester, 1988), 17–18, 33, 58, 102, 110, 275; Colin Hughes, *Lime, Lemon and Sarsaparilla: The Italian Community in South Wales, 1881–1945* (Bridgend, 1992).

[10] J. R. Alban, 'The activities of the Swansea Belgian Refugees Committee, 1914–16', *Gower*, 26 (1975); Moira Vincentelli, 'The Davies family and Belgian refugee artists and musicians in Wales', *National Library of Wales Journal*, 22/2 (1981).

[11] C. J. Williams, 'An anti-German riot in Rhyl in 1915', *Flintshire Historical Society Publications*, 26 (1973–4). For context see: Panikos Panayi, 'Germans in Britain during the First World War', *Historical Research*, 64/153 (1991).

[12] Peter Paterson, 'Freedom in Wales', *Spectator* (23 April 1983); Angus Calder, *The People's War* (London, 1969); Ruth Inglis, *The Children's War: Evacuation, 1939–1945* (London, 1989), 24–5, 30, 72; Travis L. Crosby, *The Impact of Civilian Evacuation in the Second World War* (London, 1986), 40; Clifford R. Davies, 'Early educational problems of the Second World War in the Rhyl area', *Flintshire Historical Society Publications*, 27 (1975–6); Gillian Wallis, 'North Wales receives: an account of the first government evacuation scheme, 1939–40', *Flintshire Historical Society Publications*, 32 (1989).

[13] Hughes, *Lime, Lemon*, ch. 4.

[14] See ch. 6 below. Also: Neil Evans, 'Across the universe: racial conflict and the postwar crisis in imperial Britain, 1919–1925', *Immigrants and Minorities*, 13 (1994); Geoffrey Alderman, 'Into the vortex: south Wales Jewry before 1914', *Jewish Historical Society of England* (1975); Philip N. Jones, 'Baptist chapels as an index of cultural transition in the South Wales Coalfield before 1914', *Journal of Historical Geography*, 2/4 (1976); Derec Llwyd Morgan, 'The Welsh biblical heritage', *Trans. Caenarfonshire Historical Society* (1988); Glyn Tegai Hughes, 'Dreams of a promised land' (lecture to Meirionnydd Historical and Record Society, Towyn Branch, 26 November 1971). I am very grateful to Dr Hughes for letting me see his notes. Joanne Cayford, 'In search of John Chinaman', *Llafur* 5/4 (1991); J. P May, 'The British working class and the Chinese, 1870–1911, with particular reference to the seamen's strike of 1911', unpublished University of Warwick MA thesis, 1973; May, 'The Chinese in Britain', in Colin Holmes (ed.), *Immigrants and Minorities in British Society* (London, 1978).

[15] John V. Hickey, 'The origin and development of the Irish community in Cardiff', unpublished University of Wales MA thesis, 1959; Hickey, *Urban Catholics: Urban Catholics in England and Wales from 1829 to the Present Day* (London, 1967); Peter Kellner and Christopher Hitchens, *Callaghan: The Road to No. 10* (London, 1976), 5–6.

[16] Williams, 'Foreign nationalities'; Francis, *Miners Against Fascism, passim*; Hughes, *Lime, Lemon*.

[17] Brinley Thomas, 'Wales and the Atlantic economy', in Thomas (ed.), *The Welsh Economy: Studies in Expansion* (Cardiff, 1962); Neil Evans, 'Regulating the reserve army: Arabs, Blacks and the local state in Cardiff, 1919–1945', in Kenneth Lunn (ed.), *Race and Labour in Twentieth-Century Bitain* (London, 1985); Kenneth Little, *Negroes in Britain: A Study of Race Relations in English Society* (2nd edn, London, 1972); Marika Sherwood, 'Racism and resistance: Cardiff in the 1930s and 1940s', *Llafur*, 5/4 (1991); Paul B. Rich, *Race and Empire in British Politics*

(2nd edn, Cambridge, 1990), ch. 6; Colin Holmes, *A Tolerant Country? Immigrants, Refugees and Minorities in Britain* (London, 1991), 36.

[18] Sybil Gribbons, 'An Irish city: Belfast in 1911', in David Harkness and Mary O'Dowd (eds), *The Town in Ireland* (Historical Studies, 13, Belfast, 1981); Sybil E. Baker, 'Orange and green: Belfast, 1832–1912', in H. J. Dyos and Michael Wolff (eds), *The Victorian City: Images and Realities* (London, 1973); A. C. Hepburn, 'Catholics in the north of Ireland, 1850–1921', in Hepburn (ed.), *Minorities in History* (Historical Studies, 12, 1978) and 'Work, class and religion in Belfast, 1871–1911', *Irish Social and Economic History*, 10 (1983); chs. by Fred Heatly and Brenda Collins in J. C. Beckett et al., *Belfast: The Making of the City* (Belfast, 1983).

[19] P. J. Waller, *Democracy and Sectarianism: A Political and Social History of Liverpool, 1868–1939* (Liverpool, 1981); Frank Neal, *Sectarian Violence: The Liverpool Experience, 1819–1914* (Manchester, 1988); Tony Lane, *Liverpool: Gateway of Empire* (London, 1987); Merfyn Jones, 'Rainbow city: the Irish and others in Liverpool, 1820–1914' (paper at the Lipman Seminar, 1991).

[20] Bill Murray, *The Old Firm: Sectarianism, Sport and Society in Scotland* (Edinburgh, 1984); Murray, *Glasgow's Giants: 100 Years of the Old Firm* (Edinburgh, 1988); Tom Gallagher, *Glasgow: The Uneasy Peace* (Manchester, 1987); Gallagher, *Edinburgh Divided: John Cormack and No Popery in the 1930s* (Edinburgh, 1987); Joan Smith, 'Class, skill and sectarianism in Glasgow and Liverpool, 1880–1914', in R. J. Morris (ed.), *Class, Power and Social Structure in British Nineteenth-Century Towns* (Leicester, 1986); Steve Bruce, *No Pope of Rome: Militant Protestantism in Modern Scotland* (Edinburgh, 1985); Graham Walker and Tom Gallagher (eds), *Sermons and Battle Hymns: Protestant Popular Culture in Modern Scotland* (Edinburgh, 1990).

[21] Hickey, 'Origin and development'; Philip Jenkins, 'Antipopery on the Welsh marches in the seventeenth century', *Historical Journal*, 23/2 (1980); Jenkins, ' "A Welsh Lancashire"? Monmouthsire Catholics in the eighteenth century', *Recusant History*, 15/3 (1980); Donald M. MacRaild, *Irish Migrants in Modern Britain, 1750–1922* (London, 1999).

[22] Robert Miles and Annie Phizacklea, *White Man's Country: Racism in British Politics* (London, 1984); Ira Katznelson, *Black Men, White Cities: Race, Politics and Migration in the United States, 1900–30 and Britain, 1948–68* (Oxford, 1973); Edward Pilkington, *Beyond the Mother Country: West Indians and the Notting Hill White Riots* (London, 1988); Robert Miles, 'The riots of 1958: notes on the ideological construction of "race relations" in Britain', *Immigrants and Minorities*, 3/3 (1984); Panikos Panayi, 'Middlesbrough 1961: a British race riot of the 1960s?', *Social History*, 16/2 (1991); Philip N. Jones, 'The distribution and diffusion of the coloured population of England and Wales, 1961–1971', *Trans. Institute of British Geographers*, New Series, 3/4 (1978); Ceri Peach, 'The growth and distribution of the black population in Britain, 1945–1980', in D. A. Coleman (ed.), *Demography of Immigrants and Minority Groups in the United Kingdom* (London, 1982); Leonard Bloom, 'Introduction' to K. Little, *Negroes in Britain*; P. A. S. Guhman, 'Bhuttra Sikhs in Cardiff: family organisation and kinship', *New Community* (1980).

[23] Richard T. Schaefer, 'Party affiliation and prejudice in Britain', *New Community*, 2/3 (1973); idem, 'Contacts between immigrants and Englishmen: road to tolerance of intolerance?', ibid., 2 (1973); idem, 'Regional differences in prejudice', *Regional Studies*, 9 (1975); Vaughan Robinson, 'Spatial variablity in attitudes towards race in the United Kingdom', in Peter Jackson (ed.), *Race and Racism: Essays in Social Geography* (London, 1987); Vaughan Robinson, 'Racial antipathy in south Wales and its social and demographic correlates', *New Community*, 12/1 (1984–5); Harold Carter, 'Cardiff: local, regional and national capital', in George Gordon (ed.), *Regional Cities in the UK* (London, 1986), 184; *Arcade*, 20 (7 August 1981), and 33 (5 March 1982); Martin Kettle and Lucy Hodges, *Uprising! The Police, the People and the Riots in Britain's Cities* (London, 1982). There is also a useful issue of the journal *Race and Class* on the 1981 riots (23/2–3, Autumn 1981–Winter 1982); Ceri Peach, 'A geographical perspective on the 1981 urban riots in England', *Ethnic and Racial Studies*, 9/3 (1986).

[24] Robert Miles and Anne Dunlop, 'The racialisation of politics in Britain: why Scotland is different', *Patterns of Prejudice*, 20/1 (1986); idem, 'Racism in Britain: the Scottish dimension', in Peter Jackson (ed.), *Race and Racism: Essays in Social Geography* (London, 1987); Miles and Lesley Muirhead, 'Racism in Scotland: a matter for further investigation?', in David McCrone (ed.), *Scottish Government Yearbook, 1986* (Edinburgh, 1986); anon., 'The Englishing of Scotland', *Radical Scotland*, 35 (Oct.–Nov. 1988); A. C. Hepburn, 'Minorities in history', and Nicholas Canny, 'Dominant minorities: English settlers in Ireland and Virginia, 1550–1650', both in Hepburn, *Minorities in History*; 'Rift valleys' (Channel 4 TV programme, transmitted 1991); Denis Balsom, 'The smoke behind the fires: the recent survey examining the arson campaign', *Planet*, 73 (Feb.–March 1989).

2 Slaughter and Salvation: Welsh Missionary Activity and British Imperialism

JANE AARON

Nearly two centuries ago, on 19 October 1816, a young Welsh woman barely seventeen years of age embarked on the good ship *Alacrity* bound on a great adventure. Ann Jones from Llanidloes had married Evan Evans from Llanrwst just a fortnight previously, and she now set sail with her new husband for the Cape of Good Hope, which at that time was part of Britain's most recently established colony. Motivated by the need to secure for the merchant ships of the East India Company a safe resting place on the sea route to India, the British Crown, after a series of bloody engagements with both the indigenous people of the Cape and its Dutch settlers, was finally able to fly the Union Jack over Cape Colony in 1814. Where the soldiers went, the missionaries followed. Under the auspices of the London Missionary Society, Evan Evans, fresh from his Bala ordination into the ranks of the Calvinist Methodist church, was appointed to minister the gospel to the Hottentots, or rather to the Khoikhoi, to give the people of the Cape their real name (Hottentot, which apparently denotes 'stutterer', was the name the Dutch settlers gave to the natives they encountered, whose language included an expressive pattern of clicking sounds).

Eight months after she had embarked, Ann Evans, from her new home in Bethelsdorp, a small impoverished township east of Cape Town, set about the task of attempting to convey to her family at home some impression of the world in which she now found herself. Her long letter, which was subsequently published in Wales as a fundraising missionary pamphlet (though there is no suggestion in the letter that she herself intended it to be put to such use), vividly evokes the high romance of the enterprise. She makes little herself of the perils of the journey, but one passage in particular from the letter captures the intensity of her experience, not so much in her own words, but indirectly, through her report of another woman's speech. A missionary base already established at the High Kraal had provided one resting place on the Evanses' trek into the hinterlands, and she gives her parents a detailed account of her first prayer meeting there with the Khoikhoi:

> One of the women prayed after that, and it was enough to melt the hardest heart, I think, to hear how warmly and zealously she thanked the Lord for putting it in the heart of his people in the far country to send his servants to them, poor Hottentots, the most despised nation under the whole heaven, to teach them the way of eternal life; and, O!, how she laid out her amazement that it was possible for anybody on the surface of the whole earth to possess so much love for such black, poor and wretched creatures as they were, as to leave their country, their language, their fathers and mothers, their brothers and sisters, and everything dear to nature, to come to live in the desert-lands of Africa, as the means in the hand of God to save sinners from eternal damnation; and O!, how she marvelled that we had dared to cross the great stormy sea, and cross high mountains, and go through deep rivers, to come to live in their midst, poor Hottentots, who had nothing to give us after all our dangers and labour. My heart was ready to break as I listened to her, so that I could barely prevent myself from joining with them in weeping and calling out.[1]

For whom is Ann Evans's heart nearly breaking here? For herself? As well it might, prophetically, for her adventure was certainly to cost her dear. When she returned to Wales ten years later, she accompanied a dying husband, worn out at the age of thirty-five as much by his struggles with the obstructive Cape colonists as by his work amongst the indigenous people and the diseases and hard life of the hinterland. She buried him in Llanidloes shortly after their arrival home, along with one of their children who had sickened on the voyage; the bodies of two more of her children were left behind in African graves.[2]

Or is she here weeping for the Hottentots – a people with whom she seems, from the evidence of her letter, to have fallen in love as soon as she encountered them, with all the ardency of her seventeen years? It is unlikely that she would have been deaf to the phrases in the Khoikhoi woman's speech which point to a native history of dispossession and despair. By the time Ann Evans arrived in their midst the Khoikhoi people had already suffered nearly two centuries of colonization. At the beginning of the seventeenth century, before the coming of the white man, their nomadic tribes spread throughout the Cape provinces; today only scattered groups remain, and the Khoikhoi are nearly extinct as a race. Their experience of colonization reduced them to the condition of wretchedness and abject poverty the speaker describes, and taught them to conceive of themselves as 'the most despised nation under the whole heaven'. The 1973 revised edition of the *Shorter Oxford English Dictionary* still gives as one transferred meaning of the word 'Hottentot' 'a person of inferior intellect or culture'.

The Khoikhoi woman speaks of the pain of losing homelands and relatives; it is very likely that she herself had plenty of first-hand experiences of such bereavements. While the missionaries had at least chosen to leave their native habitations voluntarily, the lands and livelihoods of the Khoikhoi had been stolen from them, their 'fathers and mothers, brothers and sisters' slaughtered by weapons whose efficiency they could not previously have dreamt of, or killed by European diseases to which they had no immunity. The Khoikhoi were exploited as cheap labourers by the colonialists, who prized them as curiosities because of their short physique – few of them were taller than five feet. In the early nineteenth century, a woman of the Khoikhoi tribe, Saartje Baartmann, was exhibited in British freak shows as the 'Hottentot Venus', and became a topic of burlesque curiosity to the street balladeers and cartoonists of the period.[3]

The culture of the Khoikhoi suffered erosion, of course, along with their people and lands. In her prayer, the Khoikhoi woman itemizes 'their language' as one of the treasures 'dear to nature' which the missionaries have had to give up; she herself, however, cannot here have been speaking in her own language. The Cape missionary stations used the first settlers' language, Dutch, in their communication with the Khoikhoi, rather than the native tongue. It is unlikely that they did so out of any deliberate disinclination to foster the indigenous tongue, for the nineteenth-century missionaries had generally a good record for using native languages, and were frequently the first to inscribe, and create a grammar for, languages which had previously only existed as an oral tongue.[4] More probably, the Cape mission's language was Dutch because, after two centuries of colonization, that language was by now in common use in any exchanges between the Khoikhoi and the white settlers. Ann Evans herself, when she wrote her letter, does not even seem to have been aware that the Khoikhoi ever had a language of their own. It was the Dutch language which she and Evan studied in preparation for their mission, during the long months on board the *Alacrity*. With a poignancy made all the more acute by the fact that she is herself writing in a minority indigenous language, she tells her parents of the great pleasure it gave her to hear 'my dear husband preach to the Hottentots for the first time in their own language' – that is, in Dutch.[5] And, of course, the message which Evan Evans delivered to the Khoikhoi in the oppressors' language would have but further eroded their native culture and the basis of their native self-respect, if they accepted it. It would have taught them that they must abandon their own gods, and with them the myths, songs, dances and rituals central to their culture, and embrace as the only true religion the professed faith of all those Dutch and British settlers who, in material terms at any rate, had most effectively brought them not to eternal life but to the brink of annihilation. Well might Ann Evans weep for the Khoikhoi, then; perhaps her emotion here is also a marker of a more complex submerged grief about the nature of her meeting with them, shaped as it was by its place within a specific historical context which, for all the unquestionable sincerity of her dedication and her personal sacrifice, now makes it difficult for us to see in this encounter an unequivocal good.

That context was, of course, the rise of the British Empire. Recently, in English cultural studies, post-colonial critics have emphasized the fact that the empire, and all it stood for, must occupy a central place in our understanding of nineteenth-century British consciousness. According to Gayatri Chakravorty Spivak, for example, 'it should not be possible to read nineteenth-century British literature without remembering that imperialism, understood as England's social mission, was a crucial part of the cultural representation of England to the English'.[6] My subject in this chapter, however, is not so much the place of the British Empire in nineteenth-century English consciousness as its place in nineteenth-century Welsh consciousness, and its role in the cultural representation of Wales to the Welsh. I have dwelt on Ann Evans's letter at such length because, as a text arising out of the missionary movement, it is representative of that type of discourse in which we find by far the most numerous references to the British Empire in Welsh nineteenth-century writing.

Before the close of the nineteenth century, gospel-bearers had been sent out from Welsh chapels to every corner of the empire, to Cape Colony, as we have seen, and also to Natal, Sierra Leone, the Sudan, Ceylon, Malacca in South-East Asia, Australia, Fiji, Jamaica, Trinidad, the West Indies, British Honduras, Newfoundland, Gibraltar (to convert the Roman Catholics), and to so many Indian provinces that it would be tedious to list them. Major bases had also been established by the Welsh Nonconformists in territories – such as China, Madagascar, northern Africa and Tahiti – which were affiliated to Britain through trading agreements though not actually annexed under the British Crown. The numbers and the costs involved in such enterprises were substantial: by 1897, the Welsh Calvinist Methodists had sent out fifty-six ordained ministers to the Khasi Hills alone. And with the missionaries went, of course, their wives and children, and later doctors, schoolteachers and nurses as well. A well-developed late nineteenth-century missionary base contained schools, hospitals, domestic dwellings for the converts as well the British-born (for the converted were often rejected from their own families and had to be housed and supported by the mission), and maybe a printing-press too, as well as the church itself, of course, all of which had to be maintained by voluntary contributions from the congregations back home.[7]

In order to encourage their readers in the impetus to give, the Welsh denominational journals of the day filled their pages with letters and reports from missionaries, and articles, stories and poems about missionaries. The secular press, too, in so far as nineteenth-century Wales can be said to have had a secular press, also naturally enough reflected the same preoccupation. A collection of tales about Welsh village life published by Sara Maria Saunders in 1897, for example, and entitled *Llon a Lleddf* (Joyous and Plaintive), is replete with references to India. A penniless girl sells her abundant hair in order to contribute her mite to the missionary collection; a widow so successfully dissembles her grief as she bids her only child Godspeed to the mission fields that he thinks she hardly cares, but the neighbours know that it has always been part of her generosity to give as if the gift meant nothing to her, and that she will never recover from this loss; a deacon who has never left the village is more familiar with every detail of the topography of the Khasi Hills than he is with his own backyard.[8] The imperial fields of the Lord were these villagers' romance, the missionaries their knights in shining armour, and each black convert a pearl that would shine forever in their heavenly crown.

References to the empire are just as rife, of course, in the English fiction of the period, but they are generally of a different order. Of course, there are missionaries in the English texts as well, but they do not usually enjoy the same kind of glamour as that which surrounds their Welsh counterparts; I am afraid that a Welsh Jane Eyre would have had to choose St John Rivers rather than Rochester as her husband if she was to retain her readers' sympathies. In typical English upper-middle-class domestic fiction, the empire features as the place to which the second son is sent to prove his manhood and repair the family fortune, not as a missionary, of course – he could hardly have repaired the family fortunes as a missionary – but as a military or civil officer. It is the place to which sad, unrequited lovers go only to re-emerge later in the novel loaded with military honours and with much enhanced eligibility; or the place in which some colonial administrator dies bequeathing to his home-based heir a fortune which will bring about the novel's requisite concluding marriage. A Welsh-language novel, even had the genre been much more extensively developed in nineteenth-century Wales than it was, could hardly have included many examples of this type of reference because membership of the imperial officer ranks, whether military or administrative, was rigidly confined to the upper middle class, a group to which few Welshmen at this time belonged. A Welsh cottager's or labourer's son of exceptional enterprise might, after 1868, be imagined as becoming a Liberal MP, or making a fortune in the dairy trade in London, but because of his parentage it would be difficult credibly to present him as joining the top-ranking empire club. Were he less ambitious, he would still statistically have been less likely than his Scottish or Irish equivalent to join the forces of empire as a voluntarily enlisted rank-and-file soldier, or as a lowly emigrant and settler, because the development of the south Wales industrial base offered the impoverished rural Welsh a new living closer to home. Consequently, in 1901, though the Welsh then made up 5 per cent of the population of the British Isles, less than 1 per cent of the British-born in Britain's overseas colonies were Welsh.[9] But when it came to missionaries, there can be little doubt that, whatever the actual ratio for specifically Welsh as opposed to British gospel-bearers, the Welsh people at home thought of their own evangelists to the empire as constituting considerably more than 1 per cent of the British total.

But the glamour which surrounds the figure of the missionary in nineteenth-century Welsh culture is too intense for it to be attributed merely to the fact that in statistical terms it constituted one of the few figures of imperial agency in which the Welsh could feel a personal involvement. Rather, I suggest, its potency arises from the missionary's redemptive role as saviour not only of the natives but also of Welsh pride in the face of the by now much-documented historical humiliations of the century. Given the awe-inspiring achievements of their English neighbours, and the mortifications induced by that neighbour's expressed disdain for the Welsh,[10] mid-nineteenth-century Welsh self-esteem would certainly have been in a very sorry plight had it not been able to take pride in the figure of the Welsh missionary as representing a far, far better mode of relating to the world at large than that of the English imperial officer. And yet the majority of the Welsh missionaries worked in fields which had only been made accessible to them by British guns, and the degree of security and prestige they enjoyed there was largely attributable to their identity as British subjects, as 'Christian soldiers' in the army of the Great White Queen.

The complex, at times contradictory, nature of the Welsh response to colonialism is apparent in some of the articles which Ieuan Gwynedd (the Revd Evan Jones) published in the first Welsh-language journal for women, Y Gymraes (The Welsh Woman), which he edited in 1850–1. In an article entitled 'Sais-addoliaeth' (The worship of the English), he pleads with his readers to resist identification with what he presents as very much the English, rather than British, ethos of imperialism. The article needs to be understood in the context of the anglicization of Wales in the nineteenth century, which Ieuan Gwynedd is here deploring. He fears that his audience will succumb to the allure of the increasingly powerful English, and reminds them that imperial glory is only gained at the expense of the colonized nations, who suffer just as the Welsh themselves did in the thirteenth century when they lost their sovereignty. His diatribe begins mildly enough. 'Personally, we have no reason to complain about the English,' he says, making use of the editorial 'we', 'but we venture to say that the spirit of the nation is such that we would not wish to see the Welsh imitating it.' Before the close of his article, however, after having listed in detail those atrocities which resulted from the aggressive 'spirit' of the English as a nation and their disparagement of other cultures, Ieuan Gwynedd is ferocious in his attack:

Are we judging our brother harshly? Let his history answer from his landing on the island of Thanet, on the borders of Kent, to his present bloody slaughters in the Punjaub and Borneo in 1849. He is the arch thief of creation. He boasts of his learning, his civilization and his religion. His learning is butchery, his civilization is robbery, and his god is himself. We are not describing individuals, but the spirit of the nation, as it manifests itself on the pages of history.[11]

And yet in later numbers of Y *Gymraes* Ieuan Gwynedd reports approvingly on the Welsh missionaries' activities in India and elsewhere.[12] There was clearly no necessary connection in his mind between English imperialism and the role of the missionaries.

Given the way in which the burgeoning empire was perceived during the first half of the nineteenth century, this is readily understandable. The slaughter of the Punjab Sikhs, to which Ieuan Gwynedd refers, was carried out not by Her Majesty's imperial army but by the militia of the East India Trading Company. Empire building was understood as being pre-eminently about increasing overseas trade. The ethos of trade was, of course, clearly distinguishable from that of Christian evangelism: in fact, there was open antagonism between the two interests. It was the evangelists largely who had aroused public protest in Britain against slavery and brought about the abolition of the British slave trade in 1807, and the freeing of slaves on British territory in 1833, with the loss, of course, of much trade revenue. Until 1813, when the evangelists in Parliament, under William Wilberforce, brought so much pressure to bear on the Government that it threatened the East India Company with the loss of its charter if it continued to ban missionaries, no missionary presence had been allowed in India: the Trading Company had outlawed them. As the Company saw it, any interference with their established religious practices was likely to provoke the Indian populace to rebellion against the white interlopers, and thus to imperil good trading relations.

For some decades after 1813, British soldiers in India continued to attempt to preserve the country's peace by checking the missionaries' endeavours to reform what they perceived as the most inhumane aspects of traditional Indian culture. A striking instance of one such collision between the interests of trade and that of the missionaries is given in *The Autobiography of Elizabeth Davis*, an oral record narrated by the intrepid traveller Betsy Cadwaladyr (to give her the name by which she knew herself) to her transcriber, the historian Jane Williams. The loyal daughter of a Calvinist Methodist preacher, Betsy had a close affinity with missionaries and a strong dislike of soldiers. She closed her long adventure-packed career by serving as a nurse under Florence Nightingale in the Crimea but makes a point in her autobiography of bluntly telling her audience that she did not volunteer out of any sympathy for the British army's plight but rather out of her insatiable wanderlust.[13] She attributes her prejudice against the military to an incident she witnessed in Madras in 1825 or thereabouts, while she was employed as a maidservant on board an independently owned merchant ship, trading between the various outposts of the empire:

> I had friends at Madras among the missionaries; and I went one day in company with Mr Elliott, Mr Cook, and Mr Benini, to see a suttee. The widow was . . . walking towards the pile [i.e. her husband's funeral pile], when Mr Cook and Mr Elliott met her, and asked her quietly whether it was her own will to be burned. She answered, 'No'. They next asked whether she would escape, if the opportunity were given her; and she answered, 'Yes'. The missionaries contrived to free a path for her, and she got off; but the English sentries stopped her. To avoid their bayonets, she threw herself into the river. The missionaries rescued her, and made an application to the governor; so that she was saved at last.[14]

Here, the chief enemy of the humane Christian viewpoint is presented as being the English soldiery, who should have known better than to allow the sacrifice of human life for the sake of preventing a possible disturbance amongst the native population. The interests of the empire understood as trade and those of the missionaries are poles apart; to participate in the work of the latter would not necessarily be to have to conceive oneself as in any way supporting the former.

But the Indian uprising of 1857, which nearly brought to an abrupt close Britain's rule in India, changed the way in which Britain conceived of its empire. The trading interest saw the mutiny as in part brought about by the natives' fear of the Christianizing presence, but the missionaries pointed out, with greater effect, that in those Indian provinces in which they had succeeded in making their presence felt less natives had rebelled. No Christian convert had raised arms against the British; had the Trading Company allowed them more scope, said the missionaries, and put Bibles in the hands of every Indian schoolchild as they had requested, the uprising might never have taken place. After Britain regained full control, India, in 1858, was placed under the direct rule of the British Crown, and the purposes of Britain in furthering its empire were now presented to the world in explicitly Christian terms. The British, it was now to be understood, ruled for the good of the colonized – those natives who had made their barbarous proclivities so disastrously clear during the uprising – and not for personal gain. According to one influential politician of the period, for example,

> the authority of the British Crown is at this moment the most powerful instrument under Providence, of maintaining peace and order in many extensive regions of the earth, and thereby assists in diffusing amongst millions of the human race, the blessings of Christianity and civilization.[15]

The missionaries, it would appear, had won the public opinion battle, but in another sense, from the point of view of someone like Ieuan Gwynedd, they had lost it, for from now on they and all they stood for would be seen as part and parcel of the ethos of British imperialism, and the providers of its overt moral justification. They would function to the public gaze as a coat of whitewash on what Joseph Conrad was later to term the 'whitened sepulchre' of imperialism.[16]

In devoutly Nonconformist nineteenth-century Wales, with the exception of some notable anti-English protesters such as Emrys ap Iwan and Michael D. Jones,[17] few voices were raised against this new version of the purposes of empire during the next decades. The travel writing of Margaret Jones of Rhosllanerchrugog, another Welsh Nonconformist maidservant, serves to provide a view of the 'heathen' more typical, perhaps, of the majority opinion in late nineteenth-century Wales than Ieuan Gwynedd's more radical perspective. Margaret Jones found employment within the household of a family of converted Jews who participated in the Christian mission to the Jews, first in Paris, then Jerusalem, and lastly in Morocco. In a characteristic passage from the second of the two books she published on her travels and experiences, she comments on the people she observed through her Moroccan window:

The influence of their tyrannical, degrading and corrupt religion (that is, Mohametanism) has worn away their civilization and their morals to a deplorable degree . . . I saw them from the window of my room beating an offender for five minutes; they thrashed him like thrashing corn. My feelings were a mixture of sadness and rejoicing. Sadness at the punishment of the sinner, and joy because I knew of a better country, a better administration, because I was born and bred in that country, and educated in the religion which is the main spring of its justice. Britain for ever![18]

She closes her commentary by assuring her audience that the only hope for the restoration of law and order in Morocco is its speedy assimilation into the British Empire and a thoroughgoing Protestant Christian mission.

Even when, in the last two decades of the century, a Home Rule movement had started in Wales, in part in emulation of the Irish 'Young Ireland' movement, not all its representatives were ready to forego their allegiance to the empire. As the leader of the Welsh Women's Liberal Association, and wife of the Liberal MP Wynford Phillipps, a member of the Cymru Fydd or 'Young Wales' group, Norah Phillipps presumably espoused the two main aims of Cymru Fydd – the Disestablishment of the Church in Wales and Home Rule. She was also in her own right a very active and effective propagator of liberal reform in Wales, particularly in the fields of women's education and women's suffrage. Yet, in an article published in *Young Wales*, the English-language mouthpiece of the Cymru Fydd movement, she has the following to say on nationalism:

It would be easy to say, 'I am Irish, Welsh, or English, therefore I will be patriotic for Ireland, Wales, or England,' or it would be easy to say, 'I care and dare for the Empire, its greatness and glory. I will be no "little Englander".' But to be truly great is to care with a passionate patriotism for this great empire – great not only in extent but far more in the intent of her civilization – and yet with joy and pride and devotion strive for the country, that part of the great whole to which we, by special love and human linking of family, language, and religion, belong.[19]

Her concept of the 'intent' of the empire – that is, its Christianizing and civilizing aim – is such that she must applaud it, and proclaim her loyalty to it, even as she is here writing within the context of a movement intent on securing more devolved powers for the people of Wales.

One unusually circumstanced group of Welsh-born people were, however, provided by their experiences with a very different view of the processes of empire, and I will close with an anecdote from the works of one of that group's best-known spokespersons, the travel writer Eluned Morgan. Eluned Morgan was born in 1870 on board the ship *Myfanwy* which took a group of Welsh emigrants to what is generally referred to as the 'Welsh colony' of Patagonia. But, of course, Patagonia was never an imperial colony, or at least not a Welsh one; it was part of an Argentine-held territory, ruled and Christianized by Spanish colonists. The Welsh settlers had acquired the right to live according to their own religious beliefs and to use their own language, but they had no administrative control over the indigenous people of the area, and did not proselytize their religion to them. Nevertheless, according to Eluned Morgan in her accounts of her Patagonian childhood, close ties formed between the Welsh and their nomadic Indian neighbours, with the Indians frequently requesting the Welsh to intercede on their behalf against the Spanish authorities' attempts to drive them out of their traditional territories. In her book *Dringo'r Andes* (Climbing the Andes), Eluned Morgan describes a chance encounter with one such persecuted Indian, who had received support from her father:

> As we talked in the tent the word 'Cristianos' came up, and I asked him whom he meant by this 'Cristianos'.
> 'The Spaniards,' he said.
> 'But are not we [i.e., the Welsh settlers in Patagonia] also Cristianos?' I said.
> 'Oh no, you are *amigos de los Indios*.' . . .
> How painful to think that the word which used to be so sacred was coupled in the pagan's heart with every cruelty and barbarism ... The Spaniard is not one jot worse than the Yank or the Englishman in this respect; destroying natives and small nations is the characteristic vice of each of them.[20]

Clearly Eluned Morgan, for all her own devoutly Christian beliefs, had come to recognize through such encounters that coupling together Christianity and empire-building degrades the former while it does nothing from the colonized's point of view to redeem the latter.

Nevertheless, the Nonconformist chapels of Wales continued to send out their emissaries to the imperial fields for the duration of British rule. And the congregations at home continued, of course, to support them, financially and morally. I cannot be the only person over fifty brought up in small-town north and west Wales whose first introduction to racial difference came with those wistful Sunday school hymns which sang of far-away children with coloured skins and nobody to speak to them of God. And the answer, of course, was 'let's send the missionaries out over the sea, they will speak to them of God'. Nor perhaps was I the only child who first consciously experienced the shock of ideological difference when, on the annual round with the missionary collecting boxes, I realized, from some unexpectedly aggressive receptions, that not everyone in the early 1960s considered the missionary movement an unequivocally good thing. Later in the 1960s India finally expelled the remaining white missionaries from its provinces, as irredeemably tainted with the stains of imperialism. Perhaps it is no coincidence that that decade, the 1960s, which laid so low the formerly haloed figure of the Welsh missionary, also saw the rise in Wales of the Welsh language movement, and the first Plaid Cymru MP. One source of national pride and of identity had gone: the vacuum had to be filled, and those far-away children, suddenly grown adult, demanding their free-dom and their own culture, taking down the Union Jack all over the globe, pointed the way. But by the late 1960s, of course, there were few committed Welsh Nonconformists left, as a percentage of the Welsh population as a whole, to feel the full impact of the trauma.

Notes

An earlier article which was substantially revised for this chapter appeared as 'Slaughter and salvation: British imperialism in nineteenth-century Welsh women's writing', in *New Welsh Review*, 38 (October 1997).

[1] Ann Evans, *Llythyr Ann Evans* . . . (Bala, 1818), 16 (my translation).

[2] G. Penar Griffith, *Hanes Bywgraffiadol o Genadon Cymreig i Wledydd Paganaidd* (Cardiff, 1897), 133–40.

[3] For an account of the 'Hottentot Venus', see Kirsti Bohata, 'The Black Venus: atavistic sexualities', in Meic Stephens (ed.), *Rhys Davies: Decoding the Hare* (Cardiff, 2001), 231–43.

[4] See Nigel Jenkins, *Gwalia in Khasia* (Llandysul, 1995) for an account of this aspect of the missionaries' work; the Welsh missionary Thomas Jones, for example, is still

esteemed in Khasia as the 'father of Khasi alphabets'; he gave the Khasi their 'written word' and in so doing kept their language alive (p. 143). But Jenkins points out that 'the missionaries' care for minority languages was often at odds with the homogenising inclinations of Empire' (p. 184).

[5] Ann Evans, *Llythyr Ann Evans*, 17–18.

[6] Gayatri Chakravorty Spivak, 'Three women's texts and a critique of imperialism', in Catherine Belsey and Jane Moore (eds), *The Feminist Reader: Essays in Gender and the Politics of Literary Criticism* (Basingstoke and London, 1995), 175.

[7] In 1890, for example, in the year of the Calvinist Methodist Missionary Society's Jubilee, Welsh Methodist chapels collected the sum of £37,326. 15s. 5d. for the cause. See John Hughes Morris, *Hanes Cenhadaeth Dramor y Methodistiaid Calfinaidd Cymreig, hyd diwedd y flwyddyn 1904* (Caernarfon, 1907), 259.

[8] Sara Maria Saunders, *Llon a Lleddf* (Holywell, 1897), 77, 56, 71.

[9] For these statistics, see P. J. Marshall (ed.), *The Cambridge Illustrated History of the British Empire* (Cambridge, 1996), 265

[10] See the notorious 'Treachery of the Blue Books', the British government's *Report of the Commission of Inquiry into the State of Education in Wales* (London, 1847), which damned the Welsh as a lazy, drunken and sexually immoral people. For a commentary on the connections between this *Report* and English imperial policy, see Gwyneth Tyson Roberts, *The Language of the Blue Books: The Perfect Instrument of Empire* (Cardiff, 1998).

[11] [Evan Jones] Ieuan Gwynedd, 'Sais-addoliaeth', *Y Gymraes*, 1 (1850), 75–6 (my translation).

[12] See, for example, 'Y Llong Genadol' (The missionary ship), ibid., 342–5.

[13] Jane Williams [Ysgafell] (ed.), *The Autobiography of Elizabeth Davis: Betsy Cadwaladyr, A Balaclava Nurse* [1857] (new edn, Dinas Powys, 1987), 153.

[14] Ibid., 78–9.

[15] Earl Grey, quoted in Marshall (ed.), *Cambridge History of British Empire*, 30.

[16] Joseph Conrad, 'Heart of Darkness' [1902], *Youth, a Narrative; and Two Other Stories* (London, 1957).

[17] See, for example, Emrys ap Iwan, 'Bully, Taffy a Paddy', and 'Sylwadau am y Rhyfel nad oedd yn Rhyfel' (Comments on the war that was no war), *Y Faner* (1880) and (1882), in D. Myrddin Lloyd (ed.), *Erthyglau Emrys ap Iwan*, i (Dinbych, 1937), 1–13, 82–9; and Michael D. Jones, 'Ymfudo a Threfedigaeth Gymreig' (Welsh emigration and colonialism), *Y Cronicl* (1850), in E. Pan Jones, *Oes a Gwaith y Prif Athraw y Parch. Michael Daniel Jones* (Bala, 1903), 63.

[18] Margaret Jones, *Morocco, a'r Hyn a Welais Yno* (Wrexham, 1883), 54 and 133 (my translation).

[19] Norah Phillipps, 'Notes on the work of Welsh Liberal women', *Young Wales*, 1 (1895), 39.

[20] Eluned Morgan, *Dringo'r Andes* (Y Fenni, 1904), 40 and 49 (my translation).

3 The Other Internationalism? Missionary Activity and Welsh Nonconformist Perceptions of the World in the Nineteenth and Twentieth Centuries*

ALED JONES

Historians of modern Wales have, rightly and understandably, shown a keen interest, for example, in Welsh socialist and proletarian traditions of internationalism. What I will try to do here is to suggest that Welsh Nonconformity, too, fostered an internationalist perspective, one that is inescapably linked with, though not necessarily reducible to, the power of the British Empire. I wish to argue that evidence of such internationalism is to be found principally in writing produced by Welsh missionaries based in north-east India between 1841 and 1966. The mission, organized by the Calvinistic Methodist Presbyterian Church of Wales, was concentrated in a region of India sharply divided by religion as well as by its physical and administrative topography, and which sat astride the highly unstable frontier between Assam and Eastern Bengal,[1] an area which, in August 1947, was to be further and brutally divided by the new Partitionist international border separating India from what was then East Pakistan, and is now Bangladesh. Relatively small in scale – rarely were there more than fifty missionary workers in the field at any one time – it employed only a tiny proportion of the 10,000 or so British missionaries who were on active service abroad in 1900. While other missionaries from Wales were at work in France, the islands of the Pacific, the Caribbean, parts of western and southern Africa, and China, those in north-east India formed the largest, most continuous project funded and organized by any Welsh-based denomination. They included evangelical preachers, doctors, nurses and teachers, and substantial numbers of them, constituting at times a clear majority, were lay women, mostly young and unmarried. The effects of their presence on the mission field were strikingly uneven, leaving a powerful and enduring mark on the Khasi Hills but making little impression on other areas of the field such as Sylhet. In Wales, too, the sounds of their evangelical fury have been strangely muted. Despite the extraordinary richness of the primary and printed records that they bequeathed to the home church, for much of the second half of the twentieth century their work attracted little sustained attention, other than from such retired missionaries as D. G. Merfyn Jones.[2] In part this may be due to the embarrassment caused by the mission's links with empire, and with the imperial arrogance associated with the idea of religious conversion in British colonies. Since the Second World War, these associations have sat uneasily with post-war constructions of Welsh national identity, whether among nationalists or the left. For both, missionaries represented the wrong kind of internationalism. I think it is time we reassessed those positions, and in doing so looked again, critically but openly, at the roles played by leading Welsh popular institutions in the expansion and consolidation of the British Empire.

The history of the Welsh mission in India has been well rehearsed, most recently in *Gwalia in Khasia* by Nigel Jenkins. The first missionary, Thomas Jones, from Aberriw, Montgomeryshire, arrived in the Khasi Hills in Assam in 1841. In the thirty years that followed his arrival, only around 500 Khasis were converted, but the extension of imperial control coupled with the growth of medical missions and schools led to greater success from the late 1870s onwards. The Khasi Christian community grew from just under 2,000 in 1881 to a little under 7,000 a decade later. By 1901 the figure had reached 16,000 and by 1905, the year of the Welsh Revival, the missionaries had established a following of some 23,000.[3] In the field, missionaries were charged with two major responsibilities. One was to take Welsh Calvinistic Methodism to the Assamese and Bengalis; the other was to keep the Welsh at home informed of their activities. This chapter will pay particular attention to the latter.

Transmission routes for missionary communications from the field back to Wales took a number of forms. Formal reports were submitted annually for publication in the *Report of the Foreign Mission*, but news also returned to Wales by means of letters, the contents of which at times filtered through to the newspaper press. News coverage of events in 1857 in particular provides an intriguing illustration of the way in which editors used missionaries effectively as foreign correspondents. The monthly denominational journal *Y Drysorfa* (The Treasury) included from 1847 a separate 'missionary chronicle' section, *Y Cronicl Cenhadol*, a periodical within a periodical, where reports from the field were regularly printed alongside other religious news and comment. Lectures and sermons given by missionaries on furlough, with occasional visits by converts, were widely publicized, as were special chapel events. Touring exhibitions of Indian villages and bazaars were intended further to excite the sympathies of their audiences. These were augmented in the 1920s by missionary films, shown in schools and chapels, such as the one shot in 1928 by Mostyn Lewis, son of the Liberal MP Sir Herbert Lewis.[4] The conversion of chapels into cinemas, albeit temporarily, signified a huge, even a shocking, shift in Nonconformist cultural sensibilities. Obituaries in newspapers also provided opportunities for the work of missionaries to be constructed as heroic, and allowed the church to appeal for more volunteers.[5] The most ubiquitous form of communication, however, was the missionary periodical press. It is certainly the most accessible to us today, yet it remains a surprisingly underused historical resource.

The Welsh mission field created its own communications media. John Pengwern Jones launched the *Friend of Sylhet* and *The Friend of the Women of Bengal* in 1899, and Helen Rowlands started *The Link* in 1933. But the most important missionary periodical was without doubt *Y Cenhadwr* (The Missionary), published wholly in Welsh between 1922 and 1974, and aimed at a popular Welsh audience at home.[6] Initially edited by the Revd J. Hughes Morris, and published as a monthly from the denomination's own press at Caernarfon, it printed a wide variety of articles, reports, essays and photographs from the mission field. Missionaries themselves contributed the vast majority of items. No circulation figures have as yet come to light, but we do know that the journal was distributed principally through the chapels and by subscription.

These forms of communication familiarized readers and audiences in Wales with images of India: one purpose was to raise funds to continue the missionary work. But what kind of world did these writings describe? The answer is more complicated than one might think. For example, there are numerous accounts in *Y Cenhadwr* where Indian religious practices, particularly Hindu beliefs, are caricatured and attacked. Take, for example, the article on Kali, one of a series on Hindu deities printed in 1924, where the author describes the goddess's nakedness, her drunken eyes, her delight in violence, her blood lust, and her orgiastic dance on the corpse of her husband, condemning in so doing the corrupting effects of her image on the morality of those who worship her, and on Hindu family life in general. Other ethnographic accounts work in similar ways, particularly those that describe dress, social codes of behaviour, diet and occupation, though rarely, to be fair, with the same virulence. In 'The Indian barber', which forms part of an ambitious series on work and street life, the missionary Dilys Edmunds describes the social and religious significance of the *napit*, but it too 'fixes' the intellectual barber in an essentialist way, and attributes his social power to the Hindu 'superstitions' which, she seeks to persuade her readers, her school for Hindu girls in Karimganj was gradually eradicating.

But while some missionaries were deriding Indian religious beliefs and social practices, others were making available to readers in Welsh translation the work of Indian and Hindu poets and priests. There can be little doubt that texts were chosen which sought to emphasize the holiness, and the proximity to Christianity, of certain aspects of other religions, as Helen Rowlands explained in her introduction to her translations of Rabindranath Tagore. But Elizabeth Williams had also earlier translated the work of the Hindu priestess Chundra Lela into Welsh in 1908,[7] while in 1924 Helen Rowlands, with Hridesh Ranjan Ghose, published the sermons of the Sadhu Sundar Sing.[8] Readers in Wales were thereby invited to read certain approved Indian religious texts, in their own language and with the approval and authority of the church. Again, however, such translations are far more likely to have been forms of appropriation, or read as signs of redemption as the Hindu neared the Christian God, rather than evidence of syncretist deviationism within the mission.

Much of *Y Cenhadwr* contains what can only be described as news journalism, especially during the 1930s and 1940s, including articles on the progress of the Congress Party, the activities of Gandhi, the proliferation of symbols of nationhood, and, in 1947, a series of extraordinary accounts of the human cost of Partition, the most notable being Helen Rowlands's reports from Karimganj, positioned on the new border between India and East Pakistan. In other accounts of journeys through the mission field, which included descriptions of landscapes, vegetation, animals, forms of transport, fields, street scenes, markets, and of the men, women and children they encountered, missionaries employed rhetorical strategies which both emphasized the otherness of India and which encouraged a sympathetic identification with it on the part of their readers. 'How different Sylhet is from Wales!' exclaimed Miss E. A. Roberts in 1902,[9] yet the very contrast was intended to produce a closer affinity. The missionaries clearly wanted readers at home to care about their work, and about the people they were in contact with. Welsh and Bengali place names are intertwined in these narratives, and comparisons are made between features of the landscape in the two regions. Such self-consciousness becomes most apparent when missionaries describe feelings of loneliness and of homesickness, of *hiraeth*, when they purport to see images of their home country projected on the landscape and the people around them. The employment of such tropes affirmed their sense of belonging to the physical as well as the mental world of their readers.

Other kinds of encounters demanded a different, more subtly nuanced use of language. An essay by Helen Rowlands entitled 'Y Glaw' (The Rain), which describes a journey taken downriver with a group of her school pupils during the flood season in Sylhet in 1925, resonated with the vibrancy of colour, the scent of flowers, the softness of skin and the sensual textures of hair and cloth. Not what you would normally expect to find in evangelical Christian writing at this time.

Missionaries also developed and adapted Welsh cultural forms in the field. In 1901 John Pengwern Jones organized the first eisteddfod in Sylhet, while Helen Rowlands had later started in Karimganj an annual eisteddfod in Bengali.[10] Hymns were written in, or translated into, indigenous languages, and these were used in much the same devotional way within the order of the service in the field as they were in the home church. J. Arthur Jones, sent to Shillong in 1910 by the *Manchester Guardian*, was struck by the combination of Indian landscape and Welsh religiosity:

> While I sat at my dinner in the dak bungalow, a familiar strain came to my ears. Mingling with the fire-flies . . . floated the minor cadences of an old Welsh tune. They were singing in the chapel which stood on the hill opposite. The timbre of the voices were a little strange, but apart from this I could have imagined myself in some Welsh village where the 'Seiat' was being held in Bethel or Saron. Yet the singers now were Khasis, a Mongolian hill folk of Assam, once worshippers of demons . . . The Khasis have adopted Welsh Methodism with scarcely a variant.[11]

And in the first issue of *Y Cenhadwr* in 1922, Thomas Charles Edwards could confidently announce that the Welsh Calvinistic

Methodists had 'to date created in India a Methodist Church in our own image'.[12] The recreation of a little Wales in India went beyond the strictly devotional. In an account of Christmas at her home for orphaned girls in Silchar in 1922, Miss E. M. Lloyd described how they had 'spent an evening in Wales!' Pictures and maps of the country had been pinned to the walls, the children were dressed in old Welsh costume, and the choir sang *Hen Wlad fy Nhadau* and a number of Welsh folk songs, 'in Welsh'.[13] While such references to the use of the language and other symbols of Welsh identity are infrequent, this account does suggest another line was being crossed, which, in a very direct way, raises the question of the colonial context of the mission. Helen Rowlands herself used the term 'a colony of Welsh people'[14] to describe the mission field.

Whether the mission formed part of the broader British imperial presence in India, or whether it was engaged in a separate process of colonization of its own, in which case it did so by taking advantage of the colonial structures of the British Empire, the link between the mission and imperialism remains established and incontrovertible. J. N. Ogilvie's descriptions of Christian missions as 'the Empire's conscience' and the 'soul of the Empire'[15] in his Duff Lecture of 1924 have been echoed by historians,[16] even though many of them have emphasized the ways in which missionaries objected to its 'treatment of subject peoples'.[17] One could make three observations on the Welsh mission as a form of cultural imperialism. The key question here is why were self-conscious members of a linguistic and cultural minority prepared to undermine the cultural autonomy of others? Nigel Jenkins suggests that they did so because they had, during the previous century, so brutally remade their own culture. They were prepared to transform others because they had transformed themselves. This is a powerful argument, though the question could be approached differently. The ambivalent, even at times contemptuous, attitudes which some missionaries held towards the leadership of the church in Wales suggest that they regarded themselves as role models for evangelists at home. It was precisely the knowledge that they had not won the war in Wales that drove the missionaries, particularly in the early decades of the twentieth century, to regard themselves as the embodiment of the evangelist spirit of early Calvinism, the true voices of the faith, whose work would promote the continued evangelization of their home country as well as their adopted one. But if they appeared as remote, even formidably austere, figures among their brethren in Wales, they may have been equally incongruous in the mission field. The highly specific nature of their theology, and its cultural and linguistic packaging, is likely to have projected an oddly fragmented or even confused image of the imperial power. On balance, it appears to me that the history of the Welsh mission, certainly in the Sylheti plains but perhaps even in the hills, is broadly consistent with Andrew Porter's evaluation of missionaries generally as being weak agents of cultural imperialism.[18]

But if missionaries were 'weak agents' in that particular sense, what appears to be clear from the evidence is that they were quite significant agents of cultural communication. In this too they addressed the same two audiences, converts and potential converts in the mission field, but also their church and their readers at home. Missionaries formed the link between the two worlds of Wales and the field, and because it was they who played that pivotal role, the relationship the two audiences was an asymmetrical one. While few Assamese or Bengalis toured Wales (and those who did were Christian), it was the missionaries themselves who introduced, through their journalism and their physical presence on furlough, cultural elements of the field. In the inter-war years, there are reports of pupils in Welsh primary schools being taught to sing folk songs in Bengali. Women-only meetings in chapels were known as zenanas. Poems and hymns were composed which eulogized the special relationship between the peoples of Wales and north-east India.[19] And, as we have seen, films, touring exhibitions and missionary journalism kept images of the field continuously in circulation.

It is possible to read this exercise in cultural communication in two ways. One is as a form of propaganda, not only for evangelization, both at home and abroad, but also for the British Empire itself. By simultaneously extolling the spiritual byproducts of empire, and by celebrating Wales's own collaborative role in Britain's imperial project, it could be argued that missionary activity was part of the ideological apparatus that sought not only to obtain the consent of Welsh Nonconformity for the empire, but also to obtain the consent of a key Welsh social institution for Wales's own colonization within it. Here, the 'multiple identities' that are embodied in missionary self-representations fold into an overarching British and imperial sense of belonging.[20] In other words, support for the mission implied support for the empire, and of Wales's collaboration with it. That is one way of reading the political fallout of missionary activity. But other readings are also possible. These spring from a fundamental element in the missionary belief system which implies that Christianity empowers both individuals and societies, and that its adoption generates social as well as ethical transformation and improvement.[21] Gustav Warneck, in his study of the relationship between missions and culture, first published in English translation in 1888, referred to Christianity, significantly, as 'the Magna Charta of humanity',[22] and James Dennis's sociological study of missions of 1897 identified this belief as a key component of Christian missionary activity worldwide. It also infused the writing of our Welsh missionaries. Only Christianity, they argued, could liberate women, provide useful education for children, and free human beings from poverty, caste and communalism, even from colonial dependency. One does not have to share that view to admit its salience as a motivating force in the Western Christian missionary enterprise. From that fundamental conviction, in this particular case, three rather important issues arise in the missionary literature which appear to have had some effect on political attitudes and forms of thinking in Wales, particularly in the period up to the Second World War.

One is the modern evolution in Wales of the concept of nationality. In the 1880s, the Young Wales movement had drawn on U Larsing's declarations of love for his Khasi Hills during his tour of Wales twenty years earlier as a model of patriotism for the Welsh to follow.[23] In 1922, in the opening issue of Y *Cenhadwr*, Thomas Charles Edwards asked whether nations could be 'moral agents'. Influenced no doubt by the political rhetoric of David Lloyd George and others during the First World War, his answer was unequivocally in the affirmative. 'The world owes more of a debt to small nations than to the great empires', he wrote. And of Wales's role as one of those 'small nations' he noted that through its missionary activity 'our lines of communications are gradually extending through the entire earth'. This, he predicted, would in turn lead to 'a new International spirit to kill the distrust and hatred of nations . . . The political importance of the Foreign Missions will become more apparent each day. On them depends the peace of the world.'[24] Shortly afterwards, in lecture notes for a furlough tour of Wales, the missionary Revd Watcyn M. Price argued that

> The world must be treated as a unit and all the nations are equal . . . We are as nationalists, as selfish as any group of politicians . . . What would

we be saying in Wales to-day if we were put in the position of India or Africa? . . . India is challenging us to be revolutionary in everything.[25]

The emphasis in these texts on the creation of a world community through Christian missionary work was, in the following decade, reiterated even by elements on the Welsh left. In 1938, David Thomas, a leading member of the Welsh ILP, saw missionaries as having raised key international questions of social injustice and imperial oppression, and having paved the way for the League of Nations.[26] In the third reading of the Indian Independence Bill on 15 July 1947, W. R. Williams welcomed Indian Independence as a vindication, and in some respects as a culmination, of the liberating work of the Welsh mission, affirming that 'Wales will be second to none in its spirit of elation and thanksgiving on this great day in the history of India'.[27] A particular reading of the missionary experience had thus entered Welsh political thinking.

Secondly, and allied to this, one could argue that the mission provided a route into the culture for anti-imperialist ideas about race, difference and power. It is clear that the experience of some Welsh missionaries in India enabled them to respond positively to the work, for example, of the English missionaries J. H. Oldham and Basil Matthews, on race and the politics of inequality. These mounted critiques of Lothrop Stoddard's national and racial chauvinism[28] and sympathetically discussed leftist analyses of racial politics in the United States. For Oldham 'racial problems . . . [were] to a large extent social, political and economic problems', and in that light he criticized the 'ethics of Empire'.[29] Both Oldham's *Christianity and the Race Problem* and Basil Matthews's *The Clash of Colour: A Study in the Problem of Race* were published in 1924, and in 1926 the debate entered the pages of *Y Cenhadwr*, with articles on 'the colour problem' which endorsed and developed Oldham's general position.[30] I cannot find any other genre of Welsh-language writing at the time that addresses the international politics of race in this way.

Finally, and this has been discussed by Margaret Strobel, Aparnu Basu and others, the belief in the liberating potential of Christianity was held to apply particularly to the condition of women.[31] As early as 1887, Sarah Jane Rees (Cranogwen), as editor of *Y Frythones* (The British Woman), had welcomed the church's decision to appoint single women as missionaries as a development that presaged a better future for Welsh women as a whole.[32] Missionary work not only provided women with greater professional opportunities than were available at home, it also gave them greater status, visibility and a degree of influence, both in the field and at home, than they might otherwise have enjoyed. It may be feasible to argue, then, that alongside the imperial message of the mission, it also helped develop new ways of thinking about nationhood, international relations and the politics of race and gender that acquired some currency, at least, in the inter-war years.

This brief exploration of the discourses of missionary writing suggests two matters of some significance. First, that we need to know much more than we now do about the Welsh mission in Assam/ Bengal, and secondly that we need to consider not only the manner in which Wales, through its missionary work, affected Indians, but also how Nonconformist evangelization in India affected the Welsh. A fuller history of the mission, and the ways in which missionary work was articulated and received back home in Wales, may cast Nonconformist Wales in the nineteenth and early twentieth centuries in a more complex light, one where the empire, and the idea of Britain itself, may be subjected to new forms of scrutiny.

Notes

*A fuller version of this chapter may be found in Aled Jones, *Welsh Missionary Journalism in India, 1880–1947* (Currents in World Christianity Position Paper 123, Cambridge, 2000).

[1] Eastern Bengal was separated from Assam and reunited with Bengal in 1912, *The Imperial Gazetteer of India*, vol. xxvi, *Atlas* (Oxford, 1909), pl. 30.

[2] Most histories are by retired missionaries, the most informative being the following 3-volume series: Ednyfed Thomas, *Bryniau'r Glaw* (Caernarfon, 1988); J. Meirion Lloyd, *Y Bannau Pell* (Caernarfon, 1989); D. G. Merfyn Jones, *Y Popty Poeth a'i Gyffiniau* (Caernarfon, 1990). See also Aled Jones, '"Meddylier am India": Tair Taith y Genhadaeth Gymreig yn Sylhet, 1887–1947', *Transactions of the Honourable Society of Cymmrodorion* (THSC), 1997, NS 4 (1998), 84–110, and Jane Aaron, 'Slaughter and salvation: British imperialism in nineteenth-century Welsh women's writing', *New Welsh Review*, 38 (October 1997), 38–46 and this volume chapter 2.

[3] B. C. Allen, CS, *Assam District Gazetteers*, vol. x, *The Khasi and Jaintia Hills, the Garo Hills and the Lushai Hills* (Allahabad, 1906), Part I, p. 66.

[4] *Y Cenhadwr* (December 1928), 236.

[5] R. J. Williams, 'Un o'r Arloeswyr: Elizabeth Williams, Sylhet', *Y Goleuad* (7 September 1917), 5. See occasional series on 'Yr Oriel Genhadol', in *Y Cenhadwr* for biographies and photographic portraits.

[6] Numbers of Welsh speakers in Wales over the age of three totalled 766,103 in 1921, peaking at 811,329 in 1931. For further details, consult L. J. Williams, *Digest of Welsh Historical Statistics* (Cardiff, 1985), i, 86–8.

[7] Elizabeth Williams, *Y Offeiriades Hindwaidd. Hanes Bywyd Chundra Lela* (1908). This text was previously translated into English by Ada Lee in 1903.

[8] Helen J. Rowlands and Hridesh Ranjan Ghose, *Sermons and Sayings of Sadhu Sundar Singh during his Visit to the Khasi Hills, Assam, March 1924* (Sylhet, 1924).

[9] Miss E. A. Roberts, 'Y Cronicl Cenhadol', *Y Drysorfa* (December 1902), 570.

[10] John Pengwern Jones introduced the eisteddfod to Sylhet in 1904, and Helen Rowlands later held eisteddfodau in Bengali in Karimganj, J. Meirion Lloyd, *Nine Missionary Pioneers: The Story of Nine Pioneering Missionaries in North-east India* (Caernarfon, 1989), 7.

[11] *Report of the Foreign Mission* (1910), xiii.

[12] Parch. T. Charles Edwards, 'Gair i Gychwyn', *Y Cenhadwr* (January 1922), 2.

[13] *Y Cenhadwr* (December 1923), 189–90. See also Susan Fleming McAllister, 'Cross-cultural dress in Victorian British missionary narratives: dressing for eternity', in John C. Hawley, *Historicizing Christian Encounters with the Other* (Basingstoke, 1998), esp. 123–4.

[14] *The Link* (March–April 1935), 18.

[15] J. N. Ogilvie, *Our Empire's Debt to Missions: The Duff Missionary Lecture 1923* (London, 1924), x, 253.

[16] Donald Harman Akenson, *The Irish Diaspora: A Primer* (Toronto, 1993), 146.

[17] Brian Stanley, *The Bible and the Flag: Protestant Missions and British Imperialism in the Nineteenth and Twentieth Centuries* (Leicester, 1990), 179.

[18] A. N. Porter, 'Cultural imperialism and Protestant missionary enterprise 1780–1914', *Journal of Imperial and Commonwealth History* (1997), 25/3, 367–91.

[19] Maldwyn C. John, *Hanes Bywyd a Gwaith Mrs Esther Lewis – Cenhades, 1887–1958* (Swansea, 1996), 15–16.

[20] See Laurence Brockliss and David Eastwood (eds), *A Union of Multiple Identities: The British Isles, c.1750–1850* (Manchester, 1997), esp. 208 on the 'more positive' British identity that emerged in the late nineteenth century with the 'experience and management of Empire'. In Scotland, '(m)issionaries unquestionably stimulated a belief in a profoundly Scottish contribution to empire-building', John M. MacKenzie, 'Essay and Reflection: On Scotland and the Empire', *International History Review*, 15 (1993), 728.

[21] James S. Dennis, *Christian Missions and Social Progress: A Sociological Study of Foreign Missions* (London, 1897), 408.

[22] Gustav Warneck, *Modern Missions and Culture: Their Mutual Relations*, trans. Thomas Smith (Edinburgh, 1888), p. xxii.

[23] S. T. Jones, 'Cymry Cymreig', *Cymry Fydd* (April 1889), 381. U Larsing was, in 1846, among the first to be converted by Welsh missionaries in Khasia. He travelled to Wales in 1860, where he died in 1863. He is buried in Chester, *Y Cenhadwr* (November 1922), 164.

[24] Charles Edwards, 'Gair i Gychwyn', 2.

[25] Revd Watcyn M. Price, 'The call of India: notes for a lecture' (n.d.), National

Library of Wales CMA GZ/53.

[26] David Thomas, *Y Ddinasyddiaeth Fawr* (Wrexham, 1938), 79–82.

[27] *Parliamentary Debates (Hansard)*, 5th series, vol. 440, col. 271. Williams was MP for Heston and Isleworth.

[28] Stoddard (1883–1950) had proposed that 'civilization is the body, the race is the soul', Lothrop Stoddard, *The Rising Tide of Colour against White World-Supremacy* (London, 1920). See also his *Revolt against Civilization: The Menace of the Under Man* (London, 1922).

[29] J. H. Oldham, *Christianity and the Race Problem* (London, 1924), 248 and 94. Oldham was Secretary to the International Missionary Council and editor of the *International Review of Missions*. See also Basil Matthews, *The Clash of Colour: A Study in the Problem of Race* (London, 1924), published by the United Council for Missionary Education. For his treatment of DuBois and Marcus Garvey, see 75–6. CMS 'Schemes of Study' are also revealing in this respect, see in particular *Indian Problems and the Christian Message: A Scheme of Study* (London, 1926) on 'the national ideal', and *India – Whither Bound? A Scheme of Study* (London, 1930), especially 'India's women: discuss "the women's movement in India holds the key to progress"', 8.

[30] *Y Cenhadwr* (March 1926), 41–4.

[31] Margaret Strobel, *European Women and the Second British Empire* (Bloomington, IN, 1991). Also Nupur Chaudhuri and Margaret Strobel (eds), *Western Women and Imperialism: Complicity and Resistance* (Bloomington, IN, 1992).

[32] Cranogwen, 'Dyfodol Merched Cymru', *Y Frythones* (July 1887), 202.

4 Apes and Cannibals in Cambria: Literary Representations of the Racial and Gendered Other[1]

KIRSTI BOHATA

The late eighteenth- and nineteenth-century project to define the distinctive ethnological and 'racial' features of the peoples of empire (as well as the various types of European) had a profound influence on the way different races, nationalities, cultures and even classes were viewed. Fundamental to this project were the supposedly empirical sciences of anthropology, such as physiology, phrenology and craniology. The forms of 'knowledge' derived from these studies became part of the popular consciousness and, despite the complex characteristics of cultures and peoples, powerful stereotypes were constructed which often denied realities or, indeed, even worked to alter reality.[2] While the theories behind the nineteenth-century project of ethnographic cartography have been discredited,[3] the images which were so enthusiastically taken up by the Victorian popular and periodical press remain in many respects meaningful signifiers into the present.

H. L. Malchow has already shown how texts such as Mary Shelley's *Frankenstein* (1818) consciously or unconsciously draw upon stereotypes of race when portraying fearful or threatening characters or scenarios.[4] Malchow's work purports to be a study of 'British' literature and, as is so often the case, this generally refers to a focus on *English* literature which fails to recognize the internal differences within this field. It is the aim of this chapter to consider how Welsh writing in English is informed by stereotypes of race and the discourses of colonialism and science. In addition, some attention will also be given to the way these discourses were implicated in the construction and management of gender identity in Wales. As will become clear, although the models discussed by Malchow are highly relevant, Welsh literature and the Welsh reader are in a more complicated position. As complicit and instrumental within the British Empire, as part of Britain, Wales and the Welsh enjoyed the status of being located well within the imperial metropole. Yet as a nation within the United Kingdom Wales finds itself outside the centre – England (or perhaps more accurately, London), its culturally and politically dominant neighbour, and therefore the Welsh themselves may be constructed as marginal or threatening Other in terms which are derived from racial, colonial discourses.

As the work of those such as Gayatri Spivak and H. L. Malchow reveals, negative stereotypes of race abound in the canonical texts of English literature, and it is not difficult to find an equal abundance of such material in Welsh writing in English. Margiad Evans (1909–58), Rhys Davies (1901–78) and Arthur Machen (1863–1947) are all significant literary presences in Welsh writing in English and, in so far as it is possible to describe any Welsh writing in English as canonical, these three writers are certainly important figures. The texts selected for discussion in this short essay, however, are merely illustrative of a much wider incidence of such imagery in Welsh writing in English. Much of this essay is concerned with gothic literature: Arthur Machen's chilling tales of the Welsh borders tend to use racial stereotyping more or less subconsciously, while Margiad Evans's story can be read to highlight the way various images of Otherness interact and inform one another. The story with which this essay concludes, 'The Chosen One' (1966) by Rhys Davies, has been included for the way the author makes deliberate and illuminating use of the discourses of anthropology in the text. Before attending to the discourses of race, gender and anthropology as they are present in these Welsh texts, however, we need first to briefly consider their wider provenance in the nineteenth-century discourses of race and empire.

It has become customary to draw attention to the similarities between patriarchy and imperialism, yet the uncomfortable premise that these two discourses firmly unite on the site of the black female body is less well documented.[5] Here one may see the discourses of racism taken to their extremes, for black women were considered to be the lowest humans in the eighteenth-century[6] hierarchy of creation known as the 'great chain of being'. The (crudely conceived) Black Woman became a highly sexualized construct and racial distinctness was asserted through the (mis)construction of black female genitalia and secondary sexual parts, particularly the buttocks, as pathological, as grotesque *deviations* from the white norm. The case of Saartje Baartman (later known as Sarah Bartmann, although her original name is not recorded) is the paradigmatic example. Baartman, who came from South Africa, was exhibited in London and Paris between 1810 and her death in 1815 as the 'Hottentot Venus'. She wore a costume which allowed the audience to appreciate her protruding buttocks and large breasts and these generated great interest among scientists and the public alike. Although she firmly resisted genital examination while she was alive, Saartje Baartman was dissected in Paris after her death and Georges Cuvier found an overdevelopment of the labia minora, which he described as the Hottentot Apron.[7] This genital formation was pathologized, in that it was seen to be abnormal and undesirable, yet it was also believed to be common to the racial group to which Baartman belonged and therefore this whole group could be considered to be pathological. Furthermore, this signifier of racial difference/pathology was linked to supposedly deviant manifestations of female sexuality, in particular those associated with an 'excessive' female libido, such as prostitution. Later in the nineteenth century, another variety of supposedly pathological female sexuality, lesbianism, came to be associated with Baartman's genitalia. Sander Gilman observes:

> The author, H. Hildebrandt [writing in 1877[8]], links this malformation [the 'Hottentot apron'] with the overdevelopment of the clitoris, which he sees as leading to those 'excesses' which 'are called "lesbian love"'. The concupiscence of the black is thus associated with the sexuality of the lesbian.[9]

Interestingly, Lisa Moore suggests that the 'over-development' of the clitoris, which Hildebrandt associates with lesbianism, was a common feature in 'the discursive representation of the [lesbian] body that came back from voyages of colonial exploration'.[10] Moore describes how the supposedly pathological sexuality of the lesbian was portrayed as a common characteristic of the 'Hindoo'. In an 1811 court case in which two women brought a libel case against the guardian of a former pupil of theirs who claimed she had witnessed the two teachers indulging in 'indecent and criminal practices',[11] the judgment finally rested on a belief that race was a primary factor in determining the sexuality of an individual. That is, in trying to account for how such a young girl might have imagined her story at all, the ' "Hindoo" background', or mixed race, of the witness (she was born in India to an Indian mother and a British father) was established as the cause of her vivid imagination and false testimony.[12]

Thus, we may see how the ostensibly unrelated discourses of race and sexuality inform and influence each other. The recognition of the inter-relation of such discourses in our rereading of 'white' texts has been one of the most significant contributions of post-colonial studies. For example, the discourses which construct upper- and middle-class white Victorian women as prone to madness, hysteria and irrationality are now understood to be entwined with those that pathologized the non-white. It makes little sense, therefore, to discuss the construction of one manifestation of Otherness – be it homo-sexuality, race, class or gender difference and so on – without simultaneously recognizing the influence of a variety of inter-related discourses of Otherness.

The interaction of the various images of cannibalism, witchcraft and lesbianism in constructions of white women as Other may be seen, for instance, in Margiad Evans's short story 'A Modest Adornment' (1948) and such interaction illustrates how racialized discourses intrude into areas which might formerly have been read in solely white gendered or gay terms.[13] The story focuses on the death of an elderly woman, a lesbian, in a state of apparent neglect and the way her lifelong partner deals with her demise. Miss Allensmore's reaction (or lack of it) to the slow death of Miss Plant is in sharp juxtaposition to the response of an elderly widow in the village who has begun to idolize Miss Plant – an affection that hints at the possibility of a less destructive homosexual, or at least homoerotic, relationship. Despite a moving ending which testifies to the old love between Miss Allensmore and Miss Plant, it is difficult for the reader to sanction Miss Allensmore's apparent selfishness during the last days of her partner's life. Indeed, Miss Allensmore might easily be read as a typical representation of a witch, so drawing on old European constructions of female Others. She lives without male company, outside of the village. She is described as a 'fat black cauldron of a woman' (235). She keeps a hoard of black cats, and even Miss Plant takes on some resemblance to a cat, with her 'great silky green eyes' in which 'there was a curious sort of threat' (235). Suggestive of another traditional witches' familiar, her bare feet are 'as dark as toads' (238). The chips she makes are 'long and warped and as gaunt as talons' (238) and her house is festooned with 'sagging black cobwebs' (238). Yet the interpretation of these features in terms of popular conceptions of the witch are complicated by the subtle but persistent images of cannibalism in the story, and these are not divorced from the fact of Miss Allensmore's sexual orientation.

Black cauldrons may be typical of witches, but large, people-sized cauldrons are also the staple of popular portrayals of (black) cannibals. Miss Allensmore's cooking habits suggest the fabled savagery of cannibals: from the kitchen comes the perpetual sound of 'furious frying or the grumpy sound of some pudding in the pot, bouncing and grunting like a goblin locked in a cupboard' (236). Miss Allensmore's appetite for food is emphasized at every opportunity, even her letters are sent by the baker, and our first glimpse of her sees her eating sweets. Elsewhere, Miss Allensmore drops grease on her naked, blackened feet (which are suggestive of the black 'savage' as well as of edible flesh); while she 'lick[s] away' an inappropriate half smile 'with the point of her tongue' (237); she regularly squats (a 'primitive' posture) or sits in front of a 'great fire' almost cooking her own body, her 'fat, soft flesh that looked as if it had been mixed with yeast, all naked and flushing' (248); even more explicitly, she is described by a villager as 'sit[ting] on top of a great fire a-frying [her]self' (245). There is the continual suggestion that Miss Allensmore has somehow devoured Miss Plant – Miss Allensmore is fat in contrast to the emaciated Miss Plant – although it is Miss Allensmore's body that is more obviously edible. The cannibalistic overtones are clear: this is a woman whose appetite is so voracious that she seems to have eaten her partner, a notion reminiscent of the purported behaviour of some South American women who were supposed to eat their lovers after sex, rather like some species of mantis.[14] The association of appetite and sexuality and the perceived excesses of these is clear, while the link between ambiguous sexuality, gender and food is established in the opening line of the story: ' "Bull's eyes are boys' sweets," said Miss Allensmore and popped one in her mouth' (235).

Yet, if the stereotypes of lesbianism, cannibalism, race and witchcraft may be seen to converge in this story, the 'authenticity' of such constructions is challenged. Miss Allensmore *is* constructed as thoroughly Other, and her refusal to conform to recognized feminine norms is accentuated by the contrast provided by Mrs Webb (Miss

Plant's caring admirer), as well as the nurse who attends Miss Plant. However, such dichotomies are problematized, and the image of Miss Allensmore as Other is subverted not only by the romantic 'subplot' (which describes the young, sensually alert Miss Plant making a slow pilgrimage, on foot, to London 'just to say to her [Miss Allensmore], "I can no longer bear to live away from you"' (259)), but also in the way the reader is subtly encouraged to reassess the nature of Miss Allensmore's appetites. For example, the disapproval of the nurse when Miss Allensmore makes chips as Miss Plant lies dying upstairs apparently links her appetite for food with 'unnatural' feelings. She seems uncaring, and cooking and eating at such a time is certainly a rejection of the customs surrounding a death; however, there is also a strong suggestion that it is the *way* that Miss Allensmore cares that is unacceptable. After Miss Plant has died, Miss Allensmore sits alone in her cottage and plays her clarinet through the night – a form of music she knows has never been understood and of which, hearing it drifting from her cottage, the villagers sternly disapprove.

The painful conclusion of the story confirms Miss Allensmore's love and not only reveals the unreliability of the narrative perspective, which may have encouraged the reader to condemn Miss Allensmore's apparently heartless behaviour, it also challenges the distortive gloss of the language of stereotype. The reader is forced to recognize that we have only glimpsed Miss Allensmore as she is characterized by village gossip – she remains throughout the story a distant, problematic and rather intangible figure. This is emphasized when Miss Allensmore returns to her cottage after Miss Plant's funeral at the end of the story; she papers over her windows and shuts herself off completely from the world, significantly excluding the reader too.

Images of witchcraft, lesbianism, cannibalism and blackness can be seen to converge around notions of excess and deviancy in 'A Modest Adornment', yet the fear of female sexuality and racial difference is not confined to these discourses alone. If the external physiology of black women provided the supposedly empirical evidence of their Otherness, then the internal organs of reproduction were no less a focus for the construction of the female body as pathological during the eighteenth and nineteenth centuries.[15] In this model of disease, the womb is seen as the cause of illness in the female body, perhaps the most extreme version of this being the phenomenon of the 'wandering womb' which could move freely around the female body and suck blood from the woman's brain (the connotations of vampirism/cannibalism are not insignificant here) rendering her weak and prone to insanity.[16] Yet, in racial terms, the womb poses perhaps the greatest threat of all in terms of its reproductive function, for it is the site of contamination, of mis-cegenation, of the corruption of the perceived purity of the races. While black women frequently, as slaves, bore the products of rape – the offspring of their white masters – it is the white woman's womb that is perceived as the greatest threat to racial purity, particularly with reference to the fears of 'black blood' going unnoticed in white society, of 'passing'.

There are all sorts of connotations attached to 'black blood'. For example, it was suggested in the eighteenth century that black people had black bile and even black blood, which caused the skin to appear black. That black bile had been considered a sign of illness since medieval times did nothing to undermine the idea that black skin was in itself a pathological indicator. Thus, black blood was believed to be the undesirable cause of black skin and, given the notions that black people were either a more primitive version of humanity or a degenerate form, the mixing of the races – the contamination of white blood – was to be feared. Thomas Jefferson, whilst noting the detrimental effects of slavery upon both slaves and slavers, justifies its continuation thus:

> Among the Romans, emancipation required but one effort. The slave, when made free, might *mix* with, without *staining* the blood of his master. But with us a second is necessary, unknown to history. When freed, he is to be removed beyond the reach of *mixture*.[17]

It is precisely this fear of 'mixture' that underlies and, indeed, provides much of the resonance, of the work of Arthur Machen. Machen's fiction concerns itself with ancient evils that predate known history and perhaps even time itself. Many of Machen's stories are set among the border hills of Wales, littered with ancient, pre-Christian *meini hirion* (megalithic stones), or else in a polite London society infiltrated by ancient pagan forces or deities. However, Machen's stories of the 1890s are dominated by very con-temporary concerns of racial purity and degeneration. In 'The Great God Pan' (1894) evil is visited upon polite society in the form of an apparently beautiful woman who is in fact the grotesque product of a coupling between a woman and the devil (although the conception seems to have been 'immaculate' rather than physical). The real threat posed by this woman lies in the invisibility of her hybridity: she *passes*. A similar union between humankind and the beings of hell is the subject of another of Machen's stories, 'The Novel of the Black Seal' (1895), where a young woman gives birth to a demonic hybrid eight months after being discovered in a distressed state alone on top of a mysterious hill. The little boy is living proof of the protagonist's belief in:

> stories of mothers who have left a child quietly sleeping, with the cottage door rudely barred with a piece of wood, and have returned, not to find the plump and rosy little Saxon, but a thin and wizened creature, with sallow skin and black piercing eyes, *the child of another race*. Then, again, there were myths darker still; the . . . hint of demons who *mingled* with the daughters of men.[18] (My emphasis.)

The sallow skin is suggestive of the unhealthy, but there is also a strong hint of racial ambiguity. The piercing eyes are signifiers of the demonic in gothic literature and here, combined with the non-white skin, suggest that races other than the idealized image of this healthy *Saxon* are themselves demonic. Given the equation of the scientist with explorer or discoverer in this story and the fact that the text suggests that the mythology of the Celts may provide a link with the forgotten people or powers sought by the scientist, the implicit suggestion is one of the English (Saxon) imperial rationalist risking all amongst the dark, forbidding and thoroughly *Other* Welsh (Celts). It seems clear that the reader is supposed to identify with the rosy Saxon rather than 'the child of another race', which may be problematic for Welsh readers who find themselves excluded from the implied audience. It might be illuminating to read the ambiguity of this issue of identification as powerfully expressive of the fears of a 'border' or 'split' identity, which appears to aspire to identify with Englishness while fearing the 'contamination' of an undesirable Welshness.

It is worth examining 'The Novel of the Black Seal' in greater detail here, as it provides a good illustration of how the gothic genre, which relies heavily upon references that are recognizable to the reader as significations of the unnatural, the uncanny or downright

evil, is heavily indebted to racist colonial discourses that give meaning to these collective signifiers of terror. Significantly, the protagonist of 'The Novel of the Black Seal' is not only a scientist, but 'an
authority of ethnology and kindred subjects' (3) and this Professor's
dedication to scientific rationalism is plainly asserted. The main part
of the story is set in Monmouthshire and the portrayal of the countryside is central to the creation of a suitably oppressive and
foreboding atmosphere; significantly, the landscape is described in
terms immediately recognizable as reminiscent of colonial texts
which portray foreign landscapes and peoples as strange and
implicitly threatening. The hills are repeatedly referred to as 'wild',
and 'savage'; rocks are of 'fantastic form'. The Professor's investigations themselves are referred to in the language of territorial
exploration and discovery; he himself admits that 'I covet the renown
of Columbus; you will, I hope, see me play the part of an explorer'
(9). And later his quest is described as an attempt to find 'the
undiscovered continent', which he believes to be peopled with 'a race
which had fallen out of the grand march of evolution' (34). The
nature of the 'lost' people is particularly fascinating – not only are
they referred to in overtly colonial terms, these primitive people are
sought in the *Welsh* countryside. In the Professor's closing statement
this scientist/explorer confesses himself to have been 'especially
drawn to consider the stories of the fairies, the good folk of the
Celtic races' (32).

Indeed, the Professor apparently does discover one of this strange
race: the child of dubious paternity who was conceived on the hills.
The boy is subject to fits during which his face becomes 'swollen and
blackened to a hideous mask of humanity' (22) and he speaks an
unintelligible language which is associated with a lack of evolution-
ary 'progress', being described as 'words . . . that might have
belonged to a tongue dead since untold ages and buried deep beneath
Nilotic mud, or in the inmost recesses of the Mexican forest' (22).
Here the conflation of the primitive and the colonial is explicit once
more, and this is furthered by the later description of a bestial race
which 'lagged so far behind the rest . . . such a folk would speak a
jargon but little removed from the inarticulate noises of brute beasts'
(34). It is interesting, then, that one word the boy uses whilst
speaking this 'primitive language' is repeated to the local Welsh-
speaking parson in order to obtain a translation. To be fair, the
Professor himself does not think it *is* a Welsh word, yet the

connotations are unavoidable and it may be assumed that the implied reader would not find the confusion between this demonic language and the exotic Welsh language, with its foreign sounding 'll's, at all incongruous.

Although Machen has been described as highly influenced by Darwinian notions of evolution,[19] it is important to note that he is still shackled by the belief in *progression* which characterized earlier constructions of the 'Great Chain of Being', and Machen's stories ultimately play upon fears of racial *degeneration* which is portrayed as the opposite or reverse of (progressive) evolution. In 'The Great God Pan', Helen, the incarnation of evil, regresses through the stages of evolution as she dies. What is significant here is the language used to describe the process (the following italicization is mine):

> Though . . . an odour of corruption choked my breath, I remained firm . . . [T]hat which was on the bed, lying there black like ink, transformed before my eyes . . . I saw the form waver from sex to sex . . . Then I saw the body *descend* to the beasts whence it *ascended*, and that which was on the *heights* go down to the *depths*, even to the *abyss* of all being . . . I watched and saw nothing but a substance as jelly. Then the *ladder was ascended* again.[20]

The repetition of the hierarchical image of creation speaks for itself. While this might not initially seem to be associated with any racial/racist imagery, the description as a whole reveals the influence of racial stereotypes. The blackness of the form lying on the bed is an obvious indicator, but so too is the malodorousness of the creature. Bad odour is yet another example of the conjunction and conflation of many discourses concerned with Others/Otherness. H. L. Malchow suggests that body odour was the focus of an obsession which failed to find a place in polite discourse and so emerges in gothic fiction associated with constructions of Otherness:

> If one also considers the strong body odor associated in racist discourse with the animalistic African or with the unpleasant odors associated with the Jew . . . as well as that ascribed to prostitutes (owing, it was thought, to the retention of semen) and to menstruating women, it is clear that scent played a role in drawing together or bridging a surprising number of nineteenth century middle-class prejudices. The discourses of racism, homophobia, misogyny, class hatred, and religious bigotry were all corroborated by this most penetrating of the physical senses.[21]

It is no surprise, then, that Miss Allensmore's home in 'A Modest Adornment' is described as housing a 'prowling smell' (239), the adjective conjuring animalistic and predatory images. The strong smell remarked upon in Machen's 'The Novel of the Black Seal', which is associated with the boy/demon, also has bestial connotations:

> There was a queer sort of smell in the study when I came down and opened the windows [relates the maid, after one of the boy's 'fits']; a bad smell it was, and I wondered what it could be. Do you know miss, I went a long time ago to the zoo in London . . . and we went into the snake house to see the snakes, and it was just the same sort of smell; very sick it made me feel . . . (28)

And if the boy and his malodourousness is, albeit tentatively, associated with the Welsh in this story, the Welsh themselves were not above invoking bad smells in a racist context. In a study of racism and immigration in Wales, Neil Evans cites the instance of a Welsh miner who asserted the need for colour segregation (or more probably exclusion) in the mines on the basis that 'black people smelled so badly that even boys couldn't work with them!'[22]

Science, and the figure of the scientist, are important ingredients of gothic (science) fiction. The influence of racial/colonial discourses which relied heavily on science – from medicine through to anthropology and ethnology and even philology – to justify and rationalize the imperial project are also to be found in other genres. The final story examined here, 'The Chosen One', by Rhys Davies, is heavily and self-consciously informed by the language and practices of (colonial) anthropology. The now infamous image of the anthropologist equipped with callipers taking cranial measurements in order to assert a hierarchical evaluation of intellectual capabilities based on skull shape and size might be seen as the epitome of the scientist as imperialist and patriarch;[23] both non-whites and women, for example, were alleged to be intellectually inferior to white men in this way. Yet brain size and intellect were not the only areas anthropologists felt able to comment upon based on their physiological observations and it is in the obviously subjective values which are stated as objective scientific truths that we may find an important aspect of the demonization of Others. In his anthropological study, *The Races of Britain* (1885), John Beddoe attempts to describe the so-called racial elements which exist on the island through the cranial statistics and the colours of eyes and hair. Nor were Beddoe and his contemporaries above commenting upon the 'character' as well as the appearance of certain groups studied, and the seamless ease with which they pass from hair colour to descriptions of obstinacy or rudeness is disturbing.

Such anthropological practices are tested and manipulated in Rhys Davies's typically curious story. In 'The Chosen One', a Welsh, working-class tenant of a cottage his family have inhabited for many generations is fighting to renew the lease with the anglicized (or possibly English?) lady of the house. The way in which the working classes are constructed as Other by the more privileged classes is certainly an important issue here, but the significance of the racial, or rather national, implications of the story ought not to be overlooked. The historical relationship between Wales and England seems to be echoed in the details we are given about the way the cottage and some land was obtained rather deceitfully from a Welsh family by the owners of the larger estate. That the aristocratic family made money through such small-scale empire-building, through the expansion of the (industrial) railways which elsewhere were a vital component of the colonial project, and that they grossly underpaid for this land while making misleading promises about the cottage lease, places the story in a colonial as well as a class context. The tenant, Rufus, displays many simian characteristics and his Welshness is contrasted with the apparent non-Welshness of the anthropologist, whose very class distances her from her Welsh surroundings. The dark curly hair, low brow and stocky build sound as if they come from a description of a Welshman in Beddoe's *Races of Britain*, and the lady of the house lives as remotely cut off from her neighbours as if she was a white settler in an African or Indian colony.[24]

Indeed, the anthropological overtones of the story are explicit; Mrs Vines has 'lived among African savages, studying their ways with her first husband',[25] has African masks adorning her walls, keeps a sheep's skull because of the 'purity' of its breeding, and views her tenant as a fascinating specimen, intensely observing his movements through binoculars. What is particularly fascinating are the descriptions of the tenant and his girlfriend in the overtly bestial terms so familiar from studies of African peoples. Rufus 'prowls' around his garden, he has 'full-fleshed lips' (1), and lives in a house Mrs Vines declares to be unfit for human habitation. She tells him

'You are almost as hairy as an ape' and shows the obligatory interest in his genitals, commenting that 'your organs are exceptionally pronounced' (31). His girlfriend, meanwhile, is distinguished by her tendency to shriek, and she is referred to by Mrs Vines as a 'jazz-dancing slut' with 'bare feet' (2). The combined reference to sexual promiscuity and the style of music and dancing which originated in black America suggest both the degeneracy of the working-class prostitute and the sensual black 'savage'. The connotations are of the primitive, the degenerate, and are described in the terms of anthropology:

> To her eye, the prognathous jaw, broad nose, and gypsy-black hair of this heavy-bodied but personable young man bore distinct atavistic elements. He possessed, too, a primitive bloom, which often lingered for years beyond adolescence with persons of tardy mental development. (12)

The prognathous jaw is associated with the mentally, racially and socially inferior; the broad nose draws parallels with the Negro, as does the racially ambiguous 'gypsy-black hair' (12). That these are racial, or hereditary, rather than accidental is emphasized by the fact that they are 'distinct *atavistic* elements' (12) (my emphasis).

In using an authorial narrative voice to describe what are effectively the anthropologist's observations, which typically run from physical appearance to assumptions of character and mental capacity, Rhys Davies draws attention to the complicity of literature with such constructions and parodies self-referential academic/scientific language used in such discourses to assert and maintain authority (Mrs Vines's letter giving notice of eviction uses language that is deliberately opaque in order to emphasize her power over her tenant). Furthermore, the story becomes almost a deconstruction of the methods of suggestion employed by some forms of literature, particularly, but by no means exclusively, the gothic. By this I mean to suggest that the anthropologist reads physical 'signs' much in the same way that a reader interprets 'literary' signs littered about the text, signs which are interpreted according to fixed conventions such as, to give a simplistic example, the association of the colour black with evil or rural isolation with an 'uncivilized' or 'savage' threat – references which are not innocently contained within an arbitrary literary convention but which continually refer back to social and cultural discourses.[26]

The intimacy of the relationship between racial stereotypes, which were the product of supposedly empirical scientific research, and the 'domestic' discourses of imperial nations becomes clear when the intriguing dialectic which exists between them is recognized. The European colonialist's perception of non-whites is often reflected in disturbing and uncanny, even horrifying, literary figures, while such images themselves, and their fantastic exploration of European fears, reflect back upon notions of the racial Other, influencing in turn our collective 'knowledge' of the non-white.

In this chapter I have focused on the way that stereotypes of the racial and gendered Other are used in Welsh writing in English to mobilize (and indeed depend for their success upon) the pre-conceptions, prejudices and associated fears of the reader. To some extent this use of racial Otherness parallels the function such constructions serve in English literature – the racist, imperial images hold sway in both literatures and Wales was, after all, part of the metropole of the British Empire. Yet, in Welsh writing in English the quasi-colonial status of Wales as peripheral nation within the United Kingdom is reflected in the way the Welsh are themselves often cast in the role of the racial Other. The Welsh reader, then, is faced with the somewhat schizophrenic experience of functioning/responding as part of the implied (metropolitan) audience usually assumed by the texts – that is, we recognize and respond to the literary motifs of the fearful Other in a certain way – while simultaneously, we realize that we are excluded from the implied audience, from the metropolis, and often actually *belong* to the group being represented as grotesquely Other.[27]

Notes

[1] This is a revised and shortened version of an essay which first appeared as 'Apes and cannibals in Cambria: images of the racial and gendered other in Gothic writing in Wales', *Welsh Writing in English: A Yearbook of Critical Essays*, 6 (2000), 119–43.

[2] See William Schneider's 'Race and empire: the rise of popular ethnography in the late nineteenth century', *Journal of Popular Culture*, 2 (1977), 98–109.

[3] See Nancy Stepan, *The Idea of Race in Science: Great Britain 1800–1960* (London, 1982).

[4] See H. L. Malchow, *Gothic Images of Race in Nineteenth Century Britain* (Stanford, CA, 1996).

[5] There is a deplorable tendency for white Western feminists to draw analogies between the experiences of 'women' and 'blacks'; apart from the racism implicit in the distinction between 'women' and 'black women', the failure to recognize gender differences in this Other category 'black' denies to ethnocentric Western feminism an important angle on constructions of white women while failing black women completely.

[6] Arthur O. Lovejoy traces the history of the idea of the Great Chain of Being back to Greece. However, he notes that 'It was in the eighteenth century that the conception of the universe as a Chain of Being, and the principles which underlay this conception – plenitude, continuity, gradation – attained their widest diffusion and acceptance.' *The Great Chain of Being: A Study of the History of an Idea* (Cambridge, MA, 1957), 183.

[7] This 'apron' was first 'observed' by Westerners in the seventeenth century and regarded as a deformity. By the late eighteenth/early nineteenth centuries there was still much confusion over whether its origins were congenital or cultural. This confusion still persists. Some academics assume congenital causes. Others suggest that cultural mores result in the manipulation of the labia to cause elongation. Some commentators also make the important point that pendulous labia – whether congenital or cultural – should not be regarded as abnormal in any way.

[8] The *OED* lists the earliest use of the word lesbian in the context of lesbian love in 1890 in *Billings Medical Dictionary*, II, 47/1. This passage is translated from German (presumably by Sander Gilman since no other is credited).

[9] Sander L. Gilman, *Difference and Pathology* (London, 1985), 89.

[10] Lisa Moore, 'Teledildonics: virtual lesbians in the fiction of Jeanette Winterson', in Elizabeth Grosz and Elspeth Probyn (eds), *Sexy Bodies: The Strange Carnalities of Feminism* (London and New York, 1995), 121

[11] Lisa Moore, ' "Something more tender still than friendship": romantic friendship in early-nineteenth century England', *Feminist Studies*, 18/3 (Fall 1992), 514.

[12] Ibid., 516

[13] Margiad Evans, 'A Modest Adornment', in *A View Across the Valley* (Dinas Powys, 1999), ed. Jane Aaron. Subsequent references appear in parentheses in the text.

[14] See Elizabeth Grosz, 'Animal sex: libido as desire and death', in Elizabeth Grosz and Elspeth Probyn (eds), *Sexy Bodies: The Strange Carnalities of Feminism*, for a discussion of how attributes from the insect world have been projected onto female sexualities, esp. p. 281; also Bram Dijkstra, *Evil Sisters: The Threat of Female Sexuality and the Cult of Manhood* (New York, 1996).

[15] See Elaine Showalter, *The Female Malady* (London, 1987) and Jane M. Ussher, *The Psychology of the Female Body* (London, 1989).

[16] See Jane M. Ussher, *Women's Madness: Misogyny or Mental Illness?* (Hemel Hempstead, 1991), 74.

[17] Thomas Jefferson, 'Laws', from *Notes on the State of Virginia*, reproduced in *Race and the Enlightenment: A Reader*, ed. Emmanual Chkwudi Eze (Oxford, 1997), 103; my emphasis.

[18] Arthur Llewellyn Machen, 'The Novel of the Black Seal', in *Tales of Horror and the Supernatural,* with an introduction by Philip van Doren Stern (London, 1949), 33; my emphasis. Subsequent references appear in parentheses in the text.

[19] See David Punter, *The Literature of Terror: A History of Gothic Fictions from 1765 to the Present Day*, ii, *The Modern Gothic* (London, 1996).

[20] Arthur Llewellyn Machen, 'The Great God Pan', in *Tales of Horror and the Supernatural*, 111–12.

[21] H. L. Malchow, *Gothic Images of Race*, 141.

[22] Neil Evans, 'Immigrants and minorities in Wales, 1840–1990: a comparative perspective', *Llafur*, 5/4, (1991), 5–26, and this volume chapter 1.

[23] The image of the calliper-wielding scientist is invoked in literary as well as the prolific historical texts relating to the nineteenth century. In Joseph Conrad's *Heart of Darkness* (1902; Penguin, 1983), the interest of the doctor (who performs a pre-embarkation medical check) in craniology is satirized, yet he remains the vehicle by which the sinister threat of 'going native', with which the novella is so concerned, is suggested.

[24] The similarity between the descriptions of Rufus in 'The Chosen One' (see below) and David Gellatie and other villagers in *Waverley* (1814; Oxford, 1981, ed. Clare Lamont), Walter Scott's classic novel about the making of 'Britain' through the union of England and Scotland, are striking. Both are described in language which is borrowed from the discourses of anthropology and similar terms to those one would expect to find in the patronizing and derogatory texts of the colonizer referring to non-whites.

[25] Rhys Davies, 'The Chosen One', *The Chosen One and Other Stories* (London, 1967), 8. Subsequent references appear in parentheses in the text.

[26] Rhys Davies plays with such signifiers and uses them with some skill, although he never really subverts them. See Kirsti Bohata, 'The black Venus: atavistic sexualities', and Daniel Williams, 'Withered roots: ideas of race in the writings of Rhys Davies and D. H. Lawrence', in Meic Stephens (ed.), *Rhys Davies: Decoding the Hare* (Cardiff, 2001).

[27] I have suggested that the construction of the Welsh as Other, as apart from and inferior to the white English hegemony, is sometimes achieved through the deployment of racist imagery. While this remains a valid thesis, the critical analysis attempted here has focused on the implications of this construction of difference for a white Welsh population, thus contributing to the construction of the Welsh nation as racially homogeneous – as white. Ironically, a non-white Welsh reader may encounter a further level of 'splitting' or displacement. See Charlotte Williams ' "I going away, I going home": mixed-"race", movement and identity', in Lynne Pearce (ed.), *Devolving Identities: Feminist Readings in Home and Belonging* (Studies in European Cultural Transition 8) (Aldershot, 2000).

5   Hughes the Congo: The Rise and Fall of the Congo Institute

IVOR WYNNE JONES

Two days before Christmas 1911, retired textile tycoons emerged from their elegant homes in Colwyn Bay to find their haven peppered with posters proclaiming: *BLACK BAPTIST'S BROWN BABY*. The eloquent alliteration of Horatio Bottomley's notorious weekly magazine *John Bull* confirmed the worst fears of a community whose inherited wealth came from Lancashire's 'dark satanic mills', built on the forced labour of America's black cotton slaves. For three months they had lived with rumours of a black baby born to an unmarried seamstress, a phenomenon that could be attributed only to the presence in the town of the African Institute, an industrial and religious training centre for the creation of self-supporting black preachers (from either side of the Atlantic) for the evangelization of black Africa. It was a pioneering venture founded in June 1887 by the Revd William Hughes, a returned Baptist missionary, but by the time the 1911 Christmas festivities were over, his Institute, dedicated to the emancipation of black Africans, was finished.

Overnight William Hughes, a member of the town council, immediate past honorary Secretary of the Royal National Eisteddfod of Wales, and a Knight of the Liberian Order of African Redemption, became a disgraced beggar, to be expunged from the histories of Wales and the Baptist Missionary Society (BMS). Alarmed by what they read in *John Bull,* local shopkeepers refused to allow any more credit with which to feed the awesome virility of his black students, ominously described in the article as 'full-blooded men of fine physique'. Although blessed with the patronage of people such as King Leopold II of the Belgians, Welsh-born explorer Sir Henry Morton Stanley, Welsh shipping and banana magnate Sir Alfred Lewis Jones, and England's lord chief justice, Lord Coleridge,

Colwyn Bay's African Institute was compelled to close its doors through which had passed men destined to become leading personalities in Pan-African Nationalism, including Mojola Agbebi, Edward Blyden and President Joseph J. Cheeseman. They came as inquisitive visitors or as resident students, and represented an extraordinary concentration of political thought in the foreign remoteness of Colwyn Bay, where the Welsh nationalism of William Hughes found expression in Pan-Africanism. Pan-Africanism was a loose set of nationalist beliefs in the unity of all black Africans, a philosophy born out of the return to Africa of American and West Indian blacks, after the foundation of the Liberian Republic in 1847.

William Hughes, the son of a tenant farmer, was born on 8 April 1856 at a remote seventeenth-century long-house farm (now a ruin) 2 miles north of Llanystumdwy, in what was then Caernarfonshire. He was always addressed as 'William-Hughes', in a fashion then commonplace in rural Wales (where the anglicized forename Hughes meant 'son of Hugh'). He never had cause to use his surname – unlike his brother Daniel Evans, who stayed at the farm until 1921. The language of this sparsely populated community, known as Ynys, was entirely Welsh, and there was never a school. He was born into an isolated world where he would be expected to spend his life as a farm labourer, with neither the money nor the education to explore beyond the fields in which he worked. His parents failed to cultivate curiosity in the occasional activity at the small Baptist chapel – Capel y Beirdd – only 350 yards away at the southern boundary of the farm, and William Hughes was seventeen years of age before he was 'converted to Christianity' after he had walked to Garndolbenmaen with friends for his first visit to a church. 'An earnest prayer at the commencement of the service decided me for Christ', said Hughes nine years later, when writing to Alfred H. Baynes, secretary of the Baptist Missionary Society.[1]

He joined Capel y Beirdd, where two years of valuable contacts made him literate, and it was at the chapel, in 1875, that he listened to a lecture on Dr Livingstone's mission in Africa, and Denbigh-born H. M. Stanley's famous greeting in 1871. While walking back to his home Hughes became a lifelong admirer of Stanley. He was told he could not become a student at the Welsh Baptist College, Llangollen, until he learnt English. Never having ventured more than 4 or 5 miles from home, he set off in April 1875 'unable to understand the simplest English sentence', and found a job as a farm labourer in

Cheshire. Eight months later he had learned enough English to move on to his finishing school – a large drapers' shop in Manchester. By 1877 he was sufficiently fluent to become a Sunday school teacher in Moss Side, where he bought a copy of *The Missionary Herald*. He was entranced by the heading 'Africa for Christ', and news of plans to set up a Baptist Mission in the Congo.[2] It was two years before the BMS team arrived at São Salvador (in July 1879), and on 14 August H. M. Stanley turned up at the mouth of the Congo River to establish 'civilised settlements [where] justice and law and order shall prevail, and murder and lawlessness, and the cruel barter for slaves, shall for ever cease'.[3]

In that autumn, when captured Zulu warriors were exhibited at Brecon for 6d. admission, when the Society for the Suppression of Vice took a bookseller to court for 'wilfully exposing in his shop window' photographs of bare-breasted Zulu women, and when Baptist missionaries were seeking a route north from São Salvador, 23-year-old William Hughes was admitted to Llangollen Baptist College. In May 1882, Principal Hugh Jones recommended the newly ordained Hughes to the BMS as 'a splendid young fellow', stating that he had linguistic limitations inhibiting his employment among the literate people of India or China, but that he was suitable for the Congo. Hughes was interviewed by the BMS in July,[4] and a month later embarked at Liverpool.[5]

When near the end of his voyage he disembarked, briefly, at the old slave market port in Landana, a detached Portuguese enclave north of the Congo River, associated with the Roman Catholic mission to Angola since the fifteenth century. Later he was to write:

One of the greatest obstacles to the success of white missionaries in Africa has been the scattering of their strength, and thus only half doing their work in several places instead of performing it completely and permanently in one locality. There are, at Landana, native craftsmen – carpenters, blacksmiths, gardeners, etc – who were redeemed from slavery in the interior, and have been trained for some part of each working day in these much needed trades, and during the rest of the day and the evenings are instructed in school studies and the faith of their teachers.[6]

Eventually to blossom at Colwyn Bay, this concept of self-supporting native missionaries was already exercising Hughes's thoughts when he stepped ashore at Banana on 22 September 1882. He travelled 93 miles up river by steamer, to the Underhill BMS base at Matadi. After a few weeks' instruction he was sent further up river and put in charge of Bayneston, which comprised a tent, a storehouse made of grass, a few fowls, some servants from the coast, and one Congolese boy, Kinkasa, whom he had brought with him from down river. Lonely and surrounded by disease and death Hughes found hope in the arrival at Bayneston of N'Kanza, a young slave boy belonging to the local chief.[7] Almost unable to walk because the soles of his feet were infested with boring parasites, N'Kanza was sent to the mission to be cured by Hughes, resulting in a bond that was later to take the boy to Colwyn Bay. By 1884 Hughes, who had moved to the main Underhill base mission, was becoming disillusioned by the international politics surrounding his work. The Germans annexed the Cameroons, and their army attacked the BMS settlement accommodating Africans of many different tribes who had been liberated by the Royal Navy while being taken into slavery. Bismarck's Berlin Conference opened in November, to carve up Africa among the Europeans, and by the time it closed in February 1885 Leopold II was king of the Congo – appointing as his first administrator Lieutenant-Colonel Sir Francis de Winton, of Maesllwch Castle, Radnorshire. Hughes was not alone in his disillusionment. In March 1885 the Revd H. K. Moolenaar (who had sailed out with Hughes) wrote to the BMS in London citing cases of cruelty to native blacks by white missionaries, but the matter was hushed up.[8] Hughes also wrote to Baynes but no hint of his suppressed letter was to be found in the report to the 93rd annual general meeting of the BMS in July 1885. Hughes had written of his engagement to Katie, daughter of the principal of Llangollen College, saying she wished to join him in the Congo.

> But because my health is so poor; because so many deaths are taking place among the missionaries; because of the many discomforts one has to contend with, together with the fact that the mission is so far only opening the way, so that none of us can refer to a station where we can establish and do missionary work, cause me to believe it would not be reasonable to take such a step,

adding that he wanted to leave the mission, accompanied by two boys, whom he would train at his own expense, for the benefit of their own people.[9]

Thus was sown the seed of Colwyn Bay's African Institute, in what could only be seen as mutiny in the eyes of the BMS establishment. While the BMS seemed content to leave Hughes to rot in the Congo he was again struck down by fever. Fortuitously, Stanley's doctor was to hand and attended him for three days and nights, telling him his only chance of life was to leave Africa. Sir Francis de Winton used his steamer to take Hughes and the boys Kinkasa and N'Kanza down river to board a ship for Liverpool.[10] 'As soon as we cleared the river and got into the ocean, the sea breeze revived me', noted Hughes, and during the voyage he decided to create a Congo Training College. While having reservations about the Welsh climate, he believed there was 'no country on earth with such religious surroundings as little Wales'.[11] Hughes and the boys turned up at the Llanelian farm run by one of his married sisters and her husband, and there they lived for many months.

Baynes refused to accept Hughes's resignation, hoping he could be persuaded to return. In an attempt to keep a rein on Hughes's radicalism, until he could be buried in the Congo, Baynes retained him on the BMS payroll as a fundraiser, to tour the Baptist churches of Wales.[12] While refusing to acknowledge the existence of Kinkasa and N'Kanza, the BMS capitalized on their star turn during Hughes's lecture tours. A Welsh poster for his 1885–6 tour announced that he would be accompanied by 'black boys', who would sing in Welsh, English and Congolese.[13] The BMS subjected Hughes to alternating threats and promises. He was told he could choose his station and be promoted to a senior missionary with better pay if he returned to the Congo, but he was warned he would be 'suppressed' if he did not go back.[14] In the autumn of 1885 he was told the BMS did not consider the many white deaths from Congo fevers to be sufficient reason for a minister to abandon his flock. In January 1886 a friendly minister warned Hughes he would be crushed by the Baptist cause.

Under these pressures he and Katie Jones were medically examined in January and February 1886, and pronounced unfit for service in Equatorial Africa. They were married in March and the BMS began erasing his memory, no doubt seeing him as a manifestation of those troublesome Welsh Baptists who argued that Wales was not properly represented in the running of the Society. The BMS recruited the support of fellow Welsh missionary Thomas Lewis when he arrived home on leave in April 1886 – accompanied by a Congolese boy. He was sent on a lecture tour, promoting the Society's official line:

'Experience has taught us all better things for Africa. These poor lads looked in despair at the snow-covered country of the white man.'[15] The BMS formally reported the severance of its links with William Hughes in May 1886.[16]

However, invitations for Hughes's lecture and the trilingual singing of his 'black boys' poured in from all parts of Wales, attracting packed congregations. During each show Kinkasa and N'Kanza sold their photographs to raise money for their keep and for Hughes's dream of an independent Welsh-based Congo Institute. In June 1887 he was appointed pastor of Llanelian Baptist church, with the promise of a second pastorate for a new church being planned for Colwyn Bay.[17] The family took up residence in Bay View Road, Colwyn Bay, calling their home Congo House two years before the first meeting of his Congo Institution Committee. In April 1890 he took over a house in Nant-y-Glyn Road which he renamed Congo Institute.

If Equatorial Africa was deleterious to the health of white missionaries, the cemetery at Llanelian Road, Colwyn Bay, suggests – wrongly – the same was true for black proselytes brought to Wales. Kinkasa began to ail in March 1887. When he died in May 1888, at an estimated age of twelve, he was certified as having succumbed to 'Congo sleeping sickness', a long slow killer. Samba, with an estimated age of fourteen, died in March 1892, due to a ruptured liver caused by a fall. N'Kanza was estimated to be sixteen when he died in April 1892 from acute heart failure caused by congestion of the liver – a problem which may have begun in Africa. Kobina Boodoo (named on his tombstone as Joseph Emmanuel Abraham) died of tuberculous meningitis in April 1909, aged twenty-one. Ernestina Morford was thirty and on a holiday visit when she died in January 1914 from acute double lobar pneumonia. During the same period Hughes lost four of his own family: daughter Edith, aged seven months, from tubercular meningitis in March 1893; wife Katie, aged thirty-three, from toxaemia and miscarriage, in August 1894; daughter Katie, aged twenty-two, from kidney failure, in May 1909; and daughter Claudia, aged thirty, in December 1918, a victim of the notorious influenza epidemic.

In July 1890 Daniel, who had been trained as a carpenter, was the first student to be returned to Africa, after a formal send-off from Tabernacl church. Hughes's only son was born at the Congo Institute in August 1890 and, as might be expected, was christened Stanley.

August 1890 saw the arrival of Kofele M'besa, a sixteen-year-old refugee from the German occupation of the former BMS mission in the Cameroons, sent by an Anglican clergyman's widow.[18] The fame of what was still a very small Colwyn Bay operation spread up and down the West African coast, and George Fraser, an orphan of a Scottish father and African mother, also arrived in 1890, at the behest of the American Baptist Missionary Union (ABMU) – whose journal, *The Baptist,* referred, on 24 January 1890, to 'the admirable Congo Training House'. Eight new students arrived in 1891, including Ernestina, the eight-year-old daughter of an African mother and the Dutch agent of the BMS at Banana. In later years she married black American missionary Joseph Morford, also trained at Colwyn Bay. Most of the students had arrived via the ABMU. In 1891 hymn-writers Dwight Lyman Moody and Ira David Sankey, both prominent in the Congo work of the ABMU, visited the institute. 'Our American friends seem to appreciate this idea more than some of our friends nearer home', wrote Hughes. Another American visitor was the Revd Daniel J. Jenkins, of Charleston, born a slave soon after the Civil War began. The institute appears to have been the inspiration for his famous orphanage, and his son visited William Hughes at Colwyn Bay in 1916, when few people wanted to know him.[19]

The institute's finances were at a low ebb in 1891, when H. M. Stanley came to the rescue with a lecture in support of the Colwyn Bay venture to an audience of 4,500 at Caernarfon's enormous eisteddfod pavilion. In July King Leopold became a patron, stoking up a long debate as to whether the Welsh Baptist Union should sever its connection with the BMS and branch out with an independent Welsh mission.

Hughes's book *Dark Africa and the Way Out* was published in March 1892. Articulating his Welsh nationalism, Hughes wrote:

It is wrong and a blunder to appoint Englishmen as judges, preachers, and magistrates over the people of Wales; even were they the best of men they would be in the wrong place . . . They are ignorant of the Welsh language, unacquainted with the affairs of the Welsh people, their poverty, history, wrongs; they cannot sympathise with the sentiments, hopes and aspirations of a conquered people . . . The English Church has failed in Wales because it came here with an English cloak upon it, attempting to teach in an unnatural way, preaching in another tongue to people who spoke Welsh.[20]

Transposing his philosophy to the 'Dark Continent', Hughes wrote: 'Our idea in training Africans as missionaries is that in all points they are like their brethren, of the same blood, the same colour, the same humour, the same language, the same in everything, excepting in education and training.' It was the start of the politicization of the Congo Institute, whose name was changed that year to the African Institute, when Hughes expanded his ambitions beyond the Congo and registered his Colwyn Bay venture as the British and African Incorporated Association.

While passing through Liverpool, the Revd Thomas Lewis Johnson, a famous black American Baptist, was given a copy of Hughes's book by Sir Alfred Jones, and travelled to Colwyn Bay in May 1892. There he found seventeen Africans in residence, and gave a public lecture in their support. 'It was very clear concerning *Dark Africa* that the way taken by Mr Hughes was *the Way Out*, and I advised my brethren in America and Africa to co-operate in his splendid work,' he wrote later.[21] December 1892 saw the return of two boys to Africa. Two students were being trained by a Colwyn Bay pharmacist, and craft apprentices included a printer, blacksmith, wheelwright, and a shipwright. All were taught gardening in the 3-acre grounds of the institute, and all were taught to preach the Gospel.[22]

Whether or not influenced by Hughes's book, Joseph Booth (1851–1932) of Melbourne set up the non-sectarian Zambesi Industrial Mission in East Africa in 1892.[23] Booth was to become a major influence on the Revd John Chilembwe (educated in Virginia in the 1890s), whose anti-white revolution in Nyasaland (Malawi) in 1915 was the first of its kind, influenced by American blacks. The third associate of this affair was Peter Nyambo, of Zambesi, a former Colwyn Bay student. Davidson Don Jabavu, of Williamstown, South Africa, another former Colwyn Bay student, was a boarder with Booth at Cape Town, in 1912.

On 20 March 1893 the Revd A. Steffens, describing himself as leader of the German Baptist Missionary Society in the Cameroons, wrote to Hughes telling him:

> It is not enough that our churches have had to suffer through the unwise behaviour of the [English] BMS, but now our youth are being stolen from us . . . We will not employ anyone who has been in a foreign country . . . We have had plenty of mournful experience of young people returning

home, bringing with them corrupt habits, like drinking beer and wine, gluttony, smoking, dancing, etc. Also, they return as gentlemen, dressed and living like Europeans, ashamed of their own language; and they are, to say the least, a disgrace to their parents and to the missionaries.

Steffens's letter continued:

The people of Victoria give us a lot of trouble because of your school. They rejected a teacher who received his education in a German school, and who is able to teach in German and Duali. They refused, too, to send their 30 children to us for education and training because they preferred to be civilised and educated in England. I hope you have some sympathy with us, and that you will leave our children alone.

'If we hear of any more boys and girls going to England we will use other means', he threatened, and while we do not know what he meant he was clearly echoing Germany's ambition for an African empire. Steffens wrote in similar terms to BMS secretary Baynes, who gleefully had it printed for general circulation.[24]

Hughes responded by setting off for West Africa at the end of June 1893. In Liberia he arranged for Rick's Institute[25] to become an affiliate of the African Institute, and established a new school for girls, which he called Russell Institute after a friend of the Colwyn Bay operation. During two weeks in the Cameroons he set up the Pembroke Institute and the Glamorgan Institute. At Bugama, New Calabar (now Nigeria), Hughes established the Alfred Jones Institute, under the care of a Sierra Leone carpenter who had worked with George Grenfell, and former Colwyn Bay student Kofele M'Besa, pending the arrival of the Revd Theophilus Scholes, a Jamaican soon to qualify at Edinburgh as a doctor of medicine.[26] Scholes, who had spent five years in the Congo with the ABMU, had visited Colwyn Bay in May 1893, and he sailed for New Calabar in July 1894.[27] Although he eventually settled in London, his writings were an important influence on Pan-Africanism, something which Jomo Kenyatta (future president of Kenya) and Ras Makonnen (a Trotskyist Guyanese who lived in Manchester) were to acknowledge as early as the 1930s.[28]

During Hughes's four months' absence the Germans found some strange BMS allies, such as the Revd Benjamin Evans, of Gadlys, a Welsh member of the BMS committee. Commencing in May 1893 he spent the next eight months attacking Hughes in the columns of *Seren Cymru*, a Welsh-language Baptist newspaper. 'No missionary belonging to us in Africa, and especially in the Congo, is in sympathy with Mr Hughes and his cause', he said in August 1893. The Revd J. Spinther James replied robustly to Steffens and Evans, and published Hughes's letters of 1885–6 that had been suppressed by the BMS.

When Hughes returned to Colwyn Bay, in October, he set about building his new African Institute, next-door to the original Congo Institute, incorporating a printing room, tailoring workshop, classrooms, full immersion baptismal font and dormitories.[29] That was the month in which a prominent group of Liverpool Baptists travelled to Colwyn Bay to discuss Hughes's motives. Well satisfied with what they saw, they arranged for a public meeting in Liverpool to raise funds for the institute, but on the day before the well-advertised assembly Hughes received a telegram saying everything had been cancelled because of serious allegations by the BMS. Three members of the Colwyn Bay committee met the local BMS superintendent under the independent chairmanship of a prominent Liverpool merchant. The allegations amounted to the letter of the Revd Mr Steffens and one from an ABMU missionary accusing Daniel, the first returned student, of being proud, untruthful and avaricious. The Colwyn Bay delegation responded with two letters from the independent native Bethel Mission at Akwa town, saying Steffens could not be trusted and that the Basel Mission was seeking to destroy them. They also produced a letter from an ABMU missionary in the Congo praising Daniel.[30]

On 9 December 1893 the *Lagos Weekly Record* carried a long feature in praise of the institute under the by-line of the Revd D. Brown Vincent, later to become an influential African nationalist under his original native name of Mojola Agbebi. 'The effort may be regarded as the first prominent contribution of Wales to the redemption of Africa', he wrote. Further West African praise came in the *Sierra Leone Weekly News* on 2 June 1894, in a report of a meeting convened at the Freetown chambers of barrister (the future Sir) Samuel Lewis, CMG, a freed Yoruba slave. The gathering resolved: 'to take some definite step in shewing the world our appreciation of this noble work which already is in earnest progress with beneficial results to Africa'.

At home, however, the BMS was still trying to 'crush' Hughes. In April 1894 Baptist ministers were instructed to dissuade children from contributing to the African Institute by promising them a tea party if they switched their efforts to the BMS. In 1895 Hughes applied for the church he had established at the Institute to be admitted into the Welsh Baptist Gymanfa, but was refused and his name was removed from the list of ministers and erased from the Baptist cause two years later. Hughes was on his own but his institute prospered in prestige (though not in funding) and helped shape modern Africa. This article does not provide the space in which to list the achievements, as missionaries and politicians, of many of the eighty-seven students who passed through Colwyn Bay – although there were a few opportunist rogues. Thoughts nurtured at Colwyn Bay led to the convening of the first international Pan-African conference in London in 1900[31] on the initiative of Trinidadian barrister H. Sylvester Williams.

The first hint of the institute's financial problems appeared in the *African Times* of 2 July 1900, with an announcement that no new students could be accepted for the forthcoming school year. A year later the Colwyn Bay operation was registered as a charitable limited company, which bought the Institute from Hughes, who used all the money to pay off his mortgage debts.[32]

The summer of 1904 brought handsome Grenadian John Lionel Franklin to Colwyn Bay as lead actor in a performance of *Uncle Tom's Cabin* at the Public Hall. He attended a service at the African Institute, where no one could have guessed that seven years later he would be Horatio Bottomley's notorious *Black Baptist* who fathered the *Brown Baby*.

Things were beginning to go awry by 18 July 1907, when Colwyn Bay residents complained that four of the students had been seen in nearby woods with white girls.[33] By this time Hughes was borrowing heavily and had begun issuing cheques that could not be met.[34] Undeterred, Hughes maintained a political profile and in 1909 wrote to the *Manchester Guardian,* protesting against the provision for a colour bar written into the South Africa Bill, then before Parliament. 'It is an insult to 360 millions of coloured people who are to be found in different parts of our Empire', he said, adding that Britain was deserting the blacks by bending to the Boers' ideas of government.[35] The Union of South Africa came into being in May 1910 and, as Hughes had foreseen, the long regime of apartheid was consolidated with the Union's Colour Bar Act in 1926.

The African Institute's last annual report was published on 10 June 1911. In October the *Colwyn Bay Times*, a weekly paper printed and published at the Institute, carried a public notice headed WARN-ING:

> We are informed that some persons in Colwyn Bay have been busy circulating a scandal respecting one of the coloured young men at the African Institute. We have investigated this matter thoroughly, and find there is no truth whatever in their report so far as this young man is concerned. Therefore, we warn such persons lest they should find themselves in the hands of the law.[36]

The Revd William Hughes was playing with words at a time when many Colwyn Bay people were beginning to question both his personal life and the activities of his black students. Someone posted a copy of his warning to *John Bull*, which sent a reporter to Colwyn Bay. A twenty-six-year-old unmarried woman from Llandudno had given birth to a boy whose skin was dark (although in maturity not readily recognizable as mixed race). She named the boy Stanley, and he was sixty-nine before he discovered his parentage, and only then when the writer showed him a photograph of John Lionel Franklin. He said it matched one he had lost during his army service in the Second World War. 'My mother did not tell me much. She never named him, but told me he was from Grenada, and had worked in Nigeria. They had spent a holiday together in Scotland. She never married, telling me she had never found anyone to match my father,' he said. [37]

The *John Bull* feature was published in two parts. It opened with a reference to the text for a Bible class at the Institute from chapter 1 of the First Book of Samuel, dealing with a man who had taken two wives, one infertile and the other giving him children. 'Anyone looking up this chapter in his Bible will be able to imagine the effect upon a mixed audience of European girls and "converted" Africans. Don't let me be misunderstood. I am not blaming these students. They are full-blooded men of fine physique,' wrote *John Bull*.[38] Colwyn Bay could hardly wait for the next instalment, in which Franklin was named and described as a 'Black scoundrel'. According to *John Bull*:

> During the summer months at Colwyn Bay some of the lady visitors act in an astonishing manner towards these natives. They may be seen seated with them on the seafront, in earnest if not affectionate conversation.

Afternoon tea parties are arranged, and when the dusk of evening arrives, 'black and white' may frequently be seen strolling together down the road behind the Institute.[39]

A County Court hearing to wind up the British & African Incorporated Association took place on 4 March 1912, when it was said that subscriptions had fallen and creditors were pressing for their money because of the *John Bull* article. A compulsory winding-up order was made and the African Institute, by then in disarray, formally closed on 21 March. On 14 March Hughes himself appeared before the Bankruptcy Court with liabilities of £4,932. He told the court: 'The attacks in *John Bull* killed the Institute, and the Institute killed me.' He was declared bankrupt.

Hughes initiated proceedings for libel against *John Bull* and the case was heard at Ruthin Assizes in June. The plaintiff said that the *John Bull* attacks were offensive and untrue; the defendants replied that they published matters of fact in the public interest – to which the judge suggested a plea of fair comment might be more appropriate. Defending himself, without the aid of counsel, Horatio Bottomley destroyed Hughes's credibility in cross-examination. Hughes had to concede the animosity of the BMS; his repeated issuing of cheques for which he had no funds; his expulsion of one unmanageable student (Josiah Batabo) yet retaining his name in the annual report as serving the institute mission in New Calabar; his inability to remember whether Okon Boco (listed as serving the institute in Old Calabar) or B. Jimsana (listed for South Africa) had also been expelled; slipshod book-keeping; no evidence of having funded any of the institute's declared forty-three out-stations in Africa; concealment from the Institute's honorary solicitor of an unfavourable auditor's report for 1910, causing the solicitor's withdrawal; and the embezzlement of Ernestina Morford's personal fund from her Dutch father. The case ended abruptly when the judge asked the jury whether there was need to continue the trial, and the foreman said they had heard enough to reach a conclusion – in favour of *John Bull*.[40] Bottomley reacted with a report stating: 'Colwyn Bay is delighted to be rid of Hughes and his niggers.'[41]

Hughes briefly resurfaced when British and French troops defeated his old German enemy in West Africa. He published a pamphlet in 1916 under the simple title of *The Cameroons*. He recalled the efforts of his African Institute to rescue indigenous students from German missionary tyranny and train them for service in their homeland, where they had become well-known preachers. 'We venture to state there would be hardly any Christians in the Cameroons at the present time but for the education and faithfulness of these men,' wrote Hughes. Epitomizing the problem of all colonial communities, Hughes said it would be unfair to the natives who, if having learnt English from the original British missionaries, and then having had to switch to the language of the German colonizers, they would have to switch again to French in any future disposal of captured enemy colonies (which was just what happened).

By 1917 Hughes had recovered sufficiently to contemplate emigrating to Africa, black Baptists from the Cameroons having sent him £30 for his fare. Fifty of the town's leading citizens signed a splendidly illuminated farewell address saying: 'After a residence of 30 years among us, during which you have rendered invaluable service to the town . . . we, the undersigned, exceedingly regret your departure.'[42] Except for the events of 1911–12, the scroll gave a detailed recitation of Hughes's career. 'Recognising your manifold services, we bid you adieu,' concluded the address, whose signatories included sixteen ministers of various denominations, the chairman of the town council, the editors of the local papers, magistrates, general practitioners, teachers and the foreman of the Urban District Council workmen. On 12 November 1917 Hughes circulated a farewell begging letter. He redated it on 9 May 1918, and circulated it again, but never left.[43] His daughter Claudia died in December 1918, the last of Hughes's immediate family, except for his estranged footballer son Stanley. He took to drink[44] and was admitted to Penrhyndeudraeth Workhouse as a pauper. He was later transferred to Conwy Workhouse where he died of heart disease on 28 January 1924. Three-quarters of a century later his name crops up on both sides of the Atlantic in any serious debate about the emancipation of black Africa, but he still awaits his niche in *The Dictionary of Welsh Biography*.

A search of the local newspapers suggests that, for the first twenty years of the institute's existence, the people of Colwyn Bay warmly embraced its young black community, albeit with an element of curiosity. Not until 1907 did the image of black students walking in the woods with local girls cause concern. Even when *John Bull*'s prejudiced investigator turned up four years later to look for the rumoured black baby, he saw local ladies happily seated on the promenade with these 'full-blooded men of fine physique', and inviting them to tea. Ironically, the Grenadian who fathered an illegitimate child was never a student at the African Institute but, having worshipped there, while passing through the town, was later employed as a travelling fundraiser. There was no fundamental racial prejudice in Victorian and Edwardian Colwyn Bay and Hughes might have been able to weather the *John Bull* storm but for his heavy debts and other weaknesses, including his fondness for the wife of a fellow minister, according to the Revd Lewis Valentine (who conducted Hughes's funeral service).[45] Hughes's son refused to discuss their estrangement, either with his relatives or with the writer, save to indicate that the 'Black baby' was the catalyst rather than the cause.

Notes

[1] One of only two letters, with additional notes on the envelope, which make up Hughes's sparse (censored?) personal file at the BMS, London.

[2] Issue of September 1877.

[3] H. M. Stanley, *The Congo and the Foundation of the Free State* (1885).

[4] BMS file.

[5] *The Missionary Herald* (August 1882).

[6] William Hughes, *Dark Africa and the Way Out* (1892), 4.

[7] Ibid., 108.

[8] J. Spinther James, *Sefydliad Colwyn Bay wedi ei Brofi trwy Dân* (Carmarthen, 1894), 84, 38.

[9] Reproduced in Welsh, eight years later, in *Seren Cymru* (3 September 1893).

[10] *Dark Africa*, 10–13.

[11] Ibid., 10.

[12] James, *Sefydliad Colwyn Bay*, 18, 32.

[13] A copy was found at the printers in Sussex Street, Rhyl, in October 1966, and shown to the writer.

[14] James, *Sefydliad Colwyn Bay*, 31–2.

[15] Thomas Lewis, *These Seventy Years* (1930).

[16] Minutes of BMS General Meeting, 11 May 1886.

[17] T. Frimston, *Bedyddwyr Cantref y Rhos* (Blaenau Ffestiniog, 1924), a history of the Baptist cause in the Colwyn Bay area, ignores the Congo Institute.

[18] *The Sower and the Seed* (10 September 1890).

[19] John Chilton, *A Jazz Nursery* (1980), 8.

[20] *Dark Africa*, 50.

[21] Thomas L. Johnson, *Twenty-eight Years a Slave* (Bournemouth, 1909), 227.

[22] *Newyddion Da* (missionary journal of the Welsh Presbyterian Church) (13 January 1893).

[23] *The Regions Beyond* (December 1894).

[24] Reprinted in *Seren Cymru* (28 July 1893).

[25] Founded in 1887 by the black community.

[26] 1893–4 annual report of the African Training Institute.

[27] *North Wales Weekly News* (6 July 1894).

[28] Imanuel Geiss, *The Pan-African Movement* (London, 1974), 207.

[29] Now demolished, the new building was not to the design of the architect's drawing shown in Hughes's book.

[30] James, *Sefydliad Colwyn Bay*, 111.

[31] Subsequent Pan-African conferences were held in London, Paris and New York, in 1919, 1921, 1923 and 1927, at Manchester in 1945, and in Accra in 1958. Pan-Africanism has since been absorbed within the Organization for African Unity.

[32] Information from the property deeds, in the possession of the writer.

[33] Produced in evidence at Ruthin Assizes in June 1912.

[34] Hughes's extensive borrowings from 1907 are listed in the Tanllan accounts book, which was shown to the writer in 1980 by Ifor Williams, grandson of Hughes's sister Sidney. One entry shows his cheque no. 6027 for £60, issued in March 1909, ostensibly to clear his debt, was returned marked 'Refer to drawer', and the debt continued to grow, never to be repaid.

[35] *Manchester Guardian* (23 August 1909).

[36] *Colwyn Bay Times* (19 October 1911).

[37] From a hitherto unpublished interview with Stanley Dale by the writer in 1980.

[38] 16 December 1911.

[39] 23 December 1911.

[40] *North Wales Weekly News* (14 and 21 June 1912); *Welsh Coast Pioneer* (13 and 20 June 1912).

[41] *John Bull* (22 June 1912).

[42] Shown to the author in 1972 by Mrs Madge Bebbington, a granddaughter of Hughes's sister Elisabeth.

[43] Copies in the possession of the writer.

[44] Information from Mrs Madge Bebbington. 'My aunt Jane Roberts would never allow us to discuss Uncle Will. She said he had made a fool of himself at the end of his life by taking to drink – a terrible crime for a Baptist.'

[45] In conversations with the writer during 1981.

6 Through the Prism of Ethnic Violence: Riots and Racial Attacks in Wales, 1826–2002[1]

NEIL EVANS

Historical work on ethnic relations in Wales has frequently focused on the riot. This has been the case for a variety of reasons. Often riots have drawn the attention of historians to an aspect of Welsh society which would otherwise have been hidden under the layers of the myth of tolerance. Secondly, major social conflicts frequently generate a large amount of comment and this enables a reconstruction of attitudes and structures of relationships to be undertaken for the past. This point shades into the third point, which is that such evidence allows the use of a social drama approach to the study of community and society. It is one in which historians have become well versed since 1945 as the study of crowds has become quite central to the subject and there is now a huge literature on crowd actions and riots.[2] It encompasses many different periods of history and is concerned with the composition, values, beliefs and actions of crowds. By providing evocative accounts of ethnic riots, historians' preoccupation with social drama has served the purpose of puncturing the idea of Welsh tolerance rather well. It also helped to place studies of minorities nearer to the centre of the discipline's concerns and meant that there was a rich literature from which to draw insights. The main drawback was that most historians saw crowd actions more generally as a form of protest and therefore as in some sense 'progressive'. Far less attention was paid to reactionary crowds, like the 'Church and King' mobs of the eighteenth century. Racist crowds were rather more like these than the rioting iron-workers of Merthyr Tydfil in 1831 or the coalminers of Tonypandy in 1910.[3]

Such historical work has changed attitudes in the social sciences. Social scientists, at least in Britain, were hindered by a lack of such actions to study in the immediate post-war period. When riots did begin to erupt in Britain in the 1980s it was often historians who offered immediate commentary in the press and journalists who drew on the rich historical studies of crowd actions to set the present in perspective.[4] American social science, with a plethora of riots throughout the twentieth century to study, coped with the challenge more effectively. Some sociologists misread the present because they misunderstood the past.[5] By contrast the historical periods in which historians discovered ethnic riots were replete with riots of all kinds and it did not seem too difficult to interpret ethnic rioting as a variation in the broader landscape. Historians of crowd action have considered crowds to have varied repertoires of behaviour which changed in different periods. It was simply necessary to assimilate racial disturbances into this framework.[6]

Approaches to ethnic history based on conflict faced particular problems, however. They were always prone to the riposte that riots were untypical events and that they revealed little about day-to-day life in Wales. Was there evidence of harmony in ethnic relations outside the violent confrontation? This issue had to be addressed, and has been done elsewhere.[7] The purpose of this chapter is to provide a specific review of what we now know about ethnic violence in Wales.

The first substantial group of immigrants to arrive in modern industrial Wales were the Irish, whose numbers began to pick up in the early nineteenth century and then rose to a crescendo during the years of the Famine migration of 1845–50. Over a period of almost sixty years, from 1826 to 1882, they were the targets of around twenty serious attacks. These fall into two broad categories. First, there were attacks which originated in the workplace; and secondly, there were wider community attacks. Behind most anti-Irish attacks there were accusations of undercutting wages, but the evidence for this is patchy at best. More often, the workplace-based attacks were efforts to expel them from jobs in times of economic hardship. These attacks came in two clusters which were associated with work in the iron-works, such as at Rhymni in 1826 and 1834, Pontypool in 1834, Nantyglo and Blaina in 1843 and Brynmawr in 1850. The second crop was associated with the early days of steam coal in the Rhondda and clustered in the years 1848–57. A riot in Aberdare in 1866 may be regarded as a reprise to these outbreaks. The latter were much more 'successful' as they prevented the Irish from establishing a foothold in this expanding industry, and by 1914 there were very few Irish-born, or Catholics, in the Rhondda Valleys. Communal riots tended to be associated with the Famine migration and were often the result of murders, religious bigotry or of economic grievances. In 1848 there were attacks on Irish communities in Llantrisant and Cardiff. The latter followed the murder of a Welshman by an Irishman and accusations that he was being hidden by the community. The Catholic church and Irish homes were then assaulted with some venom. At Pontlottyn in 1869 a crowd of around 1,000 people attacked the Irish community with such ferocity that one man died. It was the result of long-established antipathies rather than transient wage issues and illustrates a broad hostility rather than a simple economic conflict.[8]

The most famous – and the last – attack on the Irish, at Tredegar in 1882, showed the layers of hostility that could accumulate. There were economic issues: the works was converting from iron to steel production and work was scarce. The outbreak happened some two months after the Phoenix Park murders in Dublin when the Chief Secretary of Ireland and the Secretary of State were killed by Irish extremists. Also there were some local conflicts between Catholics and the Salvation Army in Tredegar. As in many riots, the spark came in the pubs. Typical were the attacks on property, with fifty homes being wrecked and fifteen people seriously injured in physical attacks.[9]

The recent research of Louise Miskell locates such actions in the repertoire of the crowd. She stresses the element of regulation of morality within them, the expression of disapproval of an alien presence. Communities rarely expressed regret at what had happened but gave vociferous support in court to those who were charged with offences. Such riots adapted the methods of the rural *ceffyl pren* (the ritual mocking of moral offenders) to industrial locations and were a variant on the attacks of the Rebecca rioters and the Scotch Cattle in the 1820s–1840s. They bridged a period when such actions had declined in the industrial and agrarian spheres but still showed life in their ethnic variation.[10]

This framework of analysis provides a means of approaching the variety of riots against the diverse ethnic groups which entered Wales in the period 1880–1920. Some conflicts were clearly motivated by questions of employment. This was the case in the series of brawls that were fought on the streets of Butetown district of Cardiff in the late nineteenth and early twentieth centuries, which were associated with economic depressions in shipping and intense conflict over jobs. Accusations of undercutting abounded, as with the anti-Irish riots, but again the case is not clear-cut. It was not always black and foreign sailors who were accused of undercutting; it could be the native-born and much of the conflict may have been about signing on the ship rather than about wage rates. Shipping was too fluid an occupation for the locals to become established in one sector and keep outsiders at bay, as happened in the iron-works and coalmines. Ships signed on their crews by the voyage, and we need to think of a constant and multifaceted struggle rather than the indigenous population defending their turf.[11]

The major riots against such incomers were communal rather than workplace-based. That is not to say that there were not elements of economic competition in them, but it *is* to say that the issues were broader than that and often involved a communal assault on an alien group. The focus of such violence was the period 1910–20, which was on the cusp of major changes. The growth of the international economy in the period 1850–1914 had been massive, and south Wales steam coal and its bunker trade had done much to fuel it – literally. It is not surprising that a diverse group of incomers became located in Wales in the process. To supplement the European seamen who had begun to appear in the mid-nineteenth century, black people and people of colour began to appear. South Wales also attracted a small proportion of the Jewish refugees from East European pogroms who began to arrive in the 1880s.

This international economy was forced out of its grooves by the world crisis of 1914–18 and it did not recover fully until after 1945. The major riots in Wales came on either side of this great divide. There were plenty of parallels elsewhere. Liverpool had five major ethnic riots in the same period, while the anti-black riots of 1917–19 occurred around the edges of the Atlantic basin – including as far west as Chicago.[12]

In south Wales these outbreaks were concentrated in two years, 1911 and 1919. In both there were associations with industrial discontent. In the summer of 1911 the Cambrian Combine strike in the Rhondda, which had started the previous autumn, was still proceeding and it was joined by the international seamen's strike, which affected all the south Wales ports. Just as this ended, a national railway strike began. A number of people died in these confrontations: one at Tonypandy and six at Llanelli in the railway strike. In Cardiff during the seamen's strike warehouses were burned down and violent picketing enforced the solidarity of the strike. There was also considerable violence in Swansea, which has not received much attention from historians.[13]

The attacks on the Chinese in Cardiff were the first of the ethnic outbreaks. The seamen's strike was solid across ethnic lines, with the exception of some of the Greeks and the Chinese – the latter were not allowed to join the union anyway. In order to win the strike the seamen needed the support of the dockers and the union constantly harped on the threat from the Chinese as a means of trying to win wider solidarity. On the day that the dockers downed tools, a Chinese crew was brought into Cardiff. There followed thirty attacks on Chinese laundries in Cardiff, located widely across the city. There had been accusations that these laundries were centres of white slave traffic in Cardiff and many other accusations of immoral behaviour were tacked on to this, such as opium smoking and gambling. Now the laundries were seen as the centres of strike-breaking. Windows were broken and property was destroyed in the attacks. This served the union's purposes as it helped maintain the solidarity of the strike, and ultimately helped the seamen to their victory. The small group of Chinese in the city – probably no more than 200 – had provided a useful scapegoat and a point around which opposition could rally.

One of the effects of the transport strike in Cardiff was to shut down the production of the eastern part of the South Wales Coalfield within three days of the strike becoming general across the waterfront in Cardiff. This added to existing industrial tensions in the area, which were cross-cut by the railway strike. Industrial conflict thus served as the backdrop to the anti-Jewish riots that occurred in the Eastern Valleys. They erupted from Tredegar, the locus of the anti-Irish riot of 1882, and spread across eastern Glamorgan and western Monmouthshire as far west as Senghennydd.

There is little real doubt that these were anti-Semitic riots, despite the efforts of some Jewish observers of the time to deny this, a strand of discussion now continued by a modern historian.[14] It is true that Jews were not the only targets and that certain splits were apparent in the local community, but the attacks started by selecting Jewish targets and only later did they involve non-Jews. Jews were attacked indiscriminately.[15] There was much condemnation of the outbreak and some expressions of philo-Semitism, but unanimity is not to be expected in such things. Much communal solidarity was expressed towards those rioters who were prosecuted, just as there had been in earlier anti-Irish riots. The fact that non-legitimated violence was used was bound to create divisions between the rioters and their supporters and the forces of order. Even the virulently anti-Irish *Cardiff and Merthyr Guardian* had condemned the riots in Cardiff in 1848 on the grounds that the Welsh should know better: they should not behave like Irishmen. The same divisions were apparent in the anti-Chinese riots in Cardiff; some observers had found the Chinese to be hard-working and law-abiding. In 1911 some people in the Valleys sheltered their Jewish neighbours rather than attack them.

Comparisons with other outbreaks at the time stress the way in which ethnic disturbances fit into a pattern. They were part of a repertoire of popular action that was being refurbished by the industrial conflicts of the period. Disputes over non-unionism in various parts of the coalfield had seen a revamping of the techniques of the *ceffyl pren* tradition in the form of whiteshirting (mockery of strike-breakers by parading them in women's petticoats). In Tonypandy in 1910 there was something of a communal uprising against the shop-keepers who were seen as taking the side of the coalowners. In Llanelli a wider community expressed its solidarity with the striking railway-men in the mass picketing which led to tragic violence, and following this the property of unpopular shopkeepers and magistrates was attacked. In Cardiff the strike of 1911 led to two other major confrontations on the streets besides the attack on the Chinese. Immigrants were only one of the targets against whom crowd action could be deployed. Perhaps to highlight the elements of ethnic conflict in these confrontations it is necessary to pick out just how unusual they were in a British context. While there was widespread hostility to Chinese seamen in Britain, the actions in Cardiff were the only recorded case of a riot against them. Similarly the anti-Jewish riots were the first since the readmission of the Jews in 1655 and the only others known of were in the East End of London in 1917. The riots which broke out in the south Wales ports in the summer of 1919 would be the worst of a wave of British outbreaks in that year.[16]

At the end of the war the economic situation again provided the context for attacks on black sailors in Barry, Newport and Cardiff. Because of shortages of merchant seamen in the First World War there had been renewed recruiting of men from the West Indies and Yemen. The black communities of the south Wales ports expanded significantly. At the end of the war white sailors were discharged from the Royal Navy and wanted their jobs back. In the main they got them and it was the newcomers who bore the brunt of unemployment. The outbreaks of 1919 were, therefore, only loosely related to the economic situation. There was a general context of industrial conflict – the post-war labour unrest, expressed in the railway strike of 1919, which was something of a dress rehearsal for the General Strike of 1926. But issues of morality once again stoked the fires of intolerance. Black men had white wives and girlfriends, and some commentators saw innocent girls as being seduced through service in boarding houses in Butetown. The black men were further accused of having shirked war duty – of having taken the high wages of merchant shipping, while white sailors fought. Certainly, wages in the merchant service were better than the paltry sums paid to the British armed services in the war, but the accusation of shirking danger was absurd. Merchant ships were just as much in the firing line as battleships and were more vulnerable. But the point is that black sailors were *seen* as profiting from the situation of others.

The trigger of the riots in Cardiff was an attack on a brake containing black men and their white wives: it was not a dispute over signing on a ship or some direct economic cause, though such an incident had triggered the similar riots in South Shields earlier in the year. Religious pressure groups, such as the Cardiff and District Citizens' Union, and the police contributed to the situation. The huge crowds that made the assaults on the black community were not entirely local but contained discharged sailors and soldiers who happened to be in the port. But there is little doubt that these represented local feeling as much as that of outsiders. The riots in Cardiff redrew the boundaries of the black community to their pre-war shape. Those who had settled in areas north of the South Wales Railway bridge were forced to leave their homes. Such displacements of population had been a feature of nineteenth-century anti-Irish riots and of the anti-Jewish riots of 1911. Control of territory was an important dimension of them, and a clear, if tacit, expression of communality. Of course, many condemned the outbreaks. There were fears that there might be retaliation in the empire, where the balance of black and white was far different from that in Britain: indeed, there were some outbreaks in the West Indies which confirmed these forebodings. But much of the discussion condemned merely the methods of the rioters: it endorsed their principles of racial purity and jobs for the white British first. As in the past with other ethnic riots, it was violence that separated them from official opinion rather than objectives.

After 1919 there were only minor affrays in the south Wales ports. In the mid-Victorian period, violence against the Irish had persisted after more general manifestations of community violence declined, whereas the reverse was true in inter-war Wales. Ethnic violence ceased in 1919, while industrial violence continued up to the General Strike of 1926. However, the mass demonstrations of the 1930s – especially mass protest against the means test in 1935 – were predominantly peaceful affairs and violence in general was removed from the repertoire of actions sanctioned by the community. Moreover, there was no echo in Wales of the disturbances associated with fascist demonstrations elsewhere in Britain, such as those which occurred in the East End of London in 1936. Fascist movements found little purchase in south Wales between the wars and failed to mobilize the kind of anti-Semitic feelings that had emerged explosively in Tredegar in 1911. Unlike the East End of London, south Wales had occasional examples of hostility to Jews but no deep-rooted tradition of anti-Semitism that could be exploited by fascist groups.[17]

By the post-war period there were few newcomers against whom to use such violence anyway. Across the Western world such ethnic riots entered a period of decline. There was a minor outbreak in Liverpool in 1948 and some of the American riots of the 1930s–1940s had this element in them. But most of the riots from the 1930s onwards in the US were ghetto rebellions in which the black population rebelled against their local exploiters in the ghetto shops and especially the police. They were very different from the riots of 1919. It took until the 1980s for such conflicts to occur in Britain. The first was in Bristol in 1980 and there were more widespread outbreaks in 1981 and 1985. There was little evidence of such an approach in Wales, though there was an outbreak in Butetown in 1981, which seems not to have spread because of a media blackout on reporting it. On that occasion, skinheads and black youths joined forces to try to lure the police into an ambush. The police anticipated this and allowed the rioters to destroy thousands of pounds' worth of property in Bute Terrace.[18] There was a more successful anti-police ambush in Butetown in 1986. This followed the pattern which had been established elsewhere: luring a police patrol into an ambush by means of a hoax 999 call and then attacking it with stones and petrol bombs.[19] Neither incident was significant on the scale of the Toxteth or Brixton riots. One reason for this is that the black community in Cardiff appears to have been less alienated from the dominant society. It was well established, intermarried, and there seems to have been far less of a rift between the generations within it compared with the English cities where such riots proliferated. Youth rebellion was less of a feature also, though it was the young people who initiated the actions that occurred. Cardiff also had less extensive areas of inner-city deprivation than many English cities.

By the 1990s violence in English cities had become concentrated in white communities and especially in outer estates rather than inner cities. The Ely riots of 1991 fitted into this pattern, but it contained one element that echoed the past. The confrontations with the police started with an attack by a white crowd on an Asian shop, following a dispute over the right to sell bread. The Pakistani family left the area and did not return. Yet much of the thrust of the events was hostility to the police and protest at deprivation. It was less straight-forwardly an anti-black communal riot than those of the past had been, despite the central element of this in the outbreak.[20]

A more disturbing and threatening trend in the 1990s was the rise in the number of ethnic assaults in Wales. It is hard to compare this with the past when no systematic data was kept and only recently have they been taken seriously by the police. We find such incidents in newspaper reports, for instance, but there is no effective means of studying them. However, their prevalence in the present guards against an assumption that, just because riots seem to be mainly a thing of the past, all is well in the realm of ethnic violence.

A new chapter in the understanding of racism in Wales opened with the murder of Mohan Singh Kullar at Cadoxton, near Neath, in December 1994. The shopkeeper was killed by a small gang of drunken youths who threw a brick at him when he investigated the disturbance they were creating; one young man got a life sentence and two others got sentences of eight and three and a half years in prison.[21] This created a sense of shock and outrage and did much to puncture the complacent attitudes that had dominated discussions of race in Wales. In this context, there was a popular reassessment of the history of race relations in Wales which drew the work of historians into the mainstream of discussion. Anti-racist cam-paigners had been arguing that it would take a racial murder to make the authorities take the threat from neo-Nazi groups in Wales seriously and this awful event had proved them, tragically, to be right.[22] In the following years a number of television programmes and press discussions, as well as the Oscar-nominated film, *Solomon a Gaenor* (which was set in the 1911 anti-Jewish riots), raised the profile of ethnic issues in political discussion and cultural awareness in Wales. It was in this context that the startling rise in the numbers of racist attacks in Wales came to be discussed.

Table 1. Racial Incidents Reported to the Police

Police Area	1988	1994–5	1995–6	1996–7	1997–8
Dyfed/Powys	0	3	23	18	17
Gwent	1	22	32	60	45
North Wales	2	3	5	4	12
South Wales	86	512	443	357	367
Provincial	2,169	6,398	7,211		
Metropolitan	2,214	5,480	5,011	5,621	5,862
Total	4,383	11,878	12,222	13,106	13,878

Source: Commission for Racial Equality Factsheets, 1997, 1999.

The centre of the problem of racial attacks – though they were present throughout Wales – was clearly in the south Wales Valleys. The journalist Steve Evans summed up the position well:

> Valleys racism, it seems, stems from particular factors. It is virtually invariably directed at local Asians rather than people from other ethnic backgrounds. The overall context is often one of deprived, run-down areas with very high unemployment but where the immigrant (black British from other areas of Britain) is relatively well off – perhaps a doctor or a pharmacist or a shopkeeper who has moved into the area precisely because he or she can see a living to be made . . . [they] might have the trappings of money, say an expensive car, in an area where money is scarce.[23]

This analysis is confirmed by the words of some of the avowed racists: 'There's white people on the dole, when there's black people . . . owning restaurants and working as doctors and taking all the money when white people should be.'[24] Such attitudes do not simply reflect economic decline and despondency – important as these are – they also involve issues of identity and social experience. The Valleys are now the least cosmopolitan part of Wales, with an overwhelming proportion of the population born locally. There is little to produce much awareness of difference or sensitivity to other cultures. Combined with this is the challenge of de-industrialization to a sense of Welsh identity. Heavy industry, and the wages it produced, was once a defining feature of Welshness.[25] In the Valleys some people have a strong sense of their Welshness but little that might provide them with any self-esteem. A sense of racial superiority fills the gap: 'We look after our race, you look after yours. I'm Celtic, I'm Welsh and proud. Our belief is we're pure; we're white and Welsh – being Welsh as well, that's a pride.'[26] This is supported by a victim of racial attacks and abuse in the area: 'The people around here think that the Valleys are the heart of Wales. That is their home town. Not anybody else's. So we're like the outsiders coming in and it's like invading their territory.' [27]

In areas like the Rhondda there are some neo-Nazi groups in existence and many signs of organized racism. Graffiti on the walls suggests that black people should leave the area ('Fuck off Coon') and some are prepared to make fascist gestures in front of the camera ('Rhondda Valley Skinheads – Sieg Heil').[28] Skinheads claim to have several hundred supporters in the Rhondda and there are suggestions that groupings of the Ku Klux Klan, Combat 18 and other equally vicious factions exist. Combat 18 has sent at least one death threat in Cardiff.[29]

Far right groups have had some presence in Wales for a couple of decades but they have never been very prominent. Most seem to have concentrated (if that is the word for small and fissiparous grouplets) around Cardiff. The growth of the National Front in the early 1970s hardly seems to have touched Wales: no candidates stood in Wales in the general elections of 1974, which proved to be its high tide in England. In the following election there were five candidates in Wales, who mustered a combined vote of 2,465 out of the 1,636,788 cast in Wales. Only in Cardiff West did the candidate poll over a thousand votes (4.1 per cent). The next highest figure was in Newport with 454 votes (0.8 per cent). In Barry, Pontypridd and Carmarthen they polled a maximum of 0.5 per cent of the vote. The candidate in Carmarthen persisted into the following election in 1983, now running under the British National Party banner, a change which garnered him precisely five votes compared with his previous outing. In 1992 a BNP candidate gathered 121 votes in Cardiff North – a mere 0.3 per cent of those cast. These figures constitute the entire parliamentary electoral history of the far right in post-war Wales.[30]

But the far right has maintained a presence in Wales through the whole of the period since the late 1970s. Ideologically this has been rather easier because of the splits in the far right since 1979. Broadly the National Front headed in two directions. One of these was the traditional centralist British approach, which kept to its major themes of anti-Semitism and antagonism to blacks, who would be compulsorily repatriated. Others were influenced by ecological currents and learned to embrace the idea of a diverse (but white!) Europe. This created the space for the recognition of ethnic differences within the UK, including support for the Welsh language, and for an attack upon English imperialism. It was the latter trend that influenced the National Front's deliberate targeting of Wales. In 1987 it invested £10,000 in work in Wales and produced some slick propaganda material. There were some articles in Welsh and support was expressed for Meibion Glyndŵr, a shadowy direct-action grouping responsible for burning second homes in rural Wales. These moves won a few dozen recruits – and quickly faced opposition on the streets from the South Wales Anti-Fascist Organisation, which disrupted concentrated recruiting drives in places like Merthyr and led to a switch to a guerrilla-like approach.

By 1990 Nick Griffin, a leading redistributivist, had moved to a smallholding in mid-Wales, and attempts were made to attach the movement to its nearest indigenously Welsh relative Cymdeithas Cyfamodwyr Cymru Rhydd (Covenanters for a Free Wales). Griffin saw potential in the 'white flight' from English conurbations: counter-urbanization driven by ethnic and racial concerns. During the BSE crisis attempts were made to recruit Welsh farmers by means of leaflets distributed at markets, with a little success. Griffin is trying to take the organization 'upmarket', with rural and respectable support, in imitation of Le Pen's Front National in France. This involves concealing much of the true nature of his party's beliefs.[31] His distaste for skinheads may explain why it is groups like the Ku Klux Klan and Combat 18 which seem to be colonizing the south Wales Valleys. The Klan has had a presence in Wales at least since the late 1980s when Alan Belshella, who was brought up in America and a was Klan member there, moved to live near Maesteg.[32]

Some of the racial violence in Wales is inspired, directly or indirectly, by groups like this. There is also considerable evidence of more routine day-to-day racial abuse in Welsh society. Some actions were potentially lethal: shots have been fired through the windows of the Immigration Advisory Service and at premises owned by Asians and Jews in South Glamorgan.[33] More recently, there has been an incident which suggests the possibility that violent groups based in disadvantaged communities of different races may clash with each other. This seems to have been the case in the riots in the north of England in 2001, and a running battle between white and Asian youths in Cardiff could be a smaller version of this.[34]

Is such hostility and exclusion, however, the sum total of race relations in contemporary Wales? Clearly, this is not the case. Most people in the Valleys are not members or supporters of vicious racist groups. Many are appalled at their presence and exhibit tolerant attitudes. People interviewed in the Rhondda about the racist attacks on Asian shopkeepers and doctors have expressed disgust at the actions of a group they brand as a minority. Some of the victims have confirmed that they have much local support and that the 'good people' feel ashamed of what has happened. The perpetrators are seen as 'stupid . . . childish'. A landlord whose pub was adorned with racist graffiti was concerned that it would get the reputation of being a racist pub. As well as the abusers we have to remember the people who are prepared to brave hostility to pursue relationships with black people. In one case in Porth a white youth who verbally defended an abused Asian restaurant owner and insisted that all people are equal was stabbed and subsequently died. A police inspector stresses that in such attacks it is the 'pillars of the community' who are being abused by the mindless.[35]

In contemporary Wales, those who indulge in ethnic violence are more marginal to their communities than they were in the past. They are associated with political groups which are far outside the mainstream. They are frequently condemned not just by the forces of order but also by many ordinary people, who find their behaviour offensive and dangerous. It is difficult for them to claim the moral superiority which the ethnic crowd once did in Wales. There is now a substantial structure of anti-racist opinion and of political action to promote racial equality which did not exist in the past. It is harder to mobilize against ethnic minorities because of this.

This is not to be complacent about the current situation. Members of ethnic minorities frequently experience racial abuse, while racial attacks and murders also occur.[36] Perhaps the very isolation of this strand of opinion encourages violence. Terrorism, after all, usually grows out of political weakness. Certainly, the communal aspect of earlier ethnic riots had some impact in constraining violence within limits acceptable to that society, which was usually short of killing people. Yet it is hard to envisage a return of the communally based attacks of the past – unless they should grow out of the hostility of two disadvantaged communities, as suggested above. For the majority, there is no longer a repertoire of violence sanctioned by the community to draw upon. Since the 1920s communal violence in general has declined and even in the miners' strikes of 1972–85 the much vaunted mass picketing was mainly a controlled pushing and shoving match with the police.[37] Those marginalized by the economic restructuring of the Valleys and other parts of Wales will continue their vicious attacks and draw some sustenance from extreme political groups. But it is harder now than in the past to present them as representative of the underlying values of their society.

Notes

[1] Thanks to Paul O'Leary for typically incisive comments on a draft and for the organizing framework which I have borrowed for the analysis.

[2] From a huge literature, the following are central: George Rudé, *The Crowd in History* (London, 1964); E. P. Thompson, 'The moral economy of the English crowd in the eighteenth century', *Past and Present*, 50 (1971); Bob Holton, 'The crowd in history: some problems of theory and method', *Social History*, 34 (1978).

[3] E. J. Hobsbawm, *Primitive Rebels* (Manchester, 1959) was one of the few studies to show a concern for such reactionary violence.

[4] The Welsh historian R. Merfyn Jones confidently predicted that the Toxteth riots of 1981 would have their logic and the selectivity of their targets displayed by subsequent research, a view amply confirmed in the event. R. Merfyn Jones, 'A land fit for Volvoes', *Arcade*, 19 (24 July 1981), 5–6.

[5] Neil Evans, 'Voices of the unheard: contemporary British urban riots in historical perspective', in Ieuan Gwynedd Jones and Glanmor Williams (eds), *Social Policy, Crime and Punishment: Essays in Memory of Jane Morgan* (Cardiff, 1994).

[6] The idea of historically specific repertoires is central to the work of the historian/sociologist Charles Tilly. For a brief introduction to his work, see his 'Major forms of collective action in Western Europe 1500–1975', *Theory and Society*, 3/3 (Fall 1976); Michael P. Hanagan, Leslie Page Moch and Wayne Te Brake (eds), *Challenging Authority: The Historical Study of Contention* (Minneapolis, 1998), editors' introduction and essay by Tilly.

[7] Neil Evans, 'Immigrants and minorities in Wales: a comparative perspective', *Llafur*, 5/4 (1991), 5–26, and ch. 1 above.

[8] Paul O'Leary, 'Anti-Irish riots in Wales, 1826–1882', *Llafur*, 5/1 (1991), 27–36.

[9] Louise Miskell, 'Reassessing the anti-Irish riot: popular protest and the Irish immigrant presence in south Wales, *c.*1826–1882', in Paul O'Leary (ed.), *The Irish in Wales* (Liverpool, forthcoming).

[10] Ibid.

[11] M. J. Daunton, 'Jack ashore: seamen in Cardiff before 1914', *Welsh History Review*, 9/2 (December 1978); Neil Evans, *Darker Cardiff: The Underside of the City, 1840–1960* (Cardiff, forthcoming) gives a slightly different and fuller analysis.

[12] Neil Evans, 'Red summers 1917–1919', *History Today*, 51/2 (February 2001).

[13] Neil Evans, ' "A tidal wave of impatience": the Cardiff general strike of 1911', in Geraint H. Jenkins and J. Beverley Smith (eds), *Politics and Society in Wales 1840–1922: Essays in Honour of Ieuan Gwynedd Jones* (Cardiff, 1988).

[14] W. D. Rubinstein, 'The anti-Jewish riots in south Wales: a re-examination', *Welsh History Review*, 18/4 (1997).

[15] This point is re-emphasized by Geoffrey Alderman, 'The anti-Jewish riots of August 1911 in south Wales: a response', *Welsh History Review*, 20 (2001).

[16] David Englander (ed.), *A Documentary History of Jewish Immigrants in Britain, 1840–1920* (Leicester, 1994), 289–98.

[17] Hywel Francis, *Miners against Fascism: Wales and the Spanish Civil War* (London, 1984); Stephen M. Cullen, 'Another nationalism: the British Union of Fascists in Glamorgan, 1932–40', *Welsh History Review*, 17/1 (1994), 105.

[18] *Arcade*, 20 (7 August 1981), 2–3.

[19] *Western Mail* (29, 30 August 1986); *South Wales Echo* (29 August, 1 September 1986).

[20] Beatrix Campbell, *Goliath: Britain's Dangerous Places* (London, 1993), ch. 1; Anne Power and Rebecca Tunstall, *Dangerous Disorder: Riots and Disturbances in Thirteen Areas of Britain, 1991–92* (York, 1997), 40.

[21] *The Times* (8 December 1994); *Western Mail* (26 October 1995).

[22] *Wales on Sunday* (24 October 1993). Paul Myers, 'Race attacks challenge idyll of welcome in Welsh valleys', *Guardian* (3 December 1994); *Western Mail* (9 June 1995); Stephen Evans, 'What's to be done about Welsh racism', *Planet*, 110 (April–May 1995), 115–16.

[23] Evans 'What's to be done', 115.

[24] National Library of Wales (NLW), S&VA, AM6989/3, 'Week-in-Week-out', 8 June 1999 – interview with skinheads in the Rhondda.

[25] R. Merfyn Jones, 'Beyond identity? The reconstruction of the Welsh', *Journal of British Studies*, 31/4 (October 1992).

[26] NLW, S&VA, AM6989/3, 'Week-in-Week-out', 8 June 1999 – interview with skinheads in the Rhondda. The interviewees confirmed Steve Evans' s view that the main focus of their anger was Asian people.

[27] NLW, S&VA, AM 3268/3, 'The way it is', BBC2, 22 October 1996 – interview with 'Jimmy'.

[28] NLW, S&VA, AM6989/3, 'Week-in-Week-out', 8 June 1999 – interview with skinheads in the Rhondda.

[29] South Glamorgan Racial Equality Council, *Annual Report, 1993–4*, 8.

[30] Beti Jones, *Etholiadau'r Ganrif: Welsh Elections, 1886–1997* (Talybont, 1999), 127–30, 131–2, 143–4.

[31] Grahame Davies, 'National Front Cymru', *Planet*, 65 (Oct./Nov. 1987), 109–11; Davies, 'National Front Cymru update', *Planet*, 66 (Dec./Jan. 1987–8), 119; Davies, 'The far right: the activities of the Welsh redistibutivists', *Planet*, 97 (Feb./March 1993); *Western Mail* (7 May 1998); Nick Ryan, 'England's green and unpleasant land', *Times Magazine* (10 April 1999).

[32] *Wales on Sunday* (24 October 1993); *Western Mail* (March 2002).

[33] South Glamorgan Racial Equality Council, *Annual Report, 1986–7*, 24; *Annual Report, 1993–4*, 8; *Annual Report, 1994–5*, 1; *Annual Report, 1995–6*, 7.

[34] *South Wales Echo* (2002).

[35] NLW, S&VA, AM 6989, 'Week-in-Week-Out', 8 June 1999; AM 3268/3, 'The way it is', BBC 2, 22 October 1996.

[36] In this context, see Kusminder Chahal and Louis Julienne, *'We Can't All Be White!' Racist Victims in the UK* (Joseph Rowntree Foundation, York, 1999), some of the fieldwork for which was carried out in Cardiff.

[37] Roger Geary, *Policing Industrial Disputes, 1893 to 1985* (paperback edn, London, 1986), chs. 5ff.

7 Playing the Game: Sport and Ethnic Minorities in Modern Wales

NEIL EVANS AND PAUL O'LEARY[1]

Organized sport is a prominent feature of modern social and cultural life. Since the late nineteenth century it has provided a mechanism for the creation of powerful and enduring group identities, focused on neighbourhood and municipality, region and nation, empire and race. Equally importantly, sport has been a means of socializing individuals into what it means to be men and women in a particular society at a particular juncture in history. This potent conjunction of gender, nationality and race makes a study of the relationship between ethnic minorities and sport a particularly rewarding one, because the formation of group identities is fundamentally about the drawing of boundaries between those who are considered members of the group and those who remain outside. This chapter provides a preliminary survey of the relationship between ethnic groups and sport in Wales, paying particular attention to the experiences of the Irish up to the 1920s and the black population thereafter.

Competitive spectator sport in its modern form in the United Kingdom emerged in the late nineteenth century.[2] Like many other leisure-time activities at this time, sport was profoundly shaped by the ethos and demands of the new industrial society, including the acceptance of agreed rules and codes of behaviour, the adoption of the time discipline of industrial capitalism on the field of play, and the establishment of hierarchical leagues for the organizing of competitions. Increasing leisure time for workers and a commensurate rise in consumer purchasing power ensured the growth and popularity of spectator sport as a mass activity. Moreover, mass communications facilitated this development, allowing the experiences of the sports field to be communicated to a wider population than could possibly be present in the flesh to witness a sporting event.

In such circumstances sport had the paradoxical ability to both unite and divide society: uniting in support of a team or sporting hero entailed the kind of rivalries with other teams and sporting idols that generated intense loyalties. Sport, as much as any other social activity, reflected tensions in the wider society. How did ethnic groups fare in such circumstances? Could they, too, take advantage of new forms of leisure to assert their own identities as well as utilizing them for integration? Or did the tensions between different ethnic groups in the workplace spill over into leisure-time activities?

During the mid-nineteenth century the Irish had been the object of intense ethnic antagonism, often spilling over into violence. Between 1826 and 1882 there were twenty cases of serious anti-Irish violence. Organized sport might have been one of the many different factors contributing to Irish integration in south Wales in the late nineteenth and early twentieth centuries.[3] Whereas in other parts of Britain sectarianism was reflected to a greater or lesser degree in sport, south Wales appears to have been remarkably free from this kind of overt ethnic tension. In Glasgow, where soccer was divided along religious lines, sectarianism was at its worst. However, in south Wales the existence of specifically Irish rugby teams, such as the Aberavon Greenstars and the Newport Hibernians, did not represent a sectarian attitude to sport so much as an expression of community or neighbourhood identity along the same lines as other local teams, some of which were organized around particular churches, neighbourhoods or public houses.

Possibly the important distinction here is that between rugby football as the dominant sporting activity in Wales rather than association football (soccer), which was the popular sporting activity in England. Dai Smith and Gareth Williams have demonstrated how sport acted as a kind of cultural solvent in industrial south Wales during those years.[4] The background to this development is significant. The pell-mell expansion of the export coal industry attracted migrants from rural Wales, England and Ireland on a remarkable scale and created a new society that lacked the kind of civic institutions that might have been able to integrate newcomers. Among the significant developments was the emergence of a Welsh international side that included players from diverse cultural backgrounds, some of whom had not been born in Wales. Famously, the *Western Mail* stated of the international player Gwyn Nicholls, who was born in Gloucestershire, that 'in everything except birth, he was a true rugby son of Wales'.[5]

During the decades immediately preceding the First World War, rugby was an institution promoting social integration in particular places and for particular groups. English incomers in the South Wales Coalfield benefited from the popularity of this form of leisure activity. It became a focus of allegiance that could overcome cultural distinctions. But sport could not transcend all such differences for all groups. These were also the decades during which there was communal violence against the Jews and the Chinese (1911) and the black community (Cardiff, 1919). Does the size of the minority matter as far as sport is concerned? Paradoxically, it might well be that the larger a minority, the easier it is to achieve recognition in sporting terms. Moreover, some sports have a greater capacity for integration than others. In Cardiff, baseball was widely associated with the Irish but provided few avenues of contact with the remainder of society.[6]

As far as the version of Welsh nationality represented by sport was concerned, the Welsh nation was white and excluded groups such as the Jews who were seen to be incompatible with the basic values of Welsh society. So there was a limit to the role to be played by sport; it can constitute meaning, but it is also influenced by other aspects of social life.

Thus, rugby became the archetypal symbol of an inclusive national identity with the capacity for uniting people of divergent backgrounds in an inclusive common identity. But it was not an all-encompassing blanket. Soccer was a later arrival, at least as a first-class game was concerned, and it owed a great deal to the actions of English incomers. The emergence of Cardiff City as a professional club in 1910 was the tip of an iceberg of football in south Wales. By then there were 268 clubs affiliated to the South Wales Association and twelve leagues. The real growth was after 1906, when there had been only five leagues and 74 clubs. What was crucial to this process was the immigration of men from north Wales, the Midlands and south-east England into south Wales.[7] They wanted to watch a sport that they were familiar with. As many as 1,000 of them might board special trains to watch Bristol City, so there was a clear demand in south Wales. It was Cardiff's role – perhaps because it, rather than the Valleys, was the spearhead of English migration into south Wales – to be the leader in this process. From the 1890s it had established a

Schools' Football League, at a time when spectators had jeered the game and stolen the ball, but this had gathered strength and was ultimately to establish close relations with Cardiff City. Symbolically it was a Bristolian, Bartley Wilson, who was the real founder of Cardiff City.[8]

Soccer, then, represented the arrival of the English in large numbers in the last surge of the expansion of the South Wales Coalfield. But rugby was already established in a position of sporting hegemony and it dictated the overall position. Soccer drew its impetus from English incomers from the Midlands and north, whereas rugby had come in from the west of England. However, rugby became absorbed into the Welsh self-image.[9] Soccer never achieved this, despite its substantial support throughout Wales. In the case of the Irish, an aspect of rugby which had the potential to cause divisions was the onset of international contests between Ireland and Wales from the season of 1881–2. Initially, these events were ill starred, with fixtures cancelled on a number of occasions during the 1880s when relationships between the governing bodies of the sport in the two countries became strained.[10] Yet these minor hiccups failed to inflame wider passions. These matches failed to have a disrupting effect, largely because of the perceived affinity between the two countries from the mid-1880s, when Welsh Liberals overwhelmingly came to support Irish nationalists in their demand for Home Rule within the United Kingdom. So pervasive was this support that when the Irish team that played against Wales at Llanelli on 7 March 1891 took the field after a series of disputed games they were greeted with sympathetic cries of 'Home Rule for Ireland'.[11] Additional evidence of rugby's integrative qualities can be found in the case of a player like William O'Neil, the son of immigrants from County Cork, who represented Wales at international level; he won eleven international caps for Wales between 1904 and 1908, during the first 'golden era' of Welsh international rugby.

The more individualist sport of boxing allowed an Irishman like Jim Driscoll to achieve both personal success and the approbation of the wider community. It has been argued that boxers occupy a special position in a society during a period of transition such as that experienced by south Wales in the years before 1914 and during subsequent decades. The sport had moved away from the illegal bare-knuckled prize fighting that had been popular previously. In fact, boxing acquired a degree of respectability previously considered unthinkable. By the end of the century, the ritual violence of the faction-fight was channelled into boxing as a formal and supervised (if not yet entirely respectable) leisure activity. Boxing held a particular attraction for working-class Irishmen.[12] By promoting boxing and other sports among young men, the Catholic clergy consciously strove to channel male aggression into disciplined sporting activity, thereby hoping to create a leisure culture which rejected alcohol. The widespread popularity of the sport was demonstrated by the enthusiastic welcome accorded John L. Sullivan, the renowned Irish-American boxer, on his visit to Cardiff in January 1888.[13]

It was this working-class culture that produced an emblematic sporting hero among the Irish in south Wales, one who embraced the raw cult of masculinity that surrounded boxing and succeeded in transcending his ethnic origins to become a hero for both Irish and Welsh. 'Peerless' Jim Driscoll was without doubt the most important sporting figure in the Irish community in south Wales in the years straddling the First World War. He was born into Cardiff's 'Little Ireland' community in 1880. He progressed from the grim experience of learning his trade as a fairground boxer to win the world featherweight title in 1909 and a coveted Lonsdale Belt in 1910–11. The nickname 'peerless' was bestowed on him by an uncharacteristically appreciative press in New York after his unsuccessful attempt to wrest the world boxing title from one of their own fighters; at home he was hailed as 'the prince of Wales'.[14] He was respected as an individual who maintained an allegiance to his Catholic religion, and he even turned down a lucrative fight with the French boxer Charles Ledoux because of his promise to attend an event at Nazareth House Catholic children's home in Cardiff. When he died in 1925 the city came to a standstill as tens of thousands of people lined the streets to pay their respects.[15]

By the early twentieth century the Irish community can be regarded as well integrated into the society of south Wales. Even some of their middle-class nationalists shared many of the assumptions about empire and imperialism that were an important feature of the political consciousness of the time. Earlier in the nineteenth century the Irish had been the butt of hostility and violence in many south Wales communities, but now they were able to take advantage of sporting activities to cement a wider integration into the emerging male mass leisure culture of the region.

Among the reasons why sport had an integrative function for the Irish in Wales was that broader cultural and political developments conspired to create a situation in which it was possible for a majority of the Welsh to perceive the Irish as brother Celts with broadly compatible political aspirations within the United Kingdom. Certainly, between the 1880s and 1914 Irish Nationalists' pursuit of self-government within the United Kingdom, as opposed to separatism, allowed Gladstonian Liberals to support the cause of Irish Home Rule. In brief, before 1914 it was possible to conceive of a self-governing Ireland remaining within the empire.

Imperialism and the discourse of race provide a crucial context for understanding the nature of sporting activity in Wales before 1914. Historians of rugby have emphasized the way in which ideas of Welshness were seen by the majority of people as being wholly compatible with an overarching British identity that was increasingly rooted in popular imperialism. This was demonstrated most clearly in the famous victory of the Welsh national team against the New Zealand All Blacks at Cardiff in 1905. The press considered the event to be one with imperial ramifications. The New Zealanders had remained undefeated during their tour of the British Isles and the *Western Mail* asserted that the Welsh team had 'come to the rescue of the Empire'.[16] The comment was accompanied by a remarkable cartoon by J. M. Staniforth depicting a Welshman carrying a rifle with fixed bayonet, representing the Welsh team, facing a grotesquely drawn black 'savage' wearing a grass skirt and carrying a rifle advancing on him. This black fighter has already killed the Scots, Irish and English in their respective trenches, while the Welshman defends the final trench under a Union Jack bearing the slogan 'Home Country'.[17]

This cartoon deserves comment for several reasons. The New Zealand team was composed of members of the white settler community ('All Blacks' referred to the colour of their strip), yet Staniforth chose to depict this sporting assault on the 'Mother Country' in overtly racial and martial terms. It is a shocking reminder of the extent to which race pervaded public discussions, even when it did not surface in such a crude manifestation as this. Even the Liberal press described the match of 1905 in overtly racial terms, although in this case they referred to the Welsh 'race'.[18] Against this background, it is important to recognize that ethnic groups such as the Irish could achieve integration in Wales partly because of the unspoken assumption that they, too, were members of the white imperial community, in spite of their Catholicism.

Viewed in this context, the Irish experience raises important questions more generally about the relationship of sport to the creation of ethnic identity and integration. Was it a question of sport promoting integration or was it a case of sport merely reinforcing a trend that already existed in other domains of society? Did sport play an active part in the process of integration or was it a passive observer of that process? After all, in the decades after 1870 the Irish experienced integration in a number of domains of social life that were, ostensibly, more important: workplace tensions began to disappear as the mass unions of the 1880s took root; in political terms, Welsh Liberals were, on the whole, much more sympathetic to Irish demands for Home Rule than were their English counterparts, who were much more seriously divided over the issue. The rise of mass spectator sport from the 1870s coincided with the period when Irish integration was taking place. Is it possible to overemphasize the role sport played in this process?

One way of addressing this general problem is by examining the extent of participation by other ethnic minorities, especially non-whites, in sporting activity in an attempt to gauge the relevant importance of sport in constituting the kinds of ethnic identities that might assist integration. It also provides an opportunity to gauge the extent of opposition to such participation. There is some evidence of an interest in sport by male members of other ethnic groups. The Jewish communities of Cardiff and Swansea played each other in an annual soccer match in the 1920s, for instance. But it is the experience of the black community which provides instructive parallels and contrasts with the Irish experience.

Irish immigrants were being integrated into south Wales society at the same time as sporting loyalties were being formed. Black newcomers, by contrast, impinged on an established situation. They consequently found it harder to make the breakthrough. The largest black community was in Cardiff's Butetown and there is evidence of sporting interests there in the inter-war period. Photographs survive of various teams playing football, cricket and other games. Most arose from particular sections of the community and were often teams solely composed of black players. There was, for instance, a soccer team called the Cardiff All Blacks (not to be confused with the New Zealand rugby team) in the late 1930s which played annual charity matches. It was not involved in regular league or other cup competitions and it is likely that this fact was the most important factor preventing the emergence of racial intolerance during these games. One of the Cardiff All Blacks players had a trial for Cardiff City FC in 1938, but he was unsuccessful; it is impossible to determine whether this was because of racism.[19] Intriguingly, the Welsh soccer team was the first of any of the representative national teams of the British Isles to field a black player. On 5 December 1931 Chepstow-born Eddie Parris, who played for Bradford Park Avenue in the second division, represented Wales against Ireland. Some of the shine of this achievement is diminished by the fact that he was probably chosen because the Welsh Football Association had difficulty in getting English League clubs to release Welsh players for international matches. This was his only international cap.[20]

Nearer home, discrimination was far more the name of the game. Many people in Butetown have recalled that only racial discrimination prevented the St Lucian seaman James Ernest from playing cricket for Glamorgan, while the young Roy Francis abandoned rugby union with Brynmawr and Abertillery for the more welcoming prospect of rugby league with Barrow in 1938. Black players were to continue for another generation to make their way in the professional game in northern England rather than in rugby union at home in Wales.[21] The professionalism of rugby league was an asset. Amateur rugby union faced the added problem of the need for a job and further possibilities of racism.

There were many who made the trip after the Second World War. Two institutions formed the basis of this progression. One was the South Church Street School. This path was blazed by Gus Risman, a man of Scottish extraction, who played only a few union games before signing for Salford in 1929. He became one of the highest scoring kickers in the history of the game, playing until 1954 and then capping this with a successful coaching career.[22] He was following a trajectory pioneered by Jim Sullivan, from the Cardiff Irish community (but not from South Church Street School), who dominated the rugby league world in the inter-war period and left all subsequent full backs in the game in his shadow.[23] Sullivan went to Wigan, the club which the greatest Welsh black player, Billy Boston, was to grace from the 1950s.

Before turning to Boston we need to look at the second of the institutions, the Cardiff International Athletic Club (sometimes abbreviated as CIACs), which was founded in 1946. The club represented a second generation of Butetown people, essentially those who had been born in Cardiff rather than those who had been born abroad. Its uniting of all peoples in sporting action was a reflection of this second-generation approach. Butetown had tended to develop a unity out of the struggles against discrimination of the 1930s and the rhetoric of racial equality which characterized the Second World War.[24] Many members were fresh from the services. The club quickly came to focus on rugby but over the years would provide cricket, soccer, baseball and basketball teams. The free-flowing rugby they played quickly built up fixture lists with second-class sides in the Valleys (there were few opponents from Cardiff) and tours in England and Ireland. The path to touring was eased by the misapprehension of some opponents that they were going to be matched against Welsh internationals! It was a community venture, sometimes taking two buses full of supporters to away fixtures. It produced many fine players and eventually a good run of success in rugby competitions, with a peak in the mid-1970s.

It was from this side that a crop of players emerged in the 1950s who would become legendary in rugby league. Their move out of Wales reveals much about racial attitudes in Wales at the time. There were no great examples of black players to follow in the union game and the only precedents were in the professional code. As early as 1888 a Maori team had toured Britain and got a cool response from the rugby teams of southern England, many of which had refused to play them. The situation was very different in the northern industrial areas which would break away in the next few years to create the Northern Union, the ancestor of rugby league. It has been suggested that in the north the working-class players identified with the socially excluded.[25] It was Wigan, in particular, which became associated with a racially integrated team by the post-war period. It had signed a Maori player as early as 1910.[26]

It was little wonder, therefore, that Billy Boston chose to go to Wigan and that Wigan saw a talent in him which meant they never expended more effort in signing any other player; they paid £3,000 for his signature. This contrasts starkly with Wales; Boston was convinced that he would never play for his country in the union game. Born in 1934 of West Indian and Irish parentage, he had played occasionally for Neath and had captained both the Welsh Boys Clubs and the Cardiff and District XV. His ambition was to play cricket for Glamorgan and rugby for Wales, but he saw little prospect of either. The cost of such attitudes of racial exclusion in south Wales was high as he was clearly one of the finest wingers (or backs in general, as he could play anywhere in the back line) to come out of Wales. His scoring record is unique: more tries than he had games (571 in 564). In Wigan he became a civic institution revered for his play, his conduct and modesty.[27]

Billy Boston was the central player in a cluster who trod similar paths. At around the same time Johnny Freeman went from the CIACs to play for Halifax. His achievements were immense, though not quite comparable to Boston's. He never gained an international cap, despite being rated by many the best winger in the world in his era. This, along with Wigan's infamous suspension of Boston in 1956 when he was made the scapegoat for a heavy cup defeat and the failure of the Great Britain team to select the outstanding Roy Francis to tour colour-barred Australia in 1946, suggest that rugby league was not entirely free of racial prejudice, however much better its record was than union.[28]

Colin Dixon also took the route from Butetown to rugby league after being 'overlooked' for a youth cap in rugby union in 1961. He went on to play 715 first-class games in rugby league for Halifax, Salford, Hull Kingston Rovers, Wales and Great Britain, scoring 177 tries, and one goal – a total of 533 points. His transfer to Salford in 1968 was for a world record fee of £15,000. Clive Sullivan, again, from the generation below Boston and Freeman (born in the 1940s rather than the 1930s), reached the very peak of the rugby league game, symbolized by his captaincy of Great Britain in the winning world cup side in 1972. He had overcome serious injuries as a child to achieve this and had once been told he would never walk, let alone play competitive sport, at the highest level.[29]

Also out of the CIACs came a champion in another sport – the boxer Joe Erskine. He played in the same side as his cousin, Johnny Freeman, and Billy Boston. However, he decided to do his combats one-to-one rather than in the collective arena. His family was famous and respected in Butetown as the keepers of a seamen's boarding house. His father was a West Indian and his mother (like most in Butetown) was from the indigenous white population. Not all have recognized Erskine's mixed-race background – he was not obviously 'black', but he was usually described at the time as coming from 'Tiger Bay', which was a way of announcing his ethnic background to the world and in 1964, when his career was over, he explicitly referred to himself as 'half-caste'. Erskine's introduction to the world of boxing came from his legendary grandmother who reportedly trained and sparred with two generations of local fighters, including her grandson. In the world of boxing, perhaps the breakthrough for black boxers had been made internationally by the 1940s. Joe Louis's fights against Max Schmelling had established the right of black men to be in the boxing ring, and even to carry the hopes of racially segregated America. In 1948 black boxers were allowed to compete for British titles.

Like Boston and Freeman, Erskine got into his chosen sport effectively through his army service. From the beginning he was compared with Jim Driscoll and he carried the aspirations of his community into the ring with him. When he won the British Empire title at Maindy Stadium in Cardiff in 1956, a runner carried the news back home to Butetown. His success was celebrated in a calypso – written, appropriately enough in Butetown's mixed community, by twin brothers of Somali descent. Erskine's career was quite short. As a boxer he had few rivals and some who saw him compared his footwork to that of Muhammad Ali, but his punch was rarely of a knockout variety and he frequently had to take hard punishment on his way to his points victories. He earned a large amount of money for the time – far more than rugby players like Boston or Freeman can have done – but he spent it on drink, women and gambling. In this, too, he echoed the frailties of the great Jim Driscoll. He died peacefully at the age of 56 in 1990 in the lonely Cardiff flat that he inhabited.[30] The fact that he chose to live in Cardiff and was a frequent visitor to the haunts of his youth speaks volumes for his commitment to his community, and he was one of the sporting heroes celebrated on the walls of the now demolished 'Bosun' pub in Butetown which had an impressive display of photographs and newspaper cuttings representing achievements in many sporting fields.

By the 1970s black sportspeople were beginning to emerge on the British stage. The subsequent prominent black sportspeople in Wales have not emerged from the tight-knit ghetto that was 1940s Butetown. Clive Sullivan had begun the breaking of the mould: he was from Splott and Ely rather than Butetown, though he had revered the young Billy Boston's ability with a cricket bat and later seen him play rugby league on TV. In other sports black players were more isolated and lacked the kind of community support which Butetown provided. Hubert 'Bull' Best (aka Tommy), who was born in Milford Haven in Pembrokeshire to a Welsh mother and a Jamaican father, made his football league debut for Chester City in October 1948. His skill on the pitch soon attracted the attention of Cardiff City FC, who secured his transfer for £7,000 and a signing-on fee of £150. He established a good rapport with spectators and stated that racist abuse merely made him strive harder to do well. He had been given a schoolboy trial for the Welsh team but had been turned down. In spite of some praise for his abilities as a professional sportsman, his achievements in club competition were limited and he was never given a place in the national team.[31] Cardiff City's next venture with a black player came a decade later when the black South African, Steve Makone, was signed from the Dutch club Hercules. He stayed for only one season (1959–60), it being felt that he was not strong enough for the British game and pitches. In what passed for wit at the time, he was known to the crowd as 'Omo'.[32] By the 1970s black players were well enough established for Clive Charles to become Cardiff's captain in 1974–5; but he came from Bow rather than from the local area. The brothers Dave and Gary Bennett were great crowd pleasers in the early 1980s after they were signed from Manchester City, the city of their birth.[33]

Rugby union took a long time to shake off the racism which had denied careers to Billy Boston, Johnny Freeman and Clive Sullivan. Nigel Walker gave up the game at the age of eighteen when he failed to be selected for the Under 19s side, despite outclassing his opponent in the final trial. He returned to play at the age of twenty-nine when his athletics career was effectively over and had a distinguished Indian summer for Wales, which leaves question marks about what he might have done in earlier days. It has to be recalled that from the 1960s to the 1980s there were many in the Welsh Rugby Union (WRU) who were prepared to welcome South African touring teams which were selected on the basis of race, to send Welsh tours to South Africa and even to defend that country's system of apartheid. It was hardly a sport which opened its arms to black players. The Springboks tour of 1970 was prevented by mass demonstrations and these were bitterly resented by the rugby establishment. Unofficial tours of South Africa continued even after that, though, of course, outside the auspices of the WRU. To many black people it must have seemed that rugby remained the carrier of imperial values that it had been at the turn of the century.

By the 1990s the breakthrough had been made. The first black player to play for Wales at rugby union was Newport-born Mark Brown of Pontypool RFC, who represented Wales six times between 1983 and 1986.[34] During the 1980s and 1990s a small number of other players followed in his footsteps, including Glenn Webbe, Nigel Walker and Colin Charvis. Their progress in the game was not necessarily smooth. Spectators threw bananas at Glenn Webbe at some club matches (a sign of disparagement more often seen in English soccer games) and the black Cardiff RFC player, Gerald Cordle, caused an uproar in 1987 when he clashed with a spectator who repeatedly abused him in a match against Aberavon Quins in the Welsh Cup.[35] By contrast, Nigel Walker, who also played for Cardiff, claims to have experienced no such problems.[36] On the whole, overt racism amongst rugby spectators appears to have been less pronounced than in soccer. This is not to say the sport has not been immune to stereotyping. A survey of Heineken League players (the highest echelon of the game in Wales) in 1993–4 revealed that fully two-thirds of black players played on the wing. This remarkable statistic, which reflects the experience of black players more generally in British rugby, has been attributed to the fact that positionally the wing is situated away from the decision-making aspects of the game.[37] Nor is racist behaviour on the pitch necessarily dead.[38]

By the 1990s there were enough black people prominent in sport in Wales for them to rate a feature in *Wales on Sunday*.[39] The four picked out as 'Welsh, gifted and black' were the athletes Colin Jackson and Nigel Walker (he had not then moved into rugby), the boxer Steve Robinson and the footballer Ryan Giggs. None of these was from Butetown. Walker was born in Cardiff of Jamaican parents and grew up in Rumney; Jackson, also born of Jamaican parents, was from Llanrumney. Giggs, whose black father, Danny Wilson, had played rugby league, is not frequently identified as a black player, though he has indicated his pride in his African background.[40] Giggs grew up in Manchester while Walker and Jackson came from the more diffuse black immigration of the 1960s rather than from the established black community in Butetown. Similar points could be made about other sporting heroes. Nathan Blake, who graced a Cardiff City shirt before going to play in the higher leagues, is from Cardiff, though not from Butetown. Rob Earnshaw, Cardiff's talented, somersaulting striker, is from Caerphilly.

By now sport has become a recognized avenue of achievement for black people in British society. Those players and competitors who play in Wales and in Welsh teams are in many ways doing what is expected of them, rather than breaking moulds. The rules for qualifying for representing a country in international competitions have become so fluid that there is hardly any surprise that black players come through. This could cause some frictions in the past. When qualifications shifted from birthplace to the current variety some wondered whether Welshness was meaningful in such a context. The short-lived magazine *Arcade* was at best insensitive (some said racist) in publishing in 1981 a photograph of the Swansea black boxer Neville Meade on its cover, with the caption 'How Welsh is Welsh sport?'[41] Now the Welsh ancestry of black players can be valuable to Welsh teams which have a small population from which to draw their talent, and games like rugby face more competition from the variety of games which are on offer. Only committed racists would deny Wales the services of Colin Charvis, who qualifies on the basis of a Cardiff-born mother, despite his East Midlands upbringing. The fact that he played for Wales via London Welsh, which he joined as a student, serves only to reveal the fluidity of post-nationality.

The real question for the future will be what happens to players after they finish playing. In rugby league many showed the way. Billy Boston became a successful publican, which in his day was the summit of many players' ambitions. Others became successful coaches. It largely remains to be seen what will happen to the black players in Wales who have come to prominence more recently. Nigel Walker has become Head of Sport at BBC Wales; Charvis is an engineer and an intellectual.[42] In the twentieth century, sport proved to be a valuable avenue of progress and of community definition for ethnic minorities in Wales. The question now is the extent to which this can be sustained, extended and built upon.[43]

Notes

[1] Our thanks to John Jenkins, Martin Johnes, Bryn Jones and Gareth Williams for their kind help with this chapter.

[2] Tony Mason, *Sport in Britain: A Social History* (London, 1988); Richard J. Holt, *Sport and the British: A Modern History* (Oxford, 1989).

[3] Paul O'Leary, *Immigration and Integration: The Irish in Wales, 1798–1922* (Cardiff, 2000).

[4] Dai Smith and Gareth Williams, *Fields of Praise: The Official History of the Welsh*

Rugby Union, 1881–1981 (Cardiff, 1980); Gareth Williams, *1905 and All That* (Llandysul, 1991). For a different perspective, see David L. Andrews and Jeremy W. Howell, 'Transforming into a tradition: rugby and the making of imperial Wales, 1890–1914', in Alan G. Ingham and John W. Loy (eds), *Sport in Social Development: Traditions, Transitions and Transformations* (Leeds, 1993), 77–96, and David L. Andrews, 'Sport and the masculine hegemony of the modern nation: Welsh rugby, culture and society, 1890–1914', in John Nauright and Timothy J. L. Chandler (eds), *Making Men: Rugby and Masculine Identity* (London, 1996), 50–69. On soccer, see Martin Johnes, 'That other game: a social history of soccer in south Wales, *c.*1906–39', unpublished University of Wales Ph.D. thesis, 1998.

[5] Smith and Williams, *Fields of Praise*, 33.

[6] Martin Johnes, ' "Poor man's cricket": baseball, class and community in south Wales, *c.*1880–1950', *International Journal of the History of Sport*, 17/4 (2000), 160.

[7] Johnes, 'That other game', 17.

[8] This section is based on an unpublished paper by Neil Evans.

[9] Brian Lile and David Farmer, 'The early development of association football in south Wales, 1890–1906', *Transactions of the Honourable Society of Cymmrodorion* (1984), 213–14; Martin Johnes, 'Irredeemably English? Football as a Welsh sport', *Planet*, 133 (February–March 1999), 72–8.

[10] Smith and Williams, *Fields of Praise*, 63.

[11] John Billot, *History of Welsh International Rugby* (Ferndale, 1970), 34.

[12] O'Leary, *Immigration and Integration*, 240.

[13] *South Wales Daily News* (4 January 1888). There is a brief mention of John L. Sullivan's visit to Cardiff in Michael T. Isenberg, *John L. Sullivan and His America* (Urbana and Chicago, 1994), 242.

[14] John O'Sullivan, 'How green was their island?', in Stewart Williams (ed.), *The Cardiff Book II* (Cardiff and Bridgend, 1974), 20–36; Dai Smith, 'Focal heroes', in his *Aneurin Bevan and the World of South Wales* (Cardiff, 1993), 328–32.

[15] *South Wales Echo* (3 February 1925); *South Wales Daily News* (4 February 1925); *Western Mail* (4 February 1925). For details of his boxing career, see Fred Deakin, *Peerless Jim Driscoll* (Stone, Staffs, 1987).

[16] *Western Mail* (18 December 1905).

[17] The cartoon is reproduced in Andrews, 'Sport and masculine hegemony', 65.

[18] *South Wales Daily News* (18 December 1905).

[19] Johnes, 'That other game', 93.

[20] Phil Vasili, *Colouring over the White Line: The History of Black Footballers in Britain* (Edinburgh, 2000), 62.

[21] Conversations between Neil Evans and several older people (including James Ernest) in Butetown, 1978–80; Robert Gate, *Gone North: Welshmen in Rugby League*, ii (Sowerby Bridge, 1988), 43–53.

[22] Robert Gate, *Gone North*, ii, 30–44; *The Independent* (19 October 1994: obituary).

[23] Gate, *Gone North*, i, 26–42.

[24] This account of the CIACs draws on notes of an interview conducted by Neil Evans with Gerald Ernest, Butetown History and Arts Centre, 21 January 2002 and the CIACs Fixture List for 1990–1, which contains a short history, pp. 10–11. For

the community in general see: Neil Evans, 'Regulating the reserve army: Arabs, blacks and the local state in Cardiff, 1919–1945', in Kenneth Lunn (ed.), *Race and Labour in Twentieth-Century Britain* (London, 1985).

[25] Tariq Ali to John Jenkins, 7 September 1998, enclosing proposal for TV documentary 'The Democratic Game'.

[26] Phil Melling, 'Billy Boston', in Huw Richards, Peter Stead and Gareth Williams (eds), *Heart and Soul: The Character of Welsh Rugby* (Cardiff, 1998), 47–58.

[27] This paragraph derives from Gate, *Gone North*, i, 108–20, and Melling, 'Billy Boston'.

[28] Gate, *Gone North*, i, 43–53 and 108–20; Melling, 'Billy Boston'; *Sports Echo* (17 February 1996).

[29] Gate, *Gone North*, i, 95–107; ii, 153–63; Joe Latus, *Hard Road to the Top: The Clive Sullivan Story* (Hull, 1973); *The Times* (9 October 1985: obituary).

[30] This account is derived from the excellent biographical file of cuttings in Cardiff Central Library, which includes articles from *Boxing News* and the *Empire News* as well as the Cardiff press.

[31] Vasili, *Colouring over the White Line*, 133–5.

[32] John Crooks, *Cardiff City Football Club: The Official History of the Bluebirds* (Harefield, Middlesex, 1992), 67, 145; reminiscences of Desmond Evans.

[33] Ibid., 99, 138, 139.

[34] John M. Jenkins, Duncan Pierce and Timothy Auty, *Who's Who of Welsh International Rugby* (Wrexham, 1991), 27.

[35] *Western Mail* (21 December 1987).

[36] See the interview with Walker in Mark Burley, 'Welsh gifted and black: a socio-cultural study of racism and sport in Cardiff', unpublished Cardiff Institute of Higher Education MA thesis, 1994, vol. II, appendix G, interview no. 1 (no pagination).

[37] Ibid., vol. I, p. 75; Joe Maguire, 'Sport, racism and British society: a sociological study of England's male Afro/Caribbean soccer and rugby union players', in Grant Jarvie (ed.), *Sport, Racism and Ethnicity* (London, 1991), 94–113.

[38] *Western Mail* (25 February 2002).

[39] *Wales on Sunday* (17 April 1994).

[40] *Observer* (1 April 2001).

[41] Gareth Jones, 'How Welsh is Welsh sport?', *Arcade* (2 October 1981); letter from R. Merfyn Jones and editor's reply, 16 October 1981.

[42] Peter Stead, 'Colin Charvis', in Huw Richards, Peter Stead and Gareth Williams (eds), *More Heart and Soul: The Character of Welsh Rugby* (Cardiff, 1999).

[43] More attention clearly needs to be paid to the current crop of Welsh athletes, including Colin Jackson, Jamie Baulch and Christian Malcolm.

8 Religious Diversity in Wales

PAUL CHAMBERS

Welsh religious belief and practice has historically been associated with Nonconformity and an egalitarian religious practice grounded in the local chapel and the Welsh language and culture. Nonconformism emerged as a significant cultural and social force in Welsh society in the late eighteenth century and was consolidated in the nineteenth century. Grounded in religious and cultural dissent and subject to constant schisms, the religious landscape of Welsh was dotted with a patchwork of small Protestant denominations, sects and independent congregations. Taken individually, these groups were diverse in matters of belief and politics. Taken together they constituted something rather more significant, what Grace Davie[1] describes as 'established dissonance', that is, a hegemonic cultural institution based on notions of community, respectability and resistance to the perceived threat of English cultural and linguistic domination. As such, Welsh Nonconformism in the nineteenth and into the twentieth century was ideally placed to function as a significant carrier of Welsh cultural identity.[2] This status was reinforced in the popular mind, both by the religious census of 1851 (which demonstrated that about 80 per cent of the worshipping population were Nonconformist) and the growing number of Welsh politicians and political leaders that emerged from Nonconformity.[3] Welsh society, therefore, was historically informed by a close relationship between Nonconformist religion, language and ethnicity. As with other societies in which there has been a close, hegemonic relationship between a particular form of religious expression and national identity, tolerance of religious diversity is often problematic.[4]

Historians of Wales generally agree that the population movements associated with the industrialization of Wales were a key factor in the growth and consolidation of Nonconformity in the newly industrialized regions. Industrialization also saw the migration into Wales of diverse ethnic groups.[5] In terms of ethnic affiliation to religious institutions, there were a number of outcomes. Initially, small Jewish worshipping communities were established in the seaports of Swansea and Cardiff. These communities prospered and Swansea saw its first synagogue erected in 1818 and Cardiff in 1847. By the second half of the nineteenth century, small Jewish communities were also to be found in Bangor, Llandudno, the ports of Newport and Porthcawl, and the newly industrialized valleys of south Wales.[6] In terms of religious organization, the distinctive feature of these small, scattered communities was their reliance on the help of older larger communities.[7] While petty prejudices and intolerance were part of the daily experience of these Jewish communities, anti-Semitism rarely spilled over into the scale and type of violence associated with early Irish settlement, the Tredegar riots of 1911 being the exception.[8] While the Jewish community in Swansea numbered 1,000 members by 1914, it rapidly declined thereafter, giving way to Cardiff as the main area of Jewish settlement. In 1968 the Jewish population of Cardiff was estimated at 3,500, but this community too has declined markedly.[9] In the long term, Judaism did not prosper in Wales and this is reflected in the fact that Wales has only three operating synagogues today.

Of more significance to the religious landscape of Wales was the migration of persons of Irish and English ethnicity. The ports of Cardiff and Swansea, Newport and Port Talbot, as well as the industrial towns of the South Wales Coalfield all saw extensive Irish immigration. The first wave of this migration also coincided with the process that was to lead to the restoration of the Roman Catholic hierarchy in England and Wales in 1850.[10] This Irish population was overwhelmingly Catholic and, in urban areas, tended to cluster around centres of worship such as St Joseph's in Swansea and St Peter's in Cardiff. While Irish immigration did much to restore the fortunes of the Roman Catholic Church in England and Wales, the hierarchies of each country responded very differently to the increasing identification of British Catholicism with Irish ethnicity.

In England, the Catholic authorities appeared reluctant to appoint significant numbers of Irish priests to serve parishes that were overwhelmingly Irish in ethnicity.[11] In Wales, where the growth of Catholicism was almost exclusively fuelled by Irish immigration, the appointment of Irish priests was less contentious, although in the mid-nineteenth century they still constituted a minority group among the clergy.[12] Concerns about the spiritual welfare of Irish Catholics in danger of lapsing or converting to Protestantism and fears about the effects of mixed marriages were addressed by the steady importation of increasing numbers of Irish clergy to serve the new Catholic parishes of industrial Wales.[13] By 1916, the picture on the ground had changed to such an extent that a separate Province of Wales could be established. Roman Catholicism in Wales, therefore, was of necessity initially Irish in tenor and as it prospered, successive waves of migrants from England and the Catholic countries of Europe both added numbers to the Church and confirmed its status in the popular mind as an 'alien' church.

This was reflected in the cultural and social experience of the Roman Catholic Church in what was an essentially Nonconformist Wales. D. Densil Morgan comments:

> Bereft of any indigenous working class tradition such as that of Lancashire and other parts of the north of England . . . Catholicism was viewed in Wales with hostility and fear. Its *mores* were strange, its rituals mystifying, and the presence among its faithful of thousands of virtually peasant Irishmen and their rough families put the church well beyond the pale. For most Welsh Christians it was a foreign and vaguely sinister institution.[14]

Irish Catholic communities in the period 1826–82 were subjected to sporadic outbursts of organized violence, not infrequently leading to many injuries and even some deaths. While these disturbances were primarily fuelled by the Irish Catholics' position as a reserve army of labour and were not unique to Wales, undoubtedly the prevailing climate of religious bigotry also played its part.[15] Gwyn A. Williams[16] suggests that, by 1900, the Irish population were well on their way to being assimilated into Welsh culture and society, but Trystan Owain Hughes characterizes the experience of Catholics, even well into the twentieth century, as one of hostility and prejudice from non-Catholics.[17]

For Irish Catholics in Wales, their patterns of settlement offset this to some extent. Residential stability facilitated the work of parish priests and combined with the increasing establishment of Catholic schools, a pattern of religious socialization based on minimal levels of religious conformity and loyalty to tribal institutions emerged. Catholics had to struggle in the face of sustained discrimination for acceptance in all areas of life. For example, the concept of Catholic education was bitterly resisted in some areas of Wales. The Nonconformist hegemony in local government meant that Free Church opposition to Catholic schools could effectively delay or block the establishment of new schools and isolated examples of this practice were to continue even after the 1944 Education Act.[18] Sectarian denunciations of 'the religion of Rome' appeared to be rooted as much in ethnicity as theology. The Church was frequently described as 'alien' and 'foreign' and even the possibility of a 'Welsh' Catholicism was frequently derided.[19] Again, the close association of Nonconformity with Welsh identity frequently led to converts to Roman Catholicism being accused of denying not only their faith but also their Welsh identity.[20] Fears about the 'dilution' of Welsh ethnicity and identity were further fuelled by the continued growth of the Catholic Church and its emergence as the second largest denomination in Wales. Indeed, as late as 1949, at a meeting of the General Assembly of the Presbyterian Church of Wales in Cardiff, the Principal of Aberystwyth Theological College stated: 'We are a reformed Church and cannot sit back and allow our country to be taken over to the Roman Catholic faith without some protest.'[21] Nevertheless, by the 1950s, the credentials of the Roman Catholic Church in Wales were becoming established within the national religious sphere.

While the Irish identity of the Church remained strong, immigration of groups of non-Irish ethnicity (notably Italian and Polish), inter-marriage and assimilation with indigenous Welsh people and culture, social and geographic mobility, and progressive secularization, were all eroding Catholicism's perceived 'ghetto' status. The Church's own relaxation of its claims to exclusivity opened the way for ecumenical initiatives with Welsh religious institutions and the promotion of the Welsh language and culture within the Church did much to counter accusations of its 'alien' status. The high-profile conversions of prominent figures in Welsh elite circles had also contributed to an increasing recognition of the 'Welsh' nature of the Church. This transformation of Catholicism's fortunes in Wales was, however, coloured by the fact that, historically, the progressive waves of Catholic immigrants had made little or no attempt to assimilate or embrace the Welsh language and culture. Given the close identification of that culture with Nonconformity and the hostility of Nonconformism to Catholics, this is understandable. Trystan Owain Hughes suggests that, ultimately, 'this Irish identity was not replaced by a specifically Welsh consciousness but rather with an anglicized one instead'.[22]

Indeed, if there was a threat to indigenous religious institutions, it did not come from Rome, but from England and from the creeping anglicization of religion. Wales was the only region of Britain to experience net immigration between 1860 and 1914, with the majority of migrants settling in Glamorgan and Monmouthshire.[23] Immigration brought anglicization, first within the commercial world but ultimately within the religious sphere.[24] For a triumphant Nonconformity that had helped shape a distinctive oppositional Welsh culture grounded in language and dissent, anglicization posed a threat to its cultural identity and linguistic independence. The Nonconformist establishment reacted in a number of ways. Politically, it sought the disestablishment of the Anglican Church in Wales, damned as it was in the popular mind by its association with land-lordism and English culture.[25] The Presbyterian Church of Wales was a prime mover in this project, but was also instrumental, through the foundation of the Forward Movement in 1885, in trying to engage with the increasingly anglicized proletariat of south-east Wales in their own language. Welsh Baptists and Independents as denominations were not so accommodating and this was reflected in the increasing emergence of English Congregational chapels catering for the new anglicized middle-class and English Baptist congregations, many sited in Monmouthshire and Glamorgan and more proletarian in character. It was becoming increasingly apparent in the industrialized regions that the use of the English language in chapel services was becoming commonplace[26] and by 1895 the English chapels were confident enough in their own strength to hold their own separate conferences.[27] The last great religious revival of 1904 can be seen as a reaction both to the increasing secularization of Welsh society and the increasing anglicization of Nonconformity in Wales. Ultimately, it failed to halt, or even slow, either process. The inheritors of the spirit of the revival were the myriad small sects of the Evangelicals and Pentecostals, English in culture and outlook and increasingly divorced from the everyday lives of Welsh people.

The political influence of Welsh Nonconformity reached its zenith in the years 1881–1920, bracketed by the Sunday Closing Act 1881 and the Welsh Church Act 1914. The disestablishment of the Anglican Church in 1920 was a hollow victory, however. The new Church in Wales was able to make a relatively smooth transition to becoming a major Welsh institution,[28] while Nonconformity increasingly struggled to maintain its social, cultural and political hegemony in Welsh life.[29] From 1920 on, and against the background of a marked decline in public religious observance, Nonconformity found itself in increasing crisis. While it still retained a strong presence and influence in Welsh society until the 1950s, the steady erosion of the Welsh language and the progressive anglicization of Wales raised significant questions about the traditional association between Nonconformism and Welsh identity. Both Anglicanism and, to a lesser extent, Roman Catholicism were able to draw on notions of a 'Celtic Church' to affirm their Welsh identity,[30] while for the new evangelical sects and denominations that were springing up, identity was primarily a question of identification with the community of the 'saved' rather than the 'nation'. In 1930 the first Welsh mosque was opened in Butetown, Cardiff. Built with a combination of local authority money and funding from the local Islamic community, it heralded the first shoots of official recognition of a new religious diversity that was increasingly to characterize parts of Wales in the second half of the twentieth century.[31] Crucially, and within the context of the preceding discussion, it opened up the possibility of new types of identity formation based on new understandings of what it is to be Welsh and religious.

If the nineteenth century was a period of religious growth, the twentieth century was largely characterized by the progressive secularization of Welsh society. Whereas the 1851 religious census suggested approximately 50 per cent of the population attended either church or chapel, the Welsh Churches Survey of 1995 suggested that approximately 9 per cent of the population now attend a place of worship.[32] Decline has been most marked in those religious institutions most closely associated with the Welsh language and culture.[33] In the period 1970–95, the Presbyterian Church of Wales closed 350 chapels and experienced a 51 per cent drop in membership, the Union of Welsh Independents closed 166 chapels and membership fell by 49 per cent, and the Baptist Union of Wales closed 163 chapels and membership fell by 58 per cent.[34] These losses are far higher than those of their nearest denominational counterparts elsewhere in Britain. Decline was less marked in the Church in

Wales. Adopting a different unit of measurement, the number of Easter communicants as a percentage of the general population over the age of fourteen years declined from 7.4 per cent in 1970 to 4.6 per cent in 1990, a drop of 38 per cent overall.[35] Conversely, the story of Roman Catholics in Wales has been one of growth and consolidation until 1970, after which decline set in.[36] Undoubtedly, the fortress model of a church forged in conditions of prejudice and discrimination, continuing ties of ethnicity, continued migration from the European Union and a higher than average birth rate, all worked to partially offset the effects of secularization in Welsh society. A series of interviews[37] carried out with Roman Catholic clergy in 1995–6 illustrated the recent decline in mass attendance and the virtual demise of Catholic social clubs. Social and geographical mobility associated with embourgeoisement, the resultant loss of social cohesion and the loosening of ties of ethnic identity were all seen as contributing factors in the weakening of a distinctive religio-ethnic subculture.

One response to this pervasive religious decline within the mainstream denominations has been a move towards ecumenicalism and greater cooperation between Christian faith groups. Beginning in the 1950s, various indigenous cooperative networks have emerged to offset the growing weakness of individual denominations. The Evangelical Movement of Wales and Associating Evangelical Churches in Wales emerged from the evangelical community, while the mainstream denominations (including the Roman Catholic Church) came together in what was eventually to become CYTUN (Churches Together in Wales).[38] Welsh ecumenicalism can be seen as both a defensive strategy in the face of secularization *and* as the institutional recognition and acceptance of the diversity and difference increasingly characterizing the religious sphere.

D. Densil Morgan suggests that, 'Just as there is no longer a single Welsh cultural identity, pluralism has become an undoubted characteristic of the religious life of the new Wales.'[39] Within the Christian sphere, new groupings of evangelical character, notably neo-Pentecostals and house churches, have become a vibrant and growing part of the religious economy.[40] Outside of the Christian sphere many world faiths are now present in Wales: Bahaism, Buddhism, Hare Krishna, Hinduism and Sikhism, and, most visibly, Islam. While it would be misleading to suggest that these non-Christian religions constitute a numerically significant presence in

Wales, nevertheless they constitute a growing sector within the religious economy.[41] Statistics are still elusive, but there is a general consensus among observers of the religious scene that Islam constitutes the largest non-Christian faith group in Wales. Cardiff (Butetown and Riverside) and Newport (Corporation Rd) have long been home to significant Muslim communities and in recent years Swansea (St Helens) has also become home to a vibrant and visible Muslim community. While these Islamic communities have until recently been phenomena associated with cities, within the last year new mosques have been established in the county boroughs of Bridgend and Rhondda Cynon Taff. In 1997 a Welsh-based Association of Muslim Professionals was established, furthering the institutionalization of Islam into Welsh culture and society.

In many ways, what we are now seeing in Wales in relation to Islam echoes the prior experience of Irish Catholics. Within the urban areas Muslim communities and businesses tend to visibly cluster around places of commerce and worship and communities have not been free from hostility and prejudice and even violence. This raises questions about just how pluralistic Welsh society really is, and whether a recognition of diversity is necessarily the same thing as a full acceptance of ethnic minority faith groups into the cultural and civic life of Wales. In terms of cooperation, or even communication, between Christian and non-Christian faith groups, there is little evidence up to now of any meaningful contact other than localized interfaith initiatives which have been dependent on the goodwill of individuals.[42] While this looks set to change in the future with the sponsorship of the National Assembly for a proposed Interfaith Council of Wales, at present non-Christian faith groups appear to be marginalized, both within the religious sphere and within the sphere of civic society. The discussion below, drawing from recent interviews with thirty faith group leaders,[43] will offer evidence of the Christocentric nature of Welsh civic society.

The process of political devolution, culminating in the establishment of the National Assembly for Wales, has given Wales the wherewithal to begin developing its own civic culture. Devolved government, it was claimed, would bring greater levels of 'accessibility, representativeness, legitimacy, openness, participation, innovation, inclusiveness and accountability'.[44] A key element in this project has been the emergent partnership between the National Assembly and the voluntary sector.[45] As voluntary associations, faith groups are an integral part of civil society.[46] In terms of their structural position within Welsh civic society, some faith groups are both working with government to deliver key services in Wales and seeking to work with politicians towards the common good.[47] In general, faith groups in Wales have welcomed political devolution and the potential opportunities it has opened up for them in terms of their public role. Indeed, sections of the Christian community (notably the Welsh-speaking denominations) enthusiastically campaigned for devolution in the run-up to the 1997 referendum.

Compared to England and Scotland, cooperative relations between faith groups and government, both formal and informal, are far more developed. The mainstream Christian denominations, represented by CYTUN, have a seat on the Voluntary Sector Partnership Council (VSPC) and monthly 'prayer breakfasts' held in Cardiff bring faith group leaders, politicians and civil servants together. Some of the interests of those non-Christian faith groups associated with ethnic minorities are articulated through the Commission for Racial Equality Wales, which also has a seat on the VSPC. In terms of formal links, evangelical Christians are less well served as a group, reflecting both the fragmented nature of Welsh evangelicalism and the well-documented reluctance of many evangelicals to engage with political institutions.[48] In terms of informal contacts between the personnel of faith groups and the Assembly, these were overwhelmingly characterized by faith group leaders as 'good'.

One factor that has contributed to a sense of engagement with the National Assembly has been its geographical proximity to the headquarters of many faith groups operating in Wales and its small size compared to Westminster. Another factor has been the willingness of Assembly Members (including the previous and present First Ministers) to make themselves accessible to faith group leaders. However, both formal and informal relations have tended to follow the historic contours of Welsh civic society. Both those historic denominations associated with a specifically Welsh brand of Nonconformist Protestantism and the Anglicans have better access than those faith groups that have historically been considered 'foreign'. The Assembly also appears to favour dialogue with the larger institutions over the type of loose organizational structures that characterize both sections of the evangelical community and non-Christian faith groups. A further dilemma (or, more properly, a set of dilemmas) for those non-Christian faith groups associated with ethnic minorities lies in the current nature of their links with the Assembly.

Despite the historic presence of non-Christian faith groups in Wales, we cannot talk about them being embedded in civic life in the same manner as some Christian faith groups. Also, as noted above, these groups do not conform organizationally to historically recognized structures such as 'church' or 'denomination', making communication difficult, although the development of indigenous organizations such as the Association of Muslim Professionals or the Hindu Cultural Association allows some faith groups to partially articulate their concerns. The most cited dilemma was the absence of any direct formal religious representation in the Assembly. While the CRE can, within its secular remit, represent their interests, it is *not* a faith-based organization. In terms of *direct* faith group participation, non-Christian religions are effectively excluded from the VSPC. Furthermore, where the Assembly engages with these groups, it does so primarily on the basis of ethnic cultural identity or 'race' rather than religious identity. As Chaney and Williams have noted elsewhere in this volume, it is effectively a race equality agenda that drives relations between the Assembly and ethnic minority groups. While not belittling the importance of this agenda, non-Christian faith groups, as *faith groups*, feel excluded from the Assembly in terms of their potential contributions and marginalized in terms of their specific religious identities. The vexed question of religious versus ethnic identity has recently been rehearsed elsewhere,[49] but suffice it to say that non-Christian faith group leaders in Wales perceive this state of affairs, when compared to their Christian counterparts, as discriminatory. Unsurprisingly, these same leaders are extremely supportive of moves towards the establishment of an Assembly-sponsored, and quasi-political, Interfaith Council for Wales, as are some evangelical Christian groups who also feel excluded from political institutions.

The interface between religious and political institutions in Wales is also taking place within the wider stage of the European Union. Growing religious diversity in Europe has been accompanied by an increasing climate of Islamophobia and civil unrest in many European cities, and a growth in state-sponsored 'anti-cult' legislation.[50] In Britain, the 'Rushdie affair' and the public discourse surrounding non-Christian faith schools reveals a secularized society apparently ill at ease with the presence of an Islamic minority and often ignorant of the religious life and needs of ethnic minority groups.[51] In France, incidents such as the *affaire du foulard* suggest that religious tolerance and pluralism are not self-evident or taken-for-granted propositions. Throughout Europe, sporadic outbursts of organized violence, both directed at ethnic minority faith groups and communities and, increasingly, emanating from those communities, serve to highlight these issues. Religious discrimination is not merely an issue of 'race', as the experience of new religious movements attests. Scientologists and Jehovah's Witnesses (and other faith groups deemed 'cults') throughout mainland Europe have been subjected to limitations on their religious liberty. The German, Italian, French, Belgian, Swiss and Greek governments have all produced negative assessments of these groups and, in many cases, hostile legislation has followed.[52] In the case of the Scientologists, members in various European states have been imprisoned, denied employment, denied basic freedoms of religious association and thought and have been subjected to a background of routine exclusion and discrimination.[53] For both ethnic minority faith groups and new religious movements, the right to freedom of conscience and religion and the right to non-discrimination on religious grounds, as protected by the existing Articles 9 and 14 of the European Convention on Human Rights, appear easily circumvented by member states and regional parliaments and assemblies. Whether this will change with the introduction of proposed new European directives on religious discrimination[54] is as yet unclear, although the track record of states and particularly of some regional governments hardly inspires confidence for the future. This makes it all the more important for the National Assembly for Wales to live up to its rhetoric of inclusivity and democratic accountability, if minority faith groups in Wales are not to be discriminated against.

Overall, religious groups in Wales have cautiously welcomed political devolution, both in terms of its potential to transform their position within civil society, and in terms of the National Assembly's stated intention to work towards a more democratic and inclusive Wales. Devolution has taken place against the background of a growing religious diversity in Welsh society which, while not as marked as that witnessed in England or other parts of Europe, is nevertheless a reality. In common with other societies where there has been a historically close relation between religious institutions and 'national' identity, religious tolerance of minority faith groups has often appeared to be only grudgingly extended. Discrimination, intolerance and even violence have all at some time formed the background to the growth of religious diversity in Wales. At the very least, minority religions have been treated as second-class citizens within the Welsh religious and civic spheres. While the progressive decline of mainstream Christianity throughout the twentieth century has opened up spaces for a more diverse religious landscape to emerge in Wales, the full acceptance of these groups remains elusive. Welsh society and institutions remain largely Christocentric in character and orientation. This is illustrated well by the current struggle of non-Christian groups to engage with political institutions on the basis of their various religious rather than cultural identities. A recognition of a religiously pluralistic Wales is one thing and a tolerance of ethnic diversity is perhaps another, but only an unqualified acceptance of the right of minority faith groups to participate within civil society can truly be termed religious tolerance.

Notes

*The research on which parts of this chapter are based was funded by the Glamorgan Policy Centre, University of Glamorgan, Wales.

[1] G. Davie, *Religion in Modern Britain* (Oxford, 1994), 95.

[2] P. Chambers, 'A very religious people? Religious decline in Wales and the consequences for Welsh identity', in G. Davie and L. Woodhead with P. Heelas (eds), *Predicting Religion: Mainstream and Margins in the West* (Aldershot, 2002).

[3] A. Thompson and P. Chambers, 'Public religion and political change in Wales', unpublished research paper presented at Bangor University, 19 December 2001.

[4] For example, see I. Merdjanova, 'In search of identity: nationalism and religion in eastern Europe', *Religion, State and Society*, 28/3 (September 2000), 233–63.

[5] N. Evans, 'Immigrants and minorities in Wales, 1840–1990: a comparative perspective', *Llafur*, 5/4 (1991), 5–26 (reprinted in chapter 1 of this volume).

[6] J. G. Campbell, 'The Jewish community in Britain', in S. Gilley and W. J. Sheils (eds), *A History of Religion in Britain* (Oxford, 1994), 436–38.

[7] U. R. Henriques, 'The conduct of a synagogue: Swansea Hebrew congregation, 1895–1914', in Henriques (ed.), *Jews of South Wales* (Cardiff, 1993), 85–110.

[8] A. Glaser, 'The Tredegar riots of August 1911', in Henriques (ed.), *Jews of South Wales*, 151–76; G. Alderman, 'The anti-Jewish riots of August 1911 in south Wales', *The Welsh History Review*, 6/4 (1972), 190–200; W. D. Rubinstein, 'The

anti-Jewish riots of 1911 in south Wales: a re-examination', *The Welsh History Review*, 18/4 (1997), 667–99.

[9] Campbell, 'Jewish community'.

[10] M. Hornsby-Smith and R. M. Lee, *Roman Catholic Opinion: A Study of Roman Catholics in England and Wales in the 1970s: Final Report* (Guildford, 1979), 14.

[11] Ibid., 21.

[12] P. O'Leary, *Immigration and Integration: The Irish in Wales 1798–1922* (Cardiff, 2000), 223–4.

[13] The Welsh hierarchy were undoubtedly helped in this by the fact that prior to mass Irish immigration, the Roman Catholic Church in Wales consisted of little more than a few recusant families living in the border areas. See D. D. Morgan, 'The essence of Welshness? Some aspects of Christian faith and national identity in Wales, *c.*1900–2000', in R. Pope (ed.), *Religion and National Identity: Wales and Scotland c. 1700–2000* (Cardiff, 2001), 151.

[14] Ibid., 150–1.

[15] P. O'Leary, 'Anti-Irish riots in Wales, 1826–1882', *Llafur*, 5/4 (1991), 27–35.

[16] G. A. Williams, *When was Wales? A History of the Welsh* (Harmondsworth, 1991), 179.

[17] T. O. Hughes, *Winds of Change: The Roman Catholic Church and Society in Wales 1916–1962* (Cardiff, 1999), 1–5.

[18] Ibid., 131–57, 223–5; G. E. Jones, *Which Nation's Schools? Direction and Devolution in Welsh Education in the Twentieth Century* (Cardiff, 1990), 100.

[19] T. O. Hughes, 'Continuity and conversion: the concept of a national church in twentieth century Wales and its relation to "the Celtic Church" ', in R. Pope (ed.), *Religion and National Identity: Wales and Scotland c.1700–2000* (Cardiff, 2001), 123–38.

[20] Hughes, *Winds of Change*, 81–5.

[21] Ibid., 151.

[22] Ibid., 180.

[23] P. Jenkins, *A History of Modern Wales: 1535–1990* (Harlow, 1992), 236–8.

[24] E. T. Davies, *Religion and Society in the Nineteenth Century* (Llandybïe, 1981), 68–71.

[25] G. A. Williams, *When was Wales?*, 228, 234.

[26] J. V. Morgan, *The Welsh Religious Revival 1904–5: A Retrospect and Criticism* (London, 1909), 254–5.

[27] W. R. Lambert, 'Some working class attitudes towards organised religion in nineteenth-century Wales', in G. Parsons (ed.), *Religion in Victorian Britain*, iv, *Interpretations* (Manchester, 1988), 110–12.

[28] C. Harris and R. Startup, *The Church in Wales: The Sociology of a Traditional Institution* (Cardiff, 1999), 1–6.

[29] R. Pope, *Building Jerusalem: Nonconformity, Labour and the Social Question in Wales, 1906–1939* (Cardiff, 1998), *passim*.

[30] Hughes, 'Continuity and conversion', 123–38.

[31] Thompson and Chambers, 'Public religion'.

[32] Bible Society, *Challenge to Change: The Results of the 1995 Welsh Churches Survey* (Swindon, 1997).

[33] D. G. Evans, *A History of Wales 1906–2000* (Cardiff, 2000), 179–88.

[34] P. Chambers, 'Factors in church growth and decline', unpublished University of Wales Ph.D. thesis, Swansea, 1999, 6.

[35] Harris and Startup, *Church in Wales*, 22.

[36] Ibid., 21

[37] Chambers, 'Factors in church growth and decline', 110–12.

[38] Thompson and Chambers, 'Public religion'.

[39] D. D. Morgan, 'Essence of Welshness', 159.

[40] See, for example, P. Chambers, 'On or off the bus: identity, belonging and schism: a case study of a neo-pentecostal house church', in S. Hunt, M. Hamilton and T. Walter (eds), *Charismatic Christianity: Sociological Perspectives* (Basingstoke, 1997).

[41] D. P. Davies, 'A time of paradoxes among the faiths', in D. Cole (ed.), *The New Wales* (Cardiff, 1990).

[42] Thompson and Chambers, 'Public religion'.

[43] Ibid.

[44] P. Chaney, T. Hall and A. Pithouse, 'New governance – new democracy', in P. Chaney, T. Hall and A. Pithouse (eds), *New Governance – New Democracy? Post-Devolution Wales* (Cardiff, 2001), 3.

[45] B. Dicks, T. Hall and A. Pithouse, 'The National Assembly and the voluntary sector: an equal partnership?', in Chaney, Hall and Pithouse (eds), *New Governance – New Democracy?*

[46] See, for example, the arguments of A. Shanks, *Civil Society, Civil Religion* (Oxford, 1995), or R. Wuthnow, *Christianity and Civil Society* (Valley Forge, 1996).

[47] A. Edwards, *Transforming Power: A Christian Reflection on Welsh Devolution* (Bangor, 2001), 23.

[48] P. Broadbent, 'Evangelicals and social justice', in *Restoring Faith in Politics* (London, 1996).

[49] P. Weller, A. Feldman and K. Purdam, *Religious Discrimination in England and Wales* (Home Office Research Study, No. 220, London, 2001).

[50] For an excellent discussion of these issues, see G. Davie, *Religion in Modern Europe* (Oxford, 2000), 115–37.

[51] This being true before the events of New York, 11 September 2001; the stakes have certainly been raised since.

[52] Davie, *Religion in Modern Europe*, 117–21.

[53] Information on human rights violations against Scientologists in Germany, France and Belgium, including a document sent to the CBSS Commissioner, December 1999; documents entitled *Discriminatory Actions and Proposed Measures Against Minority Religions by the French Government* and *Human Rights Violations: Belgium*, produced by European Human Rights Office, Church of Scientology, Brussels.

[54] Two new directives under Article 13 of the Treaty of Amsterdam 1997 provide, for the first time, an enforceable, common legal framework of minimum protection against religious discrimination, with the compliance of member states required by 2 December 2003.

9   Social Inclusion and Race Equality in Wales

CHARLOTTE WILLIAMS

Combating social exclusion has been a major element of the public policy agenda since the late 1990s. A report by the government's Social Exclusion Unit indicates that 70 per cent of all people from ethnic minority groups live in the eighty-eight most deprived districts of the UK, compared with 40 per cent of the general population.[1] In Wales the greatest concentrations of the minority population are to be found in areas of noted deprivation. In 1991 the ethnic minority population of the Objective One areas was 15,272, or 0.8 per cent of the minority population.[2] The facts of racial inequality at UK level have been clearly demonstrated.[3] Nowhere is the impact of such disparities more keenly felt than in the areas of social policy concern – health, housing, employment, poverty, education and social care. What is known about the situation of ethnic minorities in Wales? Is it indeed the case that people from these communities experience greater levels of unemployment, poorer health, poorer housing, poorer educational and occupational opportunities in Wales? To what extent are they excluded from the gamut of social opportunities? Tackling social exclusion and promoting racial equality are now firmly on the political agenda of the National Assembly for Wales (NAW).[4] This chapter explores the available evidence on the position of ethnic minorities in Wales. It will demonstrate that currently the information deserts far exceed the availability of sound and reliable streams of knowledge. It critically reviews the concept of social inclusion, pointing to the limitations of this approach in relation to the aim of achieving racial equality. The chapter concludes by pointing to some of the challenges facing the NAW in tackling racial equality.

The demographic profile of ethnic minorities in Wales throws up an immediate paradox for policy intervention. Responding to need implies some identifiable, relatively coherent category of interest as the focus for intervention. Yet to speak of the 'ethnic minority population' of Wales as if it were just such a clearly definable entity is to grossly misread the situation. The main statistical source at the time of writing remains the 1991 census. Wales's black and ethnic minority population makes up 1.5 per cent of the total population, a higher proportion than Scotland (1.3 per cent) and Ireland (0.5 per cent). Of the 41,551 people categorized as black and ethnic minority, one in two live in and around Cardiff with few concentrations elsewhere.[5] The largest ethnic groups were 'Other-other' (i.e. Black British at 7,660), Indians (6,384), Pakistanis (5,717), Chinese (4,801), Bangladeshis (3,820), Asian-Other (3,677), Black-Other (3,473) and Black-Caribbeans (3,348). The policy challenges therefore may be significantly different from other areas of Britain where there are sizeable concentrations of minority communities.

Whilst the last census indicated the former county of South Glamorgan to be one of the top ten British counties with the highest non-white population, the majority of county boroughs in Wales have ethnic minority populations of less than 2 per cent. Although there is a tendency to see the differentiation as marked by urban/rural divide, this is not the case. For instance, Cardiff and Swansea are both sizeable cities with significant minority populations and yet the profile of their minority populations is markedly different in terms of their migration histories, settlement pattern, occupational profile and so on. Leedham notes concentrations of Pakistani people in Newport, Bangladeshis in Swansea, and Cardiff with a minority population of 7.0 per cent has groups from a number of communities including long-established African and Afro-Caribbean communities in the docklands areas and Indians in Riverside and Grangetown.[6] The Chinese community is significantly more dispersed across Wales. At the last census almost 40 per cent of people from an ethnic minority in Wales ticked the category 'Chinese and others'.[7] This is undoubtedly a contentious category concealing as it did a high number of people of mixed ethnicity who may be more readily identified in the 2001 census as 'black Welsh'. Indeed it is anticipated that the 2001 census will not only go some way to correcting what is considered an underestimation of the numbers of people from an ethnic minority background in Wales but will reveal ever-increasing diversity, given for example the government's dispersal policies on refugee and asylum seekers (see Chapter 11).

To adopt a Wales-based focus to ethnic minority issues is to imply that there are some particular features of note in the Welsh context that impact on these groups and on the acknowledgement of their needs. Otherwise it would suffice to say that research generated in other parts of the UK can readily be generalized to Wales and that renewed research efforts, based on territoriality, waste resources. There may be some merit in this argument but a number of factors would suggest the value of such a focus. First, as indicated, there are key differences in the demographic profile of the ethnic minority population of Wales: its small size, diversity, dispersal and settlement patterns mark it out as distinct from England. Cardiff comprises one of the oldest black communities in Europe with third- and even fourth-generation settlement. The implications of these factors alone are instructive to other areas of Britain and to countries with newly settled communities. Secondly, it has been suggested that social, cultural and linguistic factors form an interface with issues of race and ethnicity in particular ways in Wales.[8] An example might be language ring-fencing of job opportunities or particular service provision. I have argued elsewhere that issues of race and racism have been marginal if not absent from the political agenda of Wales until very recently, with the effect that widespread apathy and complacency exists to a greater degree in Wales than in many areas of England.[9] However, by far the most compelling justification for a systematic evaluation of the position of ethnic minorities and for Welsh-based research is the establishment of the devolved Assembly for Wales and the new sense of Welsh nationhood that has been awakened by this measure of self-governance. The new Assembly's remit in relation to social policy, its mandate on equal opportunities and its responsibilities in relation to the Race Relations (Amendment) Act 2000 imply the need for up-to-date, comprehensive and readily available information concerning the circumstances of Wales's ethnic minority groups. Within a European context the Welsh government stands out for it is bound by a *unique* statutory duty that effectively requires it to *promote* equality of opportunity for *all* people in the exercise of *all* its functions. Evidence-based policy-making will be directly and immediately informed by Welsh-based research.

Across all policy domains, gaining data disaggregated for Wales by ethnic group has been near impossible. The ballpark figures provided by the 1991 census are regarded as far too blunt an instrument to guide policy development.[10] Until recently the Welsh sample in labour-force surveys has been too small to extrapolate figures by ethnicity and many public bodies in Wales have developed idiosyncratic approaches to ethnic auditing and monitoring such that no standardized statistical body of information exists.[11] The establishment of a National Statistical Framework within the Assembly and the outcomes of the 2001 census will significantly address this issue, but it will take time to determine the sophisticated tools needed to provide continuous, reliable baseline data that can be compared and combined in useful ways. This is a major challenge facing the new government.

A number of research studies have been conducted amongst minority ethnic groups in Wales. Several of the studies could be categorized as needs assessment exercises, being small-scale, parochial, lacking methodological rigour and contributing little to vigorous theoretical debate.[12] Approaches vary. Some studies adopt a cultural diversity focus, raising awareness of a particular community such as the Somalis in south Wales, the Sikhs and Gypsy and refugee communities.[13] Others eschew fine-tuned cultural differences and have focused on particular need groups such as children, older people, diabetics and women.[14] Whilst these studies provide an important focus highlighting diversity of language, norms, expectations and practices and voicing the concerns of minority groups, they have done little to shift organizational practices, power relations between majority and minority communities, or tackle the seat of racial discrimination. More recently studies are emerging that adopt a more institutional or structural approach, challenging the norms and practices of major providers of services.[15] This trend is to be welcomed. It takes cognizance of wider exclusionary forces that hinder access to services and employment opportunities vital to the aim of achieving racial equality and reflects the statutory shift towards addressing institutional discrimination.

The current legislative context provides a timely opportunity to review major areas of service delivery for minority ethnic people in Wales.

Race and housing

Housing is one of the key indicators of social exclusion. Overall owner occupation amongst ethnic minorities in Wales is lower than amongst white households (60 per cent as compared with 71 per cent) but as yet little is known about their involvement in private sector housing.[16] There is some evidence to suggest that minorities living outside of the major conurbations enjoy better socio-economic standards, better housing and more positive environments than their urban counterparts.[17] One optimistic theme that emerged from a small study in Torfaen was the positive connotation attached to rural environments by individuals from ethnic minority backgrounds who had migrated into the area for work from urban areas in England.[18] Research by Franklin and Passmore, however, suggests that the socio-economic situation of minorities in south Wales conforms to the wider UK experience.[19] The most comprehensive review to date of the housing needs of ethnic minority people was undertaken in 1999 with sponsorship from the National Assembly for Wales. The study, *From the Margins to the Centre,* aimed to evaluate the extent to which registered social landlords (RSL) and local authorities were meeting the housing needs of minorities and to assess whether there was a need for a black and ethnic minority housing strategy.[20] Overall, the study reports a picture of ethnic minority housing tenure in South Glamorgan that largely confirms the UK experience: black and ethnic minority people being more likely to live in unsatisfactory, unsafe accommodation and for longer than their white counterparts. They also experience greater difficulty in accessing suitable accommodation, experience overcrowding, are over-represented in terms of homelessness especially amongst the young[21] and are subject to degrees of racial harassment. There are, however, some interesting insights presented in this study that illustrate aspects of the situation that are specific to Wales; several of which are confirmed by other small-scale studies in Wales.[22] Frequently cited issues are the shortage of larger houses with a design and layout suitable to the living requirements of particular minority groups; the lack of information amongst minority groups about provision and services reflecting poor communication between these communities and the authorities; the dearth of specialist provision for particular need, for example, for Somali elders in Cardiff, and poor support in cases of racial harassment. Wales has just one organization providing for ethnic minority women fleeing domestic violence and no black-led social housing schemes, in contrast to their growing presence in England. At an institutional level, the study reports that, whilst most housing authorities have an equal opportunities policy in place, few have specific strategies aimed at meeting minority needs; the results of monitoring are not used to improve performance, tenant participation is poor and there is gross under-representation of black and ethnic minorities on the staff and boards of housing organizations. Of 1,066 board members in Wales only seven are from ethnic minority backgrounds.[23]

> The investigations carried out under this review confirm that Black and minority ethnic (BME) communities feel detached from mainstream housing services, and do not feel part of the management process. This sense of estrangement is reinforced by ongoing racist experiences, a lack of connection to establishment networks and cultural and communication barriers.[24]

Against this backdrop the report calls for BME-led RSLs and emphasizes the critical role of local authorities in meeting their responsibilities towards minority communities and their social inclusion. The development of a housing policy in Wales for minorities is nevertheless a complex issue, not least because of their demographic configuration. A study by Brownhill, Razzaque, Stirling and Thomas of the urban development programme in Butetown points to the racialization processes in planning policies, the ambivalent policies towards 'race' and the lack of effective minority participation in planning decisions.[25] Although the Cardiff Bay Urban District Council aimed to open up the Butetown area and link it to the rest of the city in order to break down racially based exclusion, a key impact of this policy has been a sense of loss of identity, loss of specialist facilities and 'sanctuary' provided by this historic territorial space. Elsewhere in Wales fierce debates rage about the impact of incomers on Welsh-speaking communities and the radical Welsh-language organization Cymuned has gone as far as to suggest restricted areas in Wales earmarked for Welsh speakers.[26] Local authority and RSL decision-makers walk a fine line between protecting the cultural and linguistic heritage of communities and developing restrictive policies that effectively outlaw multicultural settlement.

Health and social care

There are few studies on specific health conditions amongst minorities in Wales, but access to health and social care services is a theme that is taken up by a number of studies and policy documents.[27] It is difficult to determine any particular Welsh effect on the health care needs of minorities as opposed to those living elsewhere. However, a few key factors emerge from the studies. Wales encompasses some of the most economically deprived areas in Europe and the link between poverty and ill health is well documented.[28] The 1991 census figures suggest there is approximately double the number of long-term illnesses among minority ethnic groups compared to whites in Wales: 17.3 per cent for minorities as compared with 8.4 per cent for whites.[29] The combination of disadvantage and discrimination impacts heavily on minority communities. In addition to the most commonly cited plethora of factors that confound access to health care – communication barriers, information and knowledge barriers, cultural barriers, transport, culturally insensitive service delivery – the research suggests Wales is characterized by sluggish and tokenistic attention to minority issues. A study by Leedham on the incidence of diabetes amongst ethnic minorities[30] notes poor representation of minorities at decision-making levels of the organization, a point starkly demonstrated in a survey of secondary care practice by the NHS Equality Unit Wales in 1998:[31]

> At the level of shaping services the lack of ethnic minority input at planning and strategy levels was often highlighted during fieldwork. In this respect it appears that Wales is less advanced than England for instance.[32]

Leedham's review documents the 'absence of ethnic monitoring', 'the marginalisation as opposed to mainstreaming of ethnic minority issues' leading to piecemeal, time-limited and unsustainable initiatives and the fact that landmark documents such as *BetterWales.Com* give scant and cursory reference to ethnic minorities.[33]

Neither the Welsh Health Survey carried out in the mid-1990s nor the Atlas of Health Inequalities in Wales from 1998 gives any information on minorities. The NHS Equality Unit study of 1998[34] found considerable variability in the collection of ethnic data, making any attempt to understand the prevalence and treatment of ill health difficult. Leedham speaks of a 'pervasive colour blind approach' that permeates service delivery.[35]

A study by the Policy Research Institute on Ageing and Ethnicity (PRIAE) highlights a major difference between England and Wales as the relative absence of voluntary specialist organizations for older people from minority communities.

Our findings showed that such organizations were acting as *primary providers* in the absence of an effective response from authorities. Essentially they were a substitute for the mainstream.[36]

The relative absence of specialist organizations and an over-reliance on the small, poorly funded voluntary organizations that do exist is an identifiable theme and not confined to services for older people. The PRIAE report suggests this is a reflection of 'the general under-development in other areas of "race" relations in Wales'.[37]

In post-devolution Wales there is evidence of some considerable movement in the field of health. The NAW has commissioned an equality audit into current practices and procedures which is expected to report by mid-2002.[38] Currently only 1.8 per cent of NHS Wales employees are from a black or ethnic minority background, and 35 per cent of this group are employed in unskilled pre-registration roles.[39] The Health Strategy for Wales document proposes a programme of staff training on equality issues and procedures put in place to combat racial discrimination in the workplace. Guidelines for the appointment of chairs and non-executive directors establish the principle of equality of opportunity and fairness in making appointments to the various boards of the NHS irrespective of age, gender, ethnicity, religion or social background. [40] The strategy also states

The NHS will build on a framework to ensure that NHS organisations, managers, staff and contractors actively work to meet the expectations of patients and the public. This will cover public involvement in decisions on healthcare, the scrutiny of NHS activities, public access to information on health and healthcare services and their right to support and redress if things go wrong. These mechanisms will ensure that hitherto excluded sections of the population – including . . . members of ethnic minority populations – will have a voice and an influence.[41]

Many of the issues of neglect are replicated in the field of social care, where the paucity of research to guide evidence-based practice is alarming. The 1991 census provides information on household size and age structure from which it is possible to make some projections about social care need and the extent of informal networks. The statistics indicate a younger age profile amongst ethnic minority people in Wales and only a small proportion of ethnic minority people of retirement age (3 per cent, as compared with 21 per cent amongst the white population).[42] Ethnic minority households tend to be larger than their white counterparts (3.3 persons compared with 2.5 persons).[43] A common and pervasive myth amongst service providers has been that these households incorporate and provide support for the older person. However, studies demonstrate considerable unmet care needs amongst ethnic minority elders.[44] There exist just a handful of studies on children's needs and a few general area-based needs assessment studies to guide practice.[45] Among the themes that emerge from the research are the high levels of hidden and unmet need, low levels of knowledge of existing services and difficulties in accessing culturally appropriate care services.

Key challenges are posed for service providers by the dispersal of minorities across Wales with obvious implications for the design and delivery of services in rural areas. There is a paucity of provision in the voluntary sector – for example, Multicultural Crossroads is the only organization offering culturally matched services for older people. There are very few black-led voluntary sector organizations in Wales offering vital but limited service provision (see Chapter 12). It is to be hoped that the NAW 'Communities First' project will offer a substantial boost to this sector.[46] Yet the Welsh Council for Voluntary Action's (WCVA) response to the Communities First Strategy noted

> Organizations taking part in the consultation expressed concern about whether 'Communities First' would work for some of the most marginalized and disadvantaged communities. It was felt that black and ethnic minority groups, who often have the least access to services and support, were in danger of 'getting lost' in geographically based communities and would need an approach more specifically geared to their needs.[47]

Education

The proportion of children in the ethnic minority population is higher than in the general population (35 per cent as opposed to 20 per cent amongst whites) as is the proportion of youths (16–24).[48] There is little substantive research in this policy area. A survey of schools in Torfaen commissioned by the local authority found no evidence of ethnic monitoring, few schools with explicit policies on racial bullying and few schools equipped or explicitly geared towards multicultural education, relying instead on discrete and specialist input from voluntary sector organizations for facilities like inter-pretation and translation services.[49] In the absence of research there is no reason to believe that this state of affairs is not widespread. In terms of the experience of children from ethnic minority back-grounds, Scourfield et al. (2001) reported children coping with racism as an 'everyday possibility'.[50] Gorard's study 'Paying for "Little England"' found a number of Asian families in Wales opting for private schooling. He suggests this choice reflects a 'flight' from Welsh-language teaching.[51] This is an area for further research, as anecdotal evidence now suggests ethnic minority parents are actively choosing Welsh-medium schooling.

Following the recommendations of the MacPherson Report,[52] NAW has taken steps to develop a strategy for the implementation of multicultural education in Welsh schools. ACCAC (Qualifications, Curriculum and Assessment Authority for Wales) has produced two frameworks, one on Personal and Social Education (PSE) and one on Work Related Education, both designed to tackle prejudice and stereotyping, to promote respect of others and the valuing of cultural diversity and to ensure mainstreaming of equality across the curricu-lum.[53] There are steps being taken to develop standardized systems of ethnic monitoring and the recording of racism in schools.

A key issue is the lack of a coherent picture of minority access to educational services from nursery to post-compulsory education. The Assembly Government's 2001 education strategy, *A Paving Document: A Comprehensive Education and Lifelong Learning Programme to 2010 in Wales – The Learning Country*, states a commitment to 'press ahead with a comprehensive and regular survey of the numbers and attainments of pupils from black and ethnic minority communities in Wales so that where there are evident patterns of under achievement, resources can be better deployed to deal with them'. It commits to provide support for schools, senior managers and practitioners in setting high expectations and attainment targets for ethnic minority pupils, and for those whose first language is neither English nor Welsh and to 'provide additional financial assistance to those authorities in Wales that either are, or are likely to become, hosts for refugees and asylum seekers notably following the conflicts in Eastern Europe'.[54]

Employment

Employment is considered to be a key factor in the integration of minorities. The statistical profile that is available on the labour-market participation of ethnic minorities in Wales indicates for both ethnic minority men and women lower economic activity rates as compared to whites, less likelihood of being employed, higher levels of self-employment than whites, higher rates of unemployment and high youth unemployment.[55] Overall, 58 per cent of the non-white population are in employment, compared with 69 per cent of the white population.[56] Ethnic minorities comprise 1.6 per cent of Social Class 1 and 2 (professional, managerial and technical occupations) which undoubtedly reflects their involvement in private enterprise. However, in terms of occupational segregation there are strong ethnic disparities in the type of employment. For example, Asians tend to be represented in private sector organizations and Afro-Caribbeans in the public sector, with a virtual absence of minorities in the agricultural sector in Wales.[57] Little is known about ethnic minority involvement in enterprise although research in this area is currently under way.[58]

There is a high correlation between areas of ethnic minority settlement and high rates of unemployment and socio-economic deprivation. Looking at unemployment alone, localized statistics show huge disparities with unemployment amongst black groups running at twice the national rate and amongst Black Africans, at three times the national rate.[59] The 1991 situation will, however, provide an important benchmark against which to measure trends, set targets and monitor progress.

The NAW document *BetterWales.Com* and its successor *A Plan for Wales* argue for an ethnically diverse workforce.[60] An Equal Opportunities study for inclusion in Structural Funds 2000–2006 conducted in 1999 identified some of the key barriers to labour-market participation amongst minorities in Wales and provided some sketchy targets for economic inclusion of minorities.[61] Broadly speaking, discussions of barriers to labour-market participation focus on two main but interrelated areas: identified needs within the minority communities themselves that require capacity-building strategies, and obstacles that are the result of institutionalized racial discrimination, direct and indirect. There is significant if not rigorous empirical evidence within Wales to demonstrate the interplay of these two broad sets of factors. Whilst systematic studies are lacking, this information dearth has been filled by organizations such as NewEmploy, MEWN Cymru and Race Equality Councils (REC) operating with a type of 'practice wisdom' gained from experiences in the field and from organized 'listening exercises'. For example, a survey of the Race Equality Councils in Wales conducted within the equal opportunities study[62] confirmed many of the factors identified by other organizations, such as cultural and linguistic barriers. In addition, this consultation indicated:

- Observable differences between localities in patterns of labour-market participation. Some areas of Wales display relatively affluent socially mobile professional and managerial ethnic minority groupings or high levels of self-employment amongst minorities, with low levels of unemployment. This has produced difficulties in making cross-boundary initiatives effective as needs vary greatly.
- Concern over the numbers of highly qualified individuals working in positions that are not commensurate with their education, qualifications and experience.
- Lack of knowledge of opportunities and how to access them. Careers services unable or unwilling to take positive steps to meet the needs of minority groups.
- Lack of an appropriate infrastructure to support enterprise amongst ethnic minority groups. Weak networks, poor voluntary sector provision, weak advice giving and advocacy agencies etc., matched by an under-resourcing of agencies/initiatives aimed at addressing such inequalities.
- Lack of systemized data collection and monitoring by major public organizations, non-governmental organizations and private-sector organizations matched by a visible lack of representation of minorities in such organizations.
- Poor or non-existent equal opportunities policies and programmes of action. Lack of identified individuals responsible within organizations for taking forward action on equalities issues.
- Widespread discrimination, racial stereotyping and workplace harassment as evidenced by REC casework and increased involvement in industrial tribunals and mediation activities. For example, cases brought to the RECs reflecting blatant discrimination at the point of application for jobs, rejection on the basis of accent or

name, suspicion about language proficiency and exiting jobs on the basis of unacceptable levels of racism.
* Widespread discrimination and harassment in schools and educational institutions that remain unmonitored.
* Concern about the provisions of the Welsh Language Act and the potential impact of language policies in the recruitment, selection and promotion of people from minority groups.
* Lone parenthood and carer responsibilities coupled with lack of culturally sensitive service provision and poor childcare provision.

Employment prospects in each minority community relate to a range of factors including migration histories, the perception of employees from that minority, the economic and cultural resources of that community and geographical or local labour-market influences on demand for employees.[63] Gender is also a key differential that cuts across ethnicity.[64] Yet major studies on labour-market participation of women in Wales give little or no attention to ethnic minority women.[65]

Increasingly, it is the 'business case' for minority inclusion in the labour market that is cited in policy circles. It is argued that minority groups represent a vast and untapped potential that if harnessed would allow firms to be responsive to technological change and compete more effectively. In this sense responsibility for social integration is tied to economic inclusiveness and demonstrated through concepts of corporate responsibility and corporate citizenship. This approach is not without criticism but provides a powerful incentive to employers. The Single Programme Document and the European Equal Programme both adopt these considerations and under these schemes partnerships have been developed in Wales for projects aimed at promoting employment for ethnic minority men and women. The European Structural Funds represent a major boost to the economic inclusion of ethnic minorities because of the requirements on equal opportunity. All European aid applications must now set out impacts on ethnic minorities.

Considerable research is yet needed to develop an understanding of the economic circumstances of ethnic minority groups, in particular in assessing income levels, pay and remuneration, poverty levels and take-up of state benefits.

Policing/racial harassment

The issues of policing, racial harassment and access to justice continue to command nation-wide concern. While these issues are beyond the remit of the National Assembly they nevertheless contextualize the experience of minorities in Wales and go some way to qualifying the notion of Wales as a tolerant nation. Police forces in Wales continue to fall short of producing recruitment and retention profiles that reflect minority representation in the community, although this is now subject to specific targets under Home Office guidance. At times some startling figures on racially motivated offences have appeared in Wales (see Chapter 6). In the period 1994/5, for example, south Wales was recorded as having the third highest number of racially motivated incidents in Great Britain. These figures may be the product of more efficient policing and better recording systems than a reflection of an increase in incidents.[66] However, a Home Office study based on calculating the rates of racially motivated incidents per 1,000 of the population in 1996/7 found Gwent police force to have disproportionate numbers of such incidents and Dyfed-Powys police force attracted considerable media attention when they were rated fourth highest in England and Wales for stop and search and sixth highest for arrests of black people.[67]

A very small number of victim studies are available for Wales[68] and investigations in rural areas are slowly illustrating the dimensions of rural racism (see Chapter 10). In terms of the civil justice system a forthcoming study funded by major equality agencies in Wales will identify issues related to access to legal advice and support for ethnic minorities in employment discrimination cases.[69]

Discussion

Even by comparison with Scotland, this overview of the available research to guide policy development in Wales reveals a picture of serious neglect.[70] The dearth of information and knowledge gaps in Wales must be a cause of considerable concern. The Welsh Office Research and Development (WORD) Department (now NAW) has funded just two studies with a specific focus on ethnicity in its lifetime.[71] Until recently, the Welsh Office/NAW collected no systematic statistics disaggregated by ethnicity. Overall, this profile suggests a patterning of neglect, organizational inertia and a lack of knowledge and skills for addressing the needs of minority communities. It hints at markedly different experiences not simply between groups but also within them, mediated by factors of locality, class and gender. From this brief review of the range of policy domains it is possible to identify a number of challenges facing policy-makers in the coming decade:

- the need for ongoing, reliable and comparatively robust data, dis-aggregated by area and by ethnic group;
- the need to develop an approach to ethnic diversity that neither overcategorizes minorities nor treats them as a homogeneous entity;
- the need to find innovative ways of servicing dispersed com-munities, coordinating effort across the whole of Wales;
- the need to fund rigorous and theoretically informed research which also recognizes the frequently reported research fatigue amongst Wales's minority population;
- the need to respond to the information and knowledge deficit in relation to service provision that exists amongst minority communities;
- the need to bolster and support black-led voluntary sector activity in sustainable ways;
- the need to tackle institutional racism in white-dominated organizations;
- the need for greater representation and involvement of black and ethnic minorities on decision-making bodies.

The situation in Wales is beginning to change (see Chapter 11). There is a heightened awareness of the issues of race and ethnicity on the political agenda and an apparent commitment on the part of politicians to grapple with developing an 'ethnic' dimension to policy strategies. Responding to ethnic diversity remains a complex issue not least because of competing definitions of ethnicity. Ensuring standard and consistent definitions between different data sources is not straightforward. Further ethnic categories may not be the most useful way of responding to need in certain circumstances and may not be the key determining factor in differential use of and access to services. Social disadvantage itself has a pervasive impact on equal outcomes. What the studies do highlight is that the ethnic minority experience in Wales is considerably diverse and not coupled with disadvantage and discrimination in consistent ways. It is likely that more sophisticated analysis of the relative position of different groupings will be required to produce effective responses to inequality.

The concept of social inclusion as a strategic approach to policy development has its merits. The language of inclusion certainly has popular and political appeal. It conjures up images of cohesive and cooperative communities and as such resonates with deeply held visions of Welsh society. As a focus for tackling inequality the establishment of Social Exclusion Units has significantly contributed to the demand for systematic and rigorous statistical data for monitoring and evaluation. Several writers have, however, pointed critically to the limitations of this approach and its assumptive base. The language of inclusion has displaced more sharply focused concepts such as social justice/injustice and equality/inequality in policy discourse. The Parekh Report[72] suggests the shift in emphasis to a focus on the insider/outsider boundary of social inclusion means that concerns come to revolve around enabling individuals to traverse the margins of the exclusionary boundaries but at the same time place no real pressure for change at the centre of society, its core power relations and hierarchies. Further, the concept of social inclusion operates with rather blunt notions of who is insider and who is outsider, obfuscating fine gradations of inequality as they impact on different groups. It also has the potential to promote blanket policies that are colour and culture blind and neglect to accommodate the influence of institutional and street racism on people's experience. So, for example, universalist strategies like Communities First and the European Structural Funds may fail to acknowledge key differences in the voice, power and resources of the bidders. Wales lags behind other parts of the UK in its attention to minority issues and therefore cannot afford to subsume them too readily under the banner of social inclusion.

In addition to the forthright legislative mandate governing equality work in public organizations, a number of developments across Wales offer a new opportunity structure for tackling racial inequality. There is evidence of the establishment of equality units in major organizations including the National Health Service in Wales, Welsh local government and the National Assembly itself, aimed at promoting good practice, driving initiatives, monitoring developments and *mainstreaming* equality issues.[73] Squires has demonstrated the critical value of such units in the development of equality outcomes for women and suggests their potential value in tackling other forms of inequality.[74] In addition, Wales is unique in establishing the European Equality Partnership, a working partnership between the major equality organizations in Wales, championing equal opportunities and acting as a catalyst to political and administrative change. The Equal Opportunities Committee of NAW has prompted a number of major race equality reviews, including an internal audit,[75] and established a number of consultative links with minority communities, principally the All Wales Ethnic Minority Association (AWEMA) which has a specific brief in terms of engaging minorities in the policy process (see Chapter 11). These developments are vital and it is as yet too early to review their impact.

Full participation in a society is not simply a matter of income level, health status and educational achievement. In Wales too many of those from ethnic minorities are still shop owners, restaurant proprietors, taxi drivers and traders rather than civil servants, university professors, magistrates, chief executives and media personnel. They are substantially under-represented in the organs of governance. Their access and use of services is partial and unrewarding and their capacity to engage in civil society is hampered by forces of discrimination and harassment. The agenda of 'inclusion' starts from a very low base but the record offered by the 1991 census and research of the 1990s nevertheless represents an important touchstone for accurately measuring policy impacts, trends and developments.

Notes

[1] Social Exclusion Unit, *A New Commitment to Neighbourhood Renewal* (London, 2001), 14.

[2] See National Assembly for Wales (NAW), *Objective ONE Single Programme Document* (Cardiff, April 2000).

[3] T. Modood, R. Bethoud, J. Lakey, J. Nazroo, P. Smith, S. Virdee and S. Beishon, *Ethnic Minorities in Britain: Diversity and Disadvantage* (London, 1997).

[4] NAW, *Plan for Wales 2001* (Cardiff, 2001).

[5] C. Williams, '"Race" and racism: some reflections on the Welsh context', *Contemporary Wales*, 8 (1995), 113–31.

[6] I. Leedham, *Diabetes Health Promotion in Ethnic Minority Communities*, (Cardiff, 2000).

[7] Office of National Statistics 1996.

[8] C. Williams, '"Race" and racism'.

[9] Ibid.

[10] See Minutes of the NAW Equality of Opportunity Committee, 25 June 2000 agenda item 2.4.

[11] Papers of the Assembly's Economic Development Committee, Baseline Data for Monitoring Structural Funds, 26 January 2000: C. Williams, G. Day, T. Rees and M. Standing, *Equal Opportunities Study for Inclusion in European Structural Fund Programme Document 2000–2006: A Report for The National Assembly Office* (Cardiff, 1999).

[12] J. Evans and F. Wood, *Living in Ely: The Experience of Service Provision and Harassment among the Black and Ethnic Minority Population* (Cardiff, 1999); M. Barahu, *Making Voices Heard: Access to Services by Black and Ethnic Minority Women* (Swansea, 1997); P. Jaquest, *Needs Survey of Ethnic Minority Adults in West Glamorgan* (Swansea, 1993).

[13] Cf. D. Dando, 'Somalis in Cardiff: an urban minority', unpublished dissertation, Polytechnic of Wales, 1992; E. A. Ahmed, *Socio-Economic Disadvantages of the Somali Community in Cardiff* (Cardiff, 1998); A. Hansen and A. Hemel-Jorgensen, *Inside and Out: A Needs Analysis of the Somali Community in Cardiff* (Cardiff, 2001); P. Ghuman, 'Bhattra Sikhs in Cardiff: family and kinship organisation', *New Community* 8/3 (1980), 308–16; R. Wornell, 'The Gypsy population in Cardiff', *Contemporary Wales*, 14 (2001), 1–20; V. Robinson, 'Refugees in Wales: an invisible minority', *Contemporary Wales* (1997).

[14] J. Scourfield, H. Beynon, J. Evans and W. Shah, 'The experience of black and minority ethnic children living in the south Wales valleys', unpublished report, Cardiff School of Social Sciences, 2001; The Goal Project, *Towards A Good Old Age? The Goal Project* (Cardiff, 1994); Policy Research Institute on Ageing and Ethnicity, *Care Needs of Black and Minority Ethnic Elders in Wales* (Bradford, 2000); I. Leedham, *Diabetes Health Promotion*. Mewn Cymru, 'Making voices heard: all Wales black and ethnic minority Women's conference', Cardiff Equal Opportunities Commission, 1993.

[15] M. Coulton and C. Drury, 'Policies on ethnic, linguistic and religious needs in Wales under the Children Act 1989', *Social Work and Social Services Review*, 5/1 (1994) 47–63; NHS Wales Equality Unit, *Meeting the Health Needs of Ethnic Minority People in Wales: A Survey of Current Secondary Health Care Practice* (Cardiff, 1998); M. Nyoni, *From the Margins to the Centre: Assessing the Need for Black and Minority Ethnic Housing Strategy in Wales* (Cardiff, 2000); H. Thomas and F. Lo Piccolo, 'Best value, planning and race equality', *Planning Practice and Research*, 15/1–2 (2000), 79–94.

[16] CRE Factsheet, 'Ethnic Minorities in Wales' (2000).

[17] Valleys Race Equality Council, Annual Report 1996.

[18] C. Williams, *Ethnic Minorities in Torfaen* (Cwmbran, Torfaen County Borough Council, 1997).

[19] B. Franklin and J. Passmore, *Developing for Diversity* (Cardiff, 1998).

[20] Nyoni, *Margins to the Centre*.

[21] Barnardos Wales, 'Black Homelessness in South Wales', Report of the Conference held at Cardiff City Hall, July 1995.

[22] MEWN Cymru, 'Making Voices Heard' Conference, 1993. PRIAE, *Care Needs of Elders*. Hansen and Hemel-Jorgensen, *Inside and Out*.

[23] Nyoni, *Margins to the Centre*.

[24] Ibid., para. 14.5.

[25] S. Brownhill, K. Razzaque, T. Stirling and H. Thomas, 'Local governance and the racialisation of urban policy in the UK: the case of Urban Development Corporations', *Urban Studies*, 33/8 (1996), 1337–55.

[26] *Daily Post* (8 November 2001).

[27] For example, I. Leedham, *Diabetes Health Promotion*; E. Coyle, I. Harvey and L. Shah, *The Health and Social Care Needs of Ethnic Minorities in South Glamorgan* (Cardiff, 1993); A. Jamal, 'An assessment of the "felt" health needs of minority ethnic groups in West Glamorgan and the opportunities for health promotion', unpublished M.Sc. dissertation, University of Wales, Swansea, 1995; M. Barahu, *Making Voices Heard*; M. Coulton and S. Roberts, *Unequal Access to Health Care: The Experiences of Black and Ethnic Minorities in Swansea, Neath and Port Talbot* (Swansea, 1997); The Goal Project, *Towards a Good Old Age?*; PRIAE, *Care Needs of Elders*; NHS Wales Equality Unit, *Meeting Health Needs*.

[28] NAW, 'Better Health – Better Wales', May 1998.

[29] PRIAE, *Care Needs of Elders*.

[30] I. Leedham, *Diabetes Health Promotion*.

[31] NHS Wales Equality Unit, *Meeting Health Needs*.

[32] I. Leedham, *Diabetes Health Promotion*, 17.

[33] NAW, www.betterwales.com (Cardiff, 2000), states the aim to 'Make the particular needs of black and ethnic minority groups and disabled people a priority for the NHS and social services' (p. 31).

[34] NHS Wales Equality Unit, *Meeting Health Needs*.

[35] I. Leedham, *Diabetes Health Promotion*, 17.

[36] PRIAE, *Care Needs of Elders*, 21.

[37] Ibid., 22.

[38] NAW, Committee on Equality of Opportunity Minutes, 11 July 2000.

[39] Ibid.

[40] Ibid., 47.

[41] Ibid., 32.

[42] CRE Factsheet, 'Ethnic Minorities in Wales'.

[43] Ibid.

[44] PRIAE, *Care Needs of Elders*; The Goal Project, *Towards a Good Old Age?*

[45] Barnardos (2000); Coulton and Drury, 'Policies on needs'; Scourfield et al., 'Experience of black and minority ethnic children'; Evans and Wood, *Living in Ely*; C. Williams, *Ethnic Minorities in Torfaen*.

[46] NAW, *Communities First The Way Forward: Consultation on the Proposed Policy Framework* (Cardiff, 2001; unpaginated).

[47] WCVA, *Communities First: A Response to the Second Consultation Document* (Cardiff, 2001; unpaginated).

[48] CRE Factsheet, 'Ethnic Minorities in Wales'.

[49] C. Williams, *Ethnic Minorities in Torfaen*.

[50] H. Scourfield et al., 'Experience of black and minority ethnic children'.

[51] S. Gorard, 'Paying for "Little England" – school choice and the Welsh language', *Welsh Journal of Education*, 6/1 (1997), 19–32.

[52] W. MacPherson, *Report of the Inquiry into the Investigation of the Death of Stephen Lawrence* (London, 1999).

[53] NAW, Pre-16 Education, Schools and Early Learning Committee, 'Equality in Education Paper' (Cardiff, September 2000).

[54] NAW, *A Paving Document: A Comprehensive Education and Lifelong Learning Programme to 2010 in Wales – The Learning Country* (Cardiff, 2001; unpaginated).

[55] C. Williams et al., *Equal Opportunities Study*.

[56] All Wales Ethnic Minority Association (AWEMA), 'Response to the National Assembly for Wales' National Economic Development Strategy', May 2001.

[57] C. Williams et al., *Equal Opportunities Study*.

[58] Research into ethnic minority small and medium enterprises is currently being undertaken by Dr. Farris Myzan in the Wales Ethnic Business Centre based at University of Wales Institute, Cardiff Business School.

[59] C. Williams et al., *Equal Opportunities Study*; Hansen and Hemel-Jorgensen, *Inside and Out*.

[60] NAW, *BetterWales.Com* states the intention to 'Reduce unemployment and inactivity amongst groups which have traditionally experienced high unemployment, such . . . black and ethnic minorities', p. 29.

[61] C. Williams et al., *Equal Opportunities Study*.

[62] Ibid.

[63] T. Modood et al., *Ethnic Minorities in Britain*.

[64] T. Rees, *Women and Work: Twenty-five Years of Gender Equality in Wales* (Cardiff, 1999).

[65] D. Blackaby, N. Charles, C. Davies, P. Murphy, N. O'Leary and P. Ransome, *Women in Senior Management in Wales* (Manchester, 1999).

[66] CRE Factsheet, 'Ethnic Minorities in Wales'.

[67] Ibid.

[68] See, for example, P. Jaquest, *Needs Survey*.

[69] C. Williams, A. Griffiths, J. Borland and G. Roberts, 'Snakes and ladders: advice and support for discrimination cases in Wales' (University of Wales, Bangor, 2003).

[70] Scottish Executive, *Audit of Research on Minority Ethnic Issues in Scotland from a 'Race' Perspective* (Edinburgh, 2000).

[71] PRIAE, *Care Needs of Elders*; M. Sullivan, 'Supporting minority ethnic and young families in caring for their children: an evaluation of a Sure Start Health Development Scheme', University of Wales, Swansea, forthcoming.

[72] B. Parekh, *The Future of Multi-Ethnic Britain: The Parekh Report* (London, 2000).

[73] C. Williams, 'Can mainstreaming deliver? The equal opportunities agenda and the

National Assembly for Wales', *Contemporary Wales*, 14 (2001), 57–79.

[74] J. Squires and M. Wickham Jones, *Women in Parliament: A Comparative Analysis* (Manchester, 2001).

[75] R. McKenzie, *Lifting Every Voice: A Report and Action Programme to Address Institutional Racism at the National Assembly for Wales* (Cardiff, 2001).

10 Exploring Myths about Rural Racism: A Welsh Case Study*

VAUGHAN ROBINSON

This chapter addresses the issue of rural racism in Wales. It does so by interrogating various myths that surround the topic. These are the myths that Wales is a parochial society unaccustomed to multi-racialism, that Wales is a more tolerant society than its immediate neighbour, and that since so few of the minority ethnic population live in rural areas then racism cannot be a problem there. These contentions are explored through a mix of literature review and empirical field research, with the field material being drawn from a case study of Powys.

Popular perceptions in England are that Wales is a less cosmopolitan place than its larger neighbour, that most of the Welsh population can trace their Welsh roots back many generations, and that the Welsh have little experience of cultural diversity. Nothing could be further from the truth. Even a cursory knowledge of Welsh history and demography shows that, in many ways, Wales has been one of the most open, cosmopolitan and multicultural constituents of the UK (see Chapter 1). Despite this we have accumulated only limited knowledge to date about the nature of Wales's contemporary minority ethnic population or their experiences. Yet although little is known in Wales about its resident minority ethnic groups, one generalization that is widely accepted is that they receive a warm welcome in Wales, that is, the myth of tolerance.

In the mid-1980s I undertook a survey of attitudes towards ethnic minorities in Swansea based on a representative random sample of 232 respondents.[1] I discovered that 44 per cent of the sample could be labelled as 'showing no signs of overt hostility' to people from ethnic minorities, whilst 39 per cent were 'hostile', 12 per cent were 'strongly hostile' and 5 per cent were 'extremely hostile'. However, what is of greater significance in the present context is that overall levels of expressed racism in Swansea were not dissimilar to those found in multiracial cities in England by other researchers. In addition, the demographic groups most prone to racism in Swansea were those who were also most racist in England and elsewhere. I concluded that this showed the pervasiveness of racism in the UK, but I also noted that it meant that minorities were no more likely to be fairly treated in Wales than in England.

Whilst the Welsh myth of tolerance has been challenged by a limited amount of research, its contemporary contours have not been researched in depth, nor has the minority ethnic population yet been asked to give its views on Welsh tolerance and its experiences of life in Wales. It is these issues that are the focus of this chapter, but since the field research was deliberately set in a rural context, we need briefly to review knowledge about racial harassment and rural racism before returning to the Welsh research study.

Racial harassment

Although Asian and black people have been settling in the UK for over 400 years[2] and British society has been racialized for a similar period, racist violence and harassment has only relatively recently become the subject of detailed research. Panayi has charted the evolution of racist violence in Britain over the period 1840 to 1947[3] and the Institute of Race Relations drew attention to evidence of post-war racial victimization.[4] But it was not until the Home Office's report *Racial Attacks* in 1981 that the issue received official recognition and attempts were made to quantify its scale.[5] In that report, the government acknowledged that South Asian people were fifty times more likely to become the victims of racially motivated incidents than whites, and black Caribbeans were thirty-six times more likely. Although the data and assumptions on which that analysis was based have since been criticized,[6] it did indicate that the problem was much larger than expected, and in need of further research and monitoring. Since then, official recording of racial incidents by the police has provided one means of doing this and the British Crime Survey another. Although the former is particularly flawed,[7] it suggested that 12,000 racially motivated incidents had been reported and recorded in 1994–5. The British Crime Survey interviewed members of the public and asked them about their personal experiences of crime. The results from this suggested that racist crime was more common than had been thought. The 1992 survey, for example, estimated that 130,000 racially motivated crimes had been perpetrated against South Asians and Caribbeans in 1991. Of these, 89,000 were against South Asians and 41,000 were against Caribbeans, and racially motivated crimes formed fully 18 per cent of all crimes committed against these minorities.[8] Furthermore, it is now realized that both these sources only measure the most extreme forms of racist incidents, and that the majority of what has been patronizingly termed 'low-level' racial harassment still goes completely unrecorded. The Fourth National Survey of Ethnic Minorities undertaken by the Policy Studies Institute attempted to rectify this gap in our knowledge by asking their sample about *all* forms of racial harassment.[9] Virdee found that alongside racial attacks and damage to property, some 16 per cent of Chinese, 14 per cent of Caribbeans, 12 per cent of African Asians and 11 per cent of Pakistanis had experienced racial insults or slurs in the previous twelve months. Virdee concluded that

> in a 12 month period between 1993 and 1994, there were about 20,000 people who were racially attacked, 40,000 people who had been subjected to racially motivated property damage and 230,000 people who were racially abused or insulted. Overall then, the survey results would suggest that over a quarter of a million people were subjected to some form of racial harassment in a 12-month period.[10]

Clearly, then, racial harassment is widespread, and an everyday occurrence for members of Britain's minority ethnic population. If Virdee's estimates are correct, then one in twelve of the minority ethnic population experiences racial victimization every year.

Much less has been written about the impact of racist victimization upon people's everyday lives. Chahal and Julienne's study was one of the first to focus on this facet of racism. They undertook a national study of the impact of racism on 74 interviewees resident in urban England, Wales, Scotland and Northern Ireland. They found that not only had racist victimization 'become part of everyday experience in a variety of social situations',[11] but also that 'the impact of racist victimisation had a profound effect beyond the actual event or incident'.[12] Amongst these effects was that for people experiencing 'racist victimisation . . . [it] . . . turns normal, daily activities into assessments of personal safety and security'.[13] Examples included an interviewee who only hung her washing out after dark so as to avoid meeting her abusive neighbour, a family where children were only allowed to play in one half of the house for fear of triggering a further argument with a next-door neighbour, and a family that took their children half a mile to a public playground in preference to the one in their own street.

Rural myths

If British academics were slow to research racial harassment in general, they were even slower to focus on rural racism. Initially the issue of minority exclusion from rural areas was raised in the arts literature, through the photographs of Ingrid Pollard, but only after Jay published his seminal study of south-west England did researchers really identify rural racism as a topic worthy of study.[14] Pollard was an artist born in Guyana who visited the Lake District with friends. There she realized that she was an unwelcome visitor in a landscape which had become a metaphor for Englishness and individual freedom. She captured this sense of exclusion and not belonging in her photographs and their captions, which were later widely exhibited. Amongst these were: 'A visit to the countryside is always accompanied by a feeling of unease, dread . . .'; 'Walks through leafy glades with a baseball bat by my side'; and 'The owners of these fields, these sheep and trees want me off their green and pleasant land . . . No trespass, they want me dead . . . A slow death through eyes that slide away from me . . .'.[15]

Jay's work was more conventional but no less powerful. His was the first empirical analysis of the experiences and situation of minority ethnic people in rural areas. His survey of individuals, organizations and key decision-makers in Somerset, Dorset, Devon and Cornwall produced several findings which have since been replicated elsewhere in the UK. These were that members of the ethnic minority population in these rural areas felt embattled, under threat, isolated and vulnerable. Their response was variable with some leaving, others emphasizing their ethnicity and others trying to reduce their visibility. Most organizations and service providers felt either that there was no race problem in their area or that there was no need for them to sensitize themselves to the needs of minorities because no minorities lived in the area for which they had responsibility. In the foreword to the study, the chair of the Commission for Racial Equality (CRE) therefore concluded that:

> The essential starting point must be to question the assumption which so many appear to have accepted uncritically, that 'there is no problem here'. This report makes that belief untenable; racism in the South-West is evidently a problem, and a serious one which requires urgent attention.[16]

Additional CRE-sponsored studies have since replicated the research methodology of Jay in other rural parts of the UK and have come up with very similar conclusions.[17] Nizhar, for example, confirmed the extent and nature of racist victimization experienced by black and Asian people in rural areas and the unresponsiveness of officialdom to their needs and their problems. In addition, she also uncovered a strong belief amongst officials that special services and support mechanisms should not be provided since it was the responsibility of minorities to assimilate. As one local government officer put it, immigrants should 'give up their identity and image and take on board the white culture'.[18]

In parallel to these official research projects, others have added to the store of knowledge in three main ways. First, by studying new locations.[19] Secondly, by extending the notion of minority exclusion from those who live in rural areas to those who wish to visit rural areas.[20] Agyeman, for example, considered why 'black people' do not visit the British countryside. He argued that it was the result of four barriers: economic barriers such as the cost of getting out of towns; cultural barriers, such as the perception in many cultures that rural areas are less desirable because they are more backward; time, in that many black people have to work very long hours to earn a living wage; and racism, in that black people in the countryside were seen as 'out of place', as human aliens. They are unwelcome reminders of the multicultural and multiracial diversity of contemporary Britain'.[21] Agyeman even drew parallels between the racist attitudes of white rural dwellers who wished to see black people contained within major cities and the 'ecological racism' of conservationists who were trying to maintain the purity of the English countryside by restricting 'non-native' species to domestic gardens. Central to both beliefs was the notion that the British (English?) countryside was the repository of national spirit and identity. The third way in which the store of knowledge on rural racism has been expanded has been through a consideration of the informal and formal policy responses to rural racism. Henderson and Kaur, for example, have identified the key needs of rural minority ethnic populations and have made recommendations for how some of these might be met.[22] Local initiatives have been reported on both by Dhalech,[23] who described the progress of the Rural Race Equality Project that was set up in the south-west of England in the wake of Jay's report, and Agyeman who outlined the formation and early impact of the Black Environment Network.[24]

Lastly, there have been attempts by academics to consider not just the manifestations and nature of rural racism, but its specific causes. Philo was one of the first to argue that rural racism had to be understood in a wider context. He argued that the rural bourgeois protected their rural idyll by denying access to 'messy and non-conforming land uses' and being intolerant of 'any hint of disorder, "deviance" or "otherness"'. This led them, and the middle-class white researchers who worked in rural studies, to deny 'the real complexity of the rural population . . . and turn . . . a blind eye to the presence of all manner of "other" human groupings within this population'. These 'neglected others' included gays, lesbians, children and ethnic minorities.[25]

In his masterly ethnographic study of the Hampshire village of 'Childerley', Bell researched precisely this issue of the attempted exclusion of non-conforming groups from rural areas. He found that the key to processes of exclusion was the power of real and imagined communities. Those living in, and moving to, rural villages believed strongly that this would allow them to become part of a community, and that living in a rural community would provide clear benefits to them and their families. These included 'quietness, a slower pace, a smallness of scale, knowing everyone, helping others, tradition, refuge from the rat race, . . . freedom from material competitiveness, religious morality'.[26] In addition, rural community living provided members with a sense of belonging and identity that was thought to be absent from urban areas. Becoming 'country folk' reconnected people with an Englishness that was thought to have existed in some mythical 'Golden Age', since 'a deep tradition in western thought says that the true spirit of a nation is to be found in the country'.[27] However, as with membership of any community that is thought to offer practical benefits and social status, access must be controlled to maintain both exclusivity and 'purity'. Thus, membership of the community of 'real' 'countryfolk' had to be earned by anyone seeking entry, and this could only be achieved through 'localism', 'ruralism', 'countryism' and 'communalism'. In addition, certain people would never be allowed access to this imagined community simply because of who they were. Black and Asian people, for example, would be denied the opportunity to even earn entry, simply because their skin colour did not conform to imaginings of the past racial purity and homogeneity of the English rural idyll.[28] As a result, a positive desire to maintain something that was valued became also a negative process that denigrated and excluded those perceived not to conform.

The Victim Support Powys study

The remainder of this chapter reports research in progress that is being undertaken in the Migration Unit, University of Wales, Swansea, in conjunction with Victim Support Powys. Victim Support provides a support, advice and advocacy service for those who feel they have been victims of crime, with this service being delivered through a network of local offices staffed by professionals and volunteers.

The helpline

In 1999, Victim Support Powys in Ystradgynlais sensed that there was need for a countywide telephone helpline for those experiencing racial harassment in rural Powys. They then set about raising funds for such an initiative from a range of national and local funders and found that this process was both more difficult and more revealing than they had originally envisaged. One potential funder suggested there was no need for the initiative since there 'are no ethnic minorities in Ystradgynlais', even though he was at the time standing outside an Indian take-away, next to a filling station owned by an Asian businessman, opposite a Pakistani-owned mini-market, and facing a Chinese restaurant. Another possible funder said: 'You are surely not suggesting that we are going to have race riots in Ystrad?' Despite these responses, which illustrate the cultures of disbelief and denial that underpin thinking about race in Wales,[29] Victim Support was successful in raising funding from Powys County Council, Dyfed-Powys Police and the Home Office to establish a helpline for an initial six-month period.

During its brief existence, the helpline dealt with over a hundred enquiries even though finances allowed it to be operational for only one afternoon per week. Sixty-five people received practical help as a result of these calls. Recipients were from a range of ethnic groups and included those who had lived in Powys for a considerable number of years and those who had recently moved into the county from London, Birmingham, Coventry, Liverpool and Manchester.

The reasons why callers contacted the helpline varied. They included having experienced verbal racist abuse, physical attacks, criminal damage to property and the associated difficulty of getting planning consent for special security measures, bullying of children, exploitation at work and problems of homelessness arising from marital disputes and the absence of friends and relatives in the vicinity who could offer emergency accommodation.

A research strategy

Victim Support Powys had thus identified both that minority people in Powys did have distinctive problems and needs and that many local people and service providers denied these because they felt that ethnic minorities did not live in rural areas such as Powys. However, with the demise of the helpline, Victim Support realized they would need to provide a robust evidence-base before they could take any further initiatives in this field. They turned to the Migration Unit in the University of Wales, Swansea, to help them provide this.

In November 1999, we agreed a long-term research strategy. This had two central aims; first, to understand better the lived experience of ethnic minority people who reside outside major ethnic communities, especially those in rural areas such as Powys; second, to discover what resources, facilities and support are available to ethnic minorities in Powys, and to ascertain whether these meet expressed needs.

There are five main elements to the research strategy. The first is concerned with discovering the number and geographical distribution of ethnic minorities in Powys. The second is about discovering the statistical prevalence of racism and prejudice within Powys. The third is about understanding the significance of racism in the everyday lives of minority ethnic people who live in the county. The fourth is about ascertaining how policy-makers and service providers have responded to the perceived and expressed needs of the minority ethnic population. And the fifth is about whether the minorities feel their needs and aspirations are being met by these organizations. This chapter reports on only the second and third of these elements.

The extent of expressed racism: the white view

The first piece of research involved a statistical survey of the 'white' population of Powys to ascertain the extent of expressed prejudice and racism amongst 'local' people. We used a structured questionnaire containing thirty-four questions, some of which had previously been used either in a national study of prejudice[30] or in an international one.[31] Our questionnaire was administered in September 2000 to a sample of 154 respondents living in Powys and selected at random to fulfil sampling quotas designed to ensure a representative age and gender profile. Interviews were undertaken in seventeen different locations throughout Powys so that the sample also accurately reflected the internal geographical distribution of the county's population. In the survey we sought to identify which elements of the local population were the most prejudiced (thereby helping any future attempts to target racial awareness initiatives) and also whether the attitudes of Powys' population differed significantly, statistically, from those of other parts of the UK. The findings of this survey were as follows:

Few people in Powys regard themselves as racist

We employed a question first used on the Eurobarometer questionnaire, in which respondents were asked how racist they were on a scale of 1 (not at all racist) to 10 (very racist): 76 per cent of our sample said 'not at all racist' or 'a little racist', 19.4 per cent labelled themselves as 'quite racist', and only seven individuals thought they were 'very racist' (4.5 per cent). The mean value for the whole sample was 2.77, again falling into the 'only a little racist' category.

We can compare these results with those from the Europe-wide Eurobarometer survey. That survey found 8 per cent of British respondents and 9 per cent of all European respondents willing to categorise themselves as 'very racist', 24 per cent of both the UK and European samples described themselves as 'quite racist', and 69 per cent of the British respondents and 67 per cent of the EU respondents declared themselves 'not at all racist' or only 'a little racist'.[32] It seems clear – even allowing for any further softening in racial attitudes that might have occurred between 1997 and 2000[33] – that residents of Powys think of themselves as not being very racist.

This was confirmed by responses to our questions that asked directly whether respondents thought there was more or less prejudice in Powys against various minority ethnic groups than elsewhere in the UK. Nearly a half of all respondents thought Powys was less prejudiced, and few thought it was more prejudiced.

The Powys sample was also more optimistic about the future for race relations than the national samples in the annual British Social Attitudes Survey.[34] Even in the most optimistic year between 1983 and 1991, only 25 per cent of a national sample felt that prejudice was waning, and in most years the figure was around 18 per cent. The Powys figure was 30.5 per cent.

While people in Powys imagine themselves to be less racist than those elsewhere in the UK, the reality is that they are still prepared to express racist sentiments, and in many cases these are as extreme as those held elsewhere in the UK, if not more so

For example, 33 per cent of the Powys respondents felt that there were too many people from ethnic minorities in the UK; 29 per cent thought Britain would be better off without non-European immigrants; 18 per cent agreed that racial or ethnic minorities should have to give up their culture on arrival in the UK; 11 per cent agreed with the idea of repatriating all non-European immigrants and their British-born children; and 62 per cent felt that the UK had already reached the limit of how many people from racial or ethnic minorities it could accommodate without creating problems. For comparison, the equivalent figures for the UK sample in the Eurobarometer study were 44, 37, 26, 15 and 66 per cent.

While the Powys population imagines itself to be tolerant of minorities, it seems to think the local minority ethnic population is larger, and therefore more threatening, than is actually the case

At the last census in April 1991, the combined minority ethnic population of Powys was about 700, but our respondents estimated the figure to be 5,811 (mean value), with a range from 10 to 58,000. Seventy-two per cent overestimated the size of the minority. Thirty-one per cent thought the size of the imagined minority ethnic population to be 'a lot, but not too many' and a further 5 per cent felt it was simply 'too many'. Such overestimates are often taken as indirect measures of racism.

In summary, our survey demonstrated that, in line with the literature reviewed earlier, those residents of Powys whom we interviewed regarded themselves to be more tolerant than the UK norm. But, having imagined themselves in this way, they were paradoxically also prepared to express racist sentiments that were as extreme or more extreme than those found elsewhere in the UK.

The extent of racism: the minority ethnic view

Having quantified how tolerant the population of Powys imagined itself to be and compared this to the extremeness of some of their expressed views, it remained to explore how racist minority ethnic people found Powys to be. In many ways this is more important than how white people see themselves, since minority opinions will be based more on the behaviours they have encountered whilst living in Powys than upon the posturing of people in interviews.

To capture this other set of opinions, in spring 2000 we posted self-completion structured questionnaires to as many ethnic community associations as we had been able to identify in (or serving) Powys, asking them to distribute these to their members and collect them back in again. The questionnaire was designed to find out the extent, frequency and type of racism experienced by minority ethnic people in Powys, their expectations on moving to the county and whether these had been fulfilled. We eventually received 43 completed questionnaires, which is insufficient to analyse statistically with any degree of confidence. Instead, we chose to regard the questionnaires as qualitative data and use them to derive general themes in the experience of minorities in Powys, supported by 'typical' quotations. Where percentage figures are mentioned, these have been rounded so as not to give a false impression of statistical precision.

Our analysis concluded that ethnic minorities in Powys experienced five phenomena arising directly from their being members of different races.

A sense of being made to feel out of place or different

As was noted in the section reviewing the literature on rural racism, membership of the community of 'country folk' is jealously guarded and entry is only awarded to those who conform to the self-image of this imagined community. Those who cannot gain entry (perhaps because of their race) are deliberately 'othered' and made to feel outsiders, as Ingrid Pollard was when she visited the Lake District. There is very clear evidence of this process of 'othering' occurring in Powys, as the following quotes testify:

> We are stared at all the time as if we are alien. The expression on their faces is of horror.

> People look at you as though you are from a different planet . . . I am constantly reminded that I am different.

> I am made fun of.

> Stared at very obviously whenever I walk into anywhere or speak to anyone. Made to feel like I'm different and odd.

When such 'othering' occurs on a regular basis it can have as severe an impact upon people's mental well-being as the physical acts described by researchers such as Chahal:[35]

> It's almost as if we don't have a right to exist.
> I am made to feel worthless every day.

What is also paradoxical about this sense of heightened individual visibility is that it is at odds with the parallel belief espoused by white service providers that the minority ethnic population is so small that it becomes invisible, and therefore fails to get the services it might otherwise warrant. People of colour thus suffer for being too visible, and also for being invisible.

Lack of understanding of their cultures

We did not specifically ask questions about this issue, but responses to the many open questions on the interview schedule make it clear that this is a major issue for minority ethnic people in rural Powys. Respondents felt that not only were they made to feel different in Powys, they were also misunderstood. A common comment from those who had moved to Wales from urban England was that it was like turning the attitudinal clock back, with people being unaware of multiculturalism, and the different needs of different cultural groups. Some quotes exemplify these strongly held opinions:

> It's not so much violence but their lack of education.

> There is a major lack of awareness and education here in Wales.
>
> People tend to ignore that you have different needs.
>
> People here are ignorant of other cultures and narrow-minded.
>
> People are very uneducated about different ethnic groups.
>
> I get negative comments about my food and customs.

The gist of this was that the white population of Powys was behaving in an unacceptable manner, not out of deliberate malice, but out of an ignorance born from a societal unwillingness to accept that Wales, too, is multicultural and multi-ethnic.

Differential treatment

The lack of understanding of minority cultures and the deliberate process of 'othering' also had impacts upon how ethnic minority people in Powys were treated when interacting with local white people. Fully 70 per cent of respondents felt they were treated differently because of their ethnicity and 60 per cent thought this differential treatment took place either 'all the time' or 'occasionally'. As one person put it: 'I feel I've never been treated fairly since I've been here, especially by the services, and that can be very depressing.' Others expressed similar or more precise sentiments:

> Since moving to Wales we have lost faith in the police and the judicial system.
>
> Police turn a blind eye when I complain.
>
> It wasn't taken as serious as if a white person had been viciously attacked and nearly killed. [The police] made a conscious decision to disregard us due to our ethnic origin.
>
> People [here] are in denial about discrimination.
>
> I have asked for help from different organizations, and it has always been sub-standard: not the same as [would have been offered to] someone British/Welsh.

Overt racism

Other respondents were less forgiving in their explanations for different treatment. They felt that their differential treatment arose from a knowing and overt racism. Twenty per cent of minority ethnic respondents felt that the population of Powys was 'very racist', with one respondent simply saying 'I did not realise it would be as racist as it is'. This racism took many forms, ranging through the spectrum identified by Allport in 1954 from 'antilocution' to physical attack.[36] Name-calling was the most reported type of incident (22 respondents), followed by being ignored (14), being threatened (6), having other family members threatened (5), having property damaged (4), having family members attacked (3) and being attacked personally (1).

> When I first arrived here, I thought it was a lovely green area to live in. In time I have begun to hate living here, with all the negative views people hold regarding other cultures.

> In Wales I have experienced racism from teachers, police, solicitors, shopkeepers, old, middle-aged, and young people.

> Racial remarks all the time.

> I was bullied at work.

> Attacked verbally and physically if I speak my mind about how the Welsh treat outsiders especially ethnic people.

> I and my family have been racially attacked a few times on my business premises.

> Family members been attacked on numerous occasions.

> My sister was attacked by a British woman twice her size. Lots of people were watching her getting hit but no one helped her or stopped the attack. There was also a policeman at the time. He also did nothing for a long time, and he said in court he saw my sister start the attack.

> We have encountered 100% more violence than we did in [an English city].

A sense of isolation

Given that minority ethnic people were being excluded, victimized and attacked, it is important to know what support mechanisms they can call on in times of need. Boal has argued that three of the main functions of geographical clustering of ethnic minorities are cultural maintenance, cultural preservation and defence. He argues that only when minorities cluster can they practise their culture unhindered and develop their own institutions and facilities, pass on this culture to future generations, and defend their culture and themselves against assimilation or physical attack.[37]

We found that, because of their geographical dispersal, our respondents in Powys could call on few of these support networks. One in four of our respondents lived in localities where they were the only member of their ethnic group, and a further 40 per cent lived in places where there were 'hardly any' fellow-ethnics. As a result, almost a half of respondents would have to rely on an ethnic friend or relation who lived at a distance if they faced a 'family crisis'. In addition, nearly half our respondents never had social get-togethers with people from their own ethnic group, and a further 40 per cent only had such social gatherings occasionally. Instead, because of their physical dispersal and isolation, people from the minority ethnic population had to rely upon phone conversations to keep in touch (20 per cent calling ethnic friends or relations daily and 15 per cent calling weekly) or travelling to visit relations or friends. Twenty per cent claimed to travel to visit co-ethnics very or quite regularly and the most common journey time was '120 minutes plus', which was cited by almost half of all respondents. As one respondent put it: 'We have become insecure and isolated. The land we felt was home is now hell.'

The perceptions of minority ethnic people

Finally, we decided to undertake some qualitative in-depth interviews with members of the minority ethnic population about their experiences living in Powys. This work is still ongoing and we can report here only on the first three interviews we have undertaken, which lasted 90–120 minutes and were tape-recorded with the respondents' permission. Again, we do not claim these respondents and their lives are 'typical', although nor do we know they are untypical. One interview was with a Black-Caribbean man who had moved into Powys from England with his partner and the other two respondents were young Asian women who had also moved from England (with their parents), but had now both left the area, having reached adulthood.

Several common points came from these interviews. The first was that the perceived potential attractions of living in Powys were very much those which would have been expressed by any incomer.

Reference was made to the beauty of the landscape, the lack of pollution, the slower pace of life and the belief that rural areas had stronger and more caring communities.[38] In addition, all three respondents had some prior experience of this part of Wales through visiting relatives. None was therefore moving into the completely unknown. Our respondents had not really thought through whether racism would be more or less prevalent in Powys before moving there. Finally, all three had looked forward to the freedom that moving from an ethnic community would give them. Their comments about being able to 'get away with things' and 'be themselves' were particularly interesting, suggesting that there is a similar selectivity in ethnic migration to rural areas as there is in the white population.[39] The young man even explained that whilst in South London he 'would be just another black geezer, here I am a celebrity'.

Residence in Powys had delivered much of what our respondents had sought. They had enjoyed the physical beauty of the place and the 'quality of life' there, and they had been able to behave in ways that would not have been acceptable in ethnic areas in English cities. But life in Powys had also been a struggle. All three respondents had had to put up with very regular racist abuse, one had experienced bullying, and two had witnessed everyday racism in their fathers' shop, which had also been regularly damaged. All three also commented that attitudes were both more dated and less accepting of multiculturalism than they had experienced in the parts of England from which they had migrated to Wales.

Their responses to this racism were interestingly different, although they shared a common theme. All three resisted racism and challenged it rather than allowing themselves to become victims. Moreover, all activated whatever individual and community power they could muster. The two girls (as they had been then) both responded to racism in school by complaining to the teacher. When this failed to achieve anything, they took matters into their own hands. When next abused they punched their tormentors. Physical violence ensured that the problem did not reoccur, and the girls quickly got a reputation as people not to be messed with. The girls also described how their parents simply refused to serve customers who were racist towards them, and since theirs was the only shop in the community this sanction forced perpetrators to modify their behaviour. Lastly, the black man mobilized three alternative forms of power. He was a tall, athletic man in any case, but when he grew dreadlocks and started wearing leathers he projected a threatening image that warded off any challenges. His use of visual (Rasta) symbolism led people to stereotype him as 'hard', even when he was not. He also mobilized the power of the stereotype of black men being sexually adroit to his advantage. He argued that his exoticism in white Powys led him to be popular with local women keen to test the stereotype and with local men who both saw him as 'a good lad' and wanted to ensure that he did not poach their partners. Finally, since he was a talented musician he was both able to gain acceptance in the community by giving free lessons to local children and project an image as a 'personality'.

What these last points demonstrate is that ethnic minority people should not be seen as passive victims of racial harassment but as active agents who marshal whatever (economic, physical and symbolic) power they have access to, to challenge racism.

Conclusion

What we have discovered is that Welsh rural racism is shot through with myths and contradictions. While English commentators regard Wales as being new to multiculturalism and multiracialism, Wales has actually experienced inmigration of racially, ethnically and culturally dissimilar groups for at least a century and a half, and has been an open and cosmopolitan society since the onset of industrialization in the eighteenth century (see Chapter 1). Wales imagines itself to be a more tolerant place than England and we have shown that its population is happy to categorize itself as tolerant, when asked. Yet we have also shown that, in its actions and when asked to express specific opinions about race, immigration and ethnicity, the Welsh population appears no more, and no less, tolerant than their English neighbours. Moreover, when members of the minority ethnic population of rural Wales are asked to recount their experiences, they talk of everyday racism, a lack of understanding, being 'othered' and of overt racism, including physical attacks on themselves and their families. So as Evans demonstrates historically (see Chapter 1) we can confirm that contemporary Welsh imaginings of tolerance are just that.

What the research also shows, albeit in a tentative form at present, is that the ethnic minority population in rural Wales does not accept its allotted role as victims. Some respond by leaving, but others fight back by mobilizing what power they have and challenging racist attitudes and behaviours. They do so, however, without the support of an ethnic community, since they are not only victimized but isolated.

Finally, this study demonstrates that, with devolution, Wales has a significant opportunity to convert its imaginings into reality. Not only would this ensure a symmetry between reality and rhetoric, but it would show that Wales could lead the UK in creating a more humane and inclusive society. And not unimportantly, it would give Wales an economic edge in the post-Fordist and post-industrial era when capital, consumption and employees are so much more mobile than they once were. In this new era, an international outlook, an openness to outside influences, and an appreciation of other cultures and people is not just vital to human rights and creating an inclusive society, but it is also one of the keys to economic success.

Notes

*I would not have been able to write this chapter without the help of all at Victim Support, Ystradgynlais (especially Eileen), and without the assistance of Nissa Finney. Thanks to you all.

[1] V. Robinson, 'A study of racial antipathy in south Wales and its social and demographic correlates', New Community, 12 (1985), 116–24.

[2] R. Visram, Ayahs, Lascars and Princes (London, 1986); P. Fryer, Staying Power: the History of Black People in Britain (London, 1984).

[3] P. Panayi, Racial Violence in Britain 1840–1950 (Leicester, 1993).

[4] Institute of Race Relations, Police Against Black People (London, 1979).

[5] Home Office, Racial Attacks (London, 1981).

[6] P. Gordon, 'The police and racist violence in Britain', in T. Bjorgo and R. Witte (eds), Racist Violence and Harassment in Europe (London, 1993).

[7] S. Virdee, Racial Violence and Harassment (London, 1995).

[8] N. Aye Maung and C. Mirrlees-Black, Racially Motivated Crime: A British Crime Survey Analysis (London, 1994).

[9] T. Modood, R. Berthoud, J. Lakey, J. Nazroo, P. Smith, S. Virdee and S. Beishon, Ethnic Minorities in Britain: Diversity and Disadvantage (London, 1997).

[10] S. Virdee, 'Racial harassment', in Modood et al. (eds), Ethnic Minorities in Britain, 267.

[11] K. Chahal and L. Julienne, 'We Can't All Be White!' Racist Victimisation in the UK (York, 1999), p. vi.

[12] Ibid., p. vii.

[13] Ibid., 5.

[14] E. Jay, *'Keep them in Birmingham': Challenging Racism in South-West England* (London, 1992).

[15] I. Pollard, 'Pastoral interludes', *Third Text*, 7 (1989), 41, 42, 46.

[16] Jay, *'Keep them in Birmingham'*, 5.

[17] P. Nizhar, *No Problem? Race Issues in Shropshire* (Telford, 1995); H. Derbyshire, *Not in Norfolk: Tackling the Invisibility of Racism* (Norwich, 1994); P. DeLima, *Needs Not Numbers: An Exploration of Minority Ethnic Communities in Scotland* (London, 2001).

[18] Nizhar, *No Problem?*, 35.

[19] For example, G. Craig, B. Ahmed and F. Amery, ' "We shoot them in Newark!" The work of the Lincolnshire Forum for Racial Justice', in P. Henderson and R. Kaur (eds), *Rural Racism in the UK: Examples of Community-Based Responses* (London, 1999), 22–32; J. Rayner, 'The hidden truth behind race crimes in Britain', *Observer* (18 February 2001), 18, 8–9.

[20] S. Malik, 'Colours of the countryside – a white shade of pale', *Ecos*, 13/4 (1992), 33–40.

[21] J. Agyeman, 'Black people in a white landscape: social and environmental justice', *Built Environment*, 16/3 (1990), 232.

[22] Henderson and Kaur, *Rural Racism in the UK*.

[23] M. Dhalech, *Challenging Racism in the Rural Idyll: Final Report* (National Association of Citizen's Advice Bureaux, Exeter, 1999).

[24] Agyeman, 'Black people in a white landscape'.

[25] C. Philo, 'Neglected rural geographies: a review', *Journal of Rural Studies*, 8/2 (1992), 197, 199.

[26] M. Bell, *Childerley: Nature and Morality in a Country Village* (Chicago, 1994), 93.

[27] Ibid., 94.

[28] Cf. A. Kundnani's discussion of the new popular 'kith and kin' racism: 'In a foreign land: the new popular racism', *Race and Class*, 43/2 (2001), 41–61.

[29] V. Robinson, 'Cultures of ignorance, disbelief and denial: refugees in Wales', *Journal of Refugee Studies*, 12/1 (1999), 78–87.

[30] C. Airey, 'Social and moral values', in R. Jowell and C. Airey (eds), *British Social Attitudes: The 3rd Report* (Aldershot, 1984); K. Young, 'Class, race and opportunity', in R. Jowell (ed.), *British Social Attitudes: The 9th Report* (Aldershot, 1994).

[31] Eurobarometer, *Racism and Xenophobia in Europe* (Brussels, 1997).

[32] Ibid.

[33] On trends during these years, see V. Robinson, 'Regional variations in attitudes towards race', in P. Jackson (ed.), *Race and Racism* (London, 1987), 160–88; and Young, 'Class, race and opportunity'.

[34] Young, 'Class, race and opportunity'.

[35] Chahal and Julienne, *'We Can't All Be White!'*.

[36] G. W. Allport, *The Nature of Prejudice* (Cambridge, MA, 1954).

[37] F. Boal, 'Ethnic residential segregation', in D. Herbert and R. Johnston (eds), *Social Areas in Cities* (Chichester, 1978).

[38] Cf. Bell's findings for white incomers to Hampshire, *Childerley*.

[39] M. Parker, 'Loaded dice', *Planet*, 148 (2001), 7–12.

11 Croeso i Gymru – Welcome to Wales?[1]
Refugees and Asylum Seekers in Wales

VAUGHAN ROBINSON

The global refugee 'crisis' and the UK

For those interested in migration, the 1980s and 1990s were the decades of the refugee, with interest initially being in refugee generation (the 1980s), then refugee repatriation (early 1990s), and latterly refugee admission (or asylum seeking). While it may be an exaggeration to talk of a global refugee 'crisis' emerging in the 1980s, there is no doubt that during that decade refugee migration underwent a step-change. The number of officially recognized refugees in the world grew very rapidly, the number of countries generating refugees expanded sharply, the number and type of countries affected by refugee migrations also rose, and refugees started to flee for a much wider range of reasons.

Although it is difficult accurately to quantify the number of refugees in the world at any one point in time,[2] the United Nations High Commissioner for Refugees (UNHCR) does produce authoritative annual estimates.[3] These suggest that the global number of refugees first started to grow rapidly between 1980 and 1983, during which time numbers rose from 5.7 million to 10.9 million. There was then a second period of sharp growth beginning in 1987 and ending in 1992, when numbers further rose from 12.4 million to 18.2 million. Since then, the number has fallen back to 12.1 million,[4] although there are signs that this may have been a temporary dip.

There are several reasons why the number of refugees grew so rapidly between 1980 and 1992. First, 'misfit groups' were created by the dissolution of multi-ethnic empires into newly independent states.[5] These groups were of two types: 'minorities' were people of one identity finding themselves in a country with a different identity, thereby losing full rights and legal protection; and the 'stateless' were groups whose identity did not correspond to that of any established nation-state or minority. Zolberg argued that both these types of misfit groups would eventually become refugees, because states would purge non-conforming groups in an effort to create a strong national identity. In order to achieve this, the stateless would be expelled and minorities would be persecuted until they 'chose' to leave. Secondly, superpower rivalry was still being played out by proxy in a series of local conflicts, and these were generating refugee flight and expulsions (for example, the Afghan war). Thirdly, the 1980s saw a deregulation of air transport. This increased the availability of direct long-distance air travel and reduced its real cost. Fourthly, changes in international communications technology made it easier for potential emigrants to acquire information about possible destinations and opportunities.[6] Fifthly, the growing income gap between the developing and developed world heightened the perceived attraction of migrating to the 'West', just as legal channels of labour migration were being closed.[7] And, finally, that decade saw the growth of new forms of 'refugee' migration, including the flight of those affected by development projects (for example, dams) and/ or by ecological disasters.[8]

However, it was not just the number of refugees generated or the complexity of the causes of their flight that constituted a step-change in refugee migration in the 1980s and 1990s. In the 1970s refugees had been generated in Africa and Asia and the predominant policy response had been local integration. Refugees were resettled in neighbouring developing countries that were culturally, economically and socially similar to their country of origin. Where a powerful Western country felt some responsibility for a Third World conflict, it might have allowed entry to a small number of carefully selected 'quota' refugees on humanitarian grounds,[9] but this was the exception rather than the rule. By the 1990s, however, increasing numbers of refugees were simply bypassing official programmes, travelling to the West, and claiming asylum on arrival. For example, the number of people seeking asylum in the EU 'twelve' rose from 60,000 in 1983 to more than half a million by 1992.[10] For many Western governments this proved to be a highly threatening development. It engendered in them a fear that they were losing control of immigration, at a time when their electorates were clamouring for less immigration and tighter immigration controls. The response was draconian. Elsewhere I have described how, as the global refugee crisis finally impacted on European shores, governments and the EU erected a plethora of legislative, physical and administrative barriers designed to deny asylum seekers access to Fortress Europe.[11]

As Europe ceased to be a backwater for refugee generation and admission, some European countries experienced particularly sharp increases in the number of asylum seekers while others did not. Taking the period 1985–92, Germany experienced a 593 per cent increase in asylum applications, Spain 509 per cent and the Netherlands 360 per cent, while France saw a fall in applications and Denmark saw 'only' a 160 per cent increase. The UK was one of the countries experiencing a sharp increase (at 520 per cent) and therefore came to play a larger role in global refugee migration. Whereas Britain had accepted refugees as far back in history as the Huguenots, and been one of the main destinations for Eastern European refugees fleeing the pogroms of the 1880s and 1890s,[12] its post-war contribution to the international refugee crisis had been relatively insignificant. Each of the main groups of quota refugees accepted by the UK between 1945 and 1991 was relatively small in number (for example, 5,000 Chileans in 1974–5).[13] But, as Western governments began to lose control of refugee flight at source, so the number of people claiming asylum either 'in-country' or at 'port-of-entry' in the UK has increased. Whereas only 3,998 people claimed asylum in the UK in 1988, by 1998 this number had risen to 46,000, by 1999 to 71,160 and by 2000 it had further risen to 80,315. The UK is now one of the main destinations for asylum seekers in the EU, even if actual numbers applying for asylum are dwarfed by, for example, the number of refugees currently being accommodated by countries such as Iran (1.9 million at the beginning of 1999).

The growing sense of panic at the rise in asylum applications in the UK has impacted directly on public opinion and policy. By 1997 Britons were already expressing the view that their tolerance was being overstretched. The Eurobarometer survey in 1997 recorded that 64 per cent of British respondents agreed with the statement 'our country has reached its limits; if there were to be more people belonging to *(non-European)* minority groups we would have a problem'.[14] And the MORI poll for the *Readers' Digest* in 2000 found that '80% of adults believe that asylum seekers come to our shores because they regard Britain as a "soft touch"'. Sixty-six per cent of adults felt that there were 'too many' immigrants in Britain, and this constituted a rise of 11 percentage points over a similar survey undertaken only twelve months previously.[15] Partly because of such attitudes, the watershed 1999 Immigration and Asylum Act introduced a series of policy innovations that included a fast-track procedure quickly to remove those thought to have an unfounded claim; speeded decision-making for all others; changes to the financial support to which asylum seekers were eligible so that it came largely in the form of vouchers; and the compulsory dispersal of asylum seekers around the UK while they awaited the outcome of their application.

Refugees in Wales: recent history prior to 1999

Wales's distance from the main ports of entry to the UK has ensured that it has played a very limited part in the recent history of refugee resettlement in the UK. However, it is difficult to say how limited this part has been with any degree of certainty. One of the few government reports to discuss the geographical distribution of refugees in the UK prior to the 1999 Act calculated that fully 85 per cent of all such people lived in London.[16] However, the absence of official data on the socio-demographics of asylum seekers and refugees makes it almost impossible to get any accurate idea of the real distribution of these groups or the number found in any particular region or locality. As one author wrote, when lamenting the paucity of official data and research, 'reliable official data on the size or distribution of refugee groups within the United Kingdom are not available in the public domain'.[17]

However, despite the absence of official data, three studies do give us snapshots of the refugee population in the early and late 1990s and help us ascertain which national groups migrated to Wales, where they lived in Wales, their demographics and some of the key issues that faced them.

The first of these was a piece of research commissioned by the Welsh Refugee Council (WRC) to produce some estimates of the size of the refugee population of Wales.[18] This study began by trying to use census data to produce maximum numbers for different national groups in Wales. It then attempted to use data from nongovernmental organizations (NGOs) to consider how many 'quota' refugees had been resettled in Wales by central government. 'Quota' refugees can be distinguished from 'spontaneous' refugees. The latter travel individually and then make an individual application for asylum on arrival. Quota refugees, on the other hand, are given group asylum before departure from their home country (or from camps in third countries), are transported to the UK en masse, and are then the recipients of a government welfare and resettlement programme. In recent times, the UK government has committed itself to five refugee quotas, of 28,608 Ugandan Asians in 1973, 5,000 Chileans in 1975, 12,000 Vietnamese over the period 1979–84, 4,000 Bosnians in 1992, and 4,300 Kosovars in 1999. In each case, the government delegated responsibility for reception and resettlement to NGOs, which were funded and overseen by the Home Office.

The government policies associated with the arrival of each of these groups have been evaluated by the Migration Unit at University of Wales, Swansea, and in three of the five cases data have also been acquired from NGOs about the geographical distribution of those refugees resettled through government schemes. These data showed that the Ugandan Asians initially, and also subsequently, concentrated themselves in areas that had sizeable pre-existing Asian communities in England (for example, Leicester and London). Wales was not a favoured destination.

The Vietnamese represent a rather different case, since they were given little choice over their place of resettlement and were also deliberately dispersed throughout Britain in small groups of four to ten families. Robinson and Hale's data demonstrated that the Vietnamese were widely dispersed throughout the UK, and that some 602 were resident in Wales in 1981.[19] Their analysis also showed that the Vietnamese subsequently regrouped within major English conurbations via a process of rapid and extensive secondary migration. As a result, the number of Vietnamese in Wales had fallen to 282 by 1991. More recently, the Bosnians have also experienced government attempts to manipulate their geographical distribution, with refugees being resettled in the specific targeted 'cluster areas' of Scotland, north-east England, West Yorkshire, West Midlands, East Midlands and London.[20] Wales was not designated a cluster area and therefore did not receive Bosnian quota refugees. Based on these various analyses of quota programmes, it was consequently concluded that:

> it is clear that Wales has not been a favoured destination for the resettlement of quota refugees in the 1970s, 1980s and 1990s. Government

intervention in resettlement has ensured a manufactured geographical outcome in which Wales has had little part to play. Where small groups of individuals have been resettled in the Principality, they have tended not to remain, but have sought residence, instead, within larger communities of their countryfolk, usually within English cities. For example, the Vietnamese community in Swansea, which began with 14 families, had shrunk by 1989 to only eight families.[21]

Finally, I attempted to derive my own estimates of the size and distribution of the refugee population in Wales by undertaking my own survey. This involved a questionnaire survey of organizations which might have been expected to have come into contact with refugees, or which might represent them. In all, 329 questionnaires were distributed to county council departments, district authorities, housing associations, the police, training and enterprise councils, job centres, Red Cross branches, refugee groups, NGOs, and institutions of further and higher education across the whole of Wales. Ninety items of correspondence were received from these organizations, giving a response rate of over 27 per cent. In ten cases where the information provided by respondents was either incomplete or of some interest, organizations were telephoned for further details, and an additional eight organizations which came to light during the research were also telephoned rather than sent a questionnaire. The results of this survey were interesting and illuminating.

Although all those statutory and non-statutory bodies which were likely to come into contact with refugees and asylum seekers were sent a questionnaire, very few had actually had any contact with such people at all. Only thirteen organizations out of the 329 approached (4.0 per cent) claimed to have had any contact with refugees and, with two exceptions, the number of people involved was very small. The results of the survey are mapped in Figure 1. They demonstrate that the majority of known asylum seekers/refugees in 1997 were concentrated in Cardiff (67 per cent of the total), Newport (16 per cent) and Swansea (12 per cent). Outside these clusters, there were only small numbers, or even individuals, drawn from a variety of ethnic groups, and occasionally associated with places of learning (Lampeter, Pontypridd, Port Talbot). Seventy per cent of all refugee households were Somali, 9.3 per cent were Vietnamese, 7 per cent were Iranian, 6 per cent were Sudanese, and 5.6 per cent were Iraqis. Fifteen different nationality groups were represented.

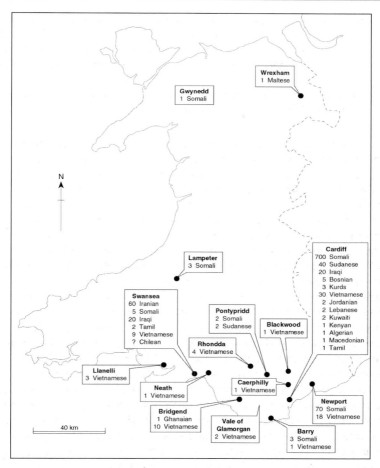

Figure 1. The estimated distribution of refugees/asylum seekers in 1997

From this survey I concluded that the size of the refugee/asylum seeker population of Wales was around 1,016 households, containing perhaps 3,565 individuals. If this were correct, it would mean that Wales contained about 3.6 per cent of all the 100,000 refugees estimated by the UNHCR to be living in the UK at that time. Since Wales contained around 5.3 per cent of the entire population of the UK, refugees were therefore significantly under-represented in Wales.

However, this report did warn that there were a number of reasons why this figure might have been an underestimate. These were that refugees might have chosen deliberately or accidentally not to represent themselves as such when they came into contact with organizations; that those providing services might then not have been able to distinguish between refugees and other members of the ethnic minority population; that refugees might have opted to resolve their own difficulties rather than seek assistance from others, and might therefore never come to the attention of public bodies; that refugees might not have contacted service providers because they did not value the services which they provided; or that 'refugees' may not have recognized the validity of this label or might feel they have passed beyond it.

The second piece of research which considered the refugee population of Wales prior to the 1999 Immigration and Asylum Act was Save the Children's study of the Somali community of Cardiff in 1994.[22] As noted above, the Somalis represented probably the largest single group of refugees in Wales and were concentrated in the two settlements of Cardiff and Newport. As such, they deserve an extended discussion. Save the Children described how Somali settlement in Cardiff dates back to the turn of the century, when Somali seamen worked on board ships that were exporting Welsh coal. Further male migrants arrived in the 1950s, attracted by the booming economy and the availability of work. However, it was not really until the 1960s that a 'community' came into being, when women started to join the men, and families were formed or reformed. This community was then further augmented in the 1980s by continued family reunion and the flight of single refugees anxious to escape the deteriorating political conditions in Somalia.

By 1994 Save the Children claimed that the Somali community in Cardiff numbered some 4,000, of which perhaps 2,000 were recently arrived refugees. The community was interconnected by extensive family networks and by the fact that most people originated from the same part of Somalia, namely Somaliland. Save the Children identified several key issues facing the Somali community at that time. These were: difficulties getting refugee status; problems bringing wives and children to the UK; the way in which language was acting as a barrier to access to services and entitlements; high rates of unemployment; an unwillingness on the part of service providers to recognize the specialist health needs of people who had experienced civil war; the need for facilities for women; the need to secure and expand the Somali Advice and Information Centre and also establish a Somali Community Centre; and the unmet demand from those seeking to enter self-employment for advice. Save the Children then went on to make three general recommendations. These were that the statutory and voluntary sectors should:

- invest in projects which develop the skills and capacities of the community, and in so doing provide routes out of poverty;
- improve access to mainstream services through the appointment of more Somali-speaking staff;
- allocate resources to the development of culturally sensitive services targeting specific groups in the Somali community.[23]

The final piece of research which sheds light on the refugee population of Wales prior to the 1999 Act is my article of 1999.[24] I reported the second phase of my research for the Welsh Refugee Council, which was concerned with whether service providers were aware of the needs of refugees and had successfully responded to these. In order to collect primary data on the scale and type of targeted service provision, a second questionnaire survey was organized. This involved a longer self-completion questionnaire sent out to 225 organizations which might reasonably have had contact with refugees. This list included county councils, district authorities, training and enterprise councils, job centres, charities, racial equality councils, health trusts, social housing providers, institutions of further and higher education and advice centres. Ethnic community groups were not contacted since the survey was attempting to quantify awareness of refugee needs, and refugee groups were assumed to be well aware of their own needs.

Seventy-seven replies were received, of which seventy-two contained usable data. The key results of this survey were that: only eight organizations provided services for refugees/asylum seekers; only two organizations intended to expand their service provision for refugees, with one intending to improve health care provision and another intending to organize an event designed to raise awareness of the plight of refugees; 40 per cent of organizations stated that refugees were an extremely low priority for them and only 3 per cent of respondents saw them as a central priority; 40 per cent felt that refugees had neither become more nor less important as an institutional priority over the last five years and 6 per cent felt that refugees had become much less of a priority, even though that period had seen a sharp increase in the number of asylum seekers entering the UK. The most common services provided for refugees were translating and advice on immigration or welfare issues, and organizations seemed to have made little effort to sensitize themselves to the needs of refugees. Only two organisations had deliberately employed refugees. Only four (7 per cent) had appointed targeted staff, but not all these staff had then received specialist training. Over half of all bodies sought no consultation whatsoever with refugee communities or their representatives, and only two organizations arranged regular formal consultation. And 82 per cent of organizations had never had any direct contact with the WRC.

I concluded my 1999 survey by arguing that attitudes towards refugees and asylum seekers in Wales were shaped by three 'cultures'.[25] The first of these was a 'culture of ignorance' deriving from the absence of any data on the distribution of refugees or their socio-demographics. This allowed some organizations to avoid their responsibilities, and even where organizations wished to bring about change, they found this very difficult because they were working in an information vacuum that hobbled decision-making. One organization that had been questioned even said they had no contact with refugees because they provided services only for the mentally unwell, assuming therefore that refugees were all mentally healthy. This displayed an alarming ignorance of the prevalence of post-traumatic stress disorder amongst refugees. Another organization said they would not expect to have any contact with refugees because they dealt only with old and lonely people, as if refugees were all young! Less easily remedied was the 'culture of disbelief' amongst service providers who argued that there was no need for action in Wales because there were no refugees in Wales or in their particular locality. Instead, refugees were seen as an English 'problem' which was restricted to that country's major metropolitan areas. This 'culture of disbelief' was widespread within Wales, with many organizations claiming that refugee needs were an unimportant issue for them without having taken the trouble to consult with refugee groups or indeed ascertain whether there was a local refugee population. Finally, there was the 'culture of denial', which assumed that racism and exclusion were less virulent in Wales than in England, and therefore that refugees did not face any unusual or noteworthy problem living in Wales.

The 1999 Asylum Act and Wales

As has already been noted, the 1999 Immigration and Asylum Act marked a sea change in British asylum policy but it also marked a turning point for Wales. For the first time Wales became an official reception area for asylum seekers while they awaited the outcome of their application.

Although authorities in the south-east of England had been dispersing asylum seekers informally since 1996, Wales did not become involved in this. It was not until December 1998, when the Home Secretary encouraged local authorities to formulate an official nation-wide dispersal policy, that Wales first became involved and it was declared one of the ten consortia responsible for dispersing up to 2,600 asylum seekers per month from the south-east of England.[26] However, delays in setting up this voluntary scheme led the Home Secretary to intervene in December 1999 and impose a centrally planned and managed dispersal policy run by a new division of the Home Office called NASS (National Asylum Support Service).

The new system was to work as follows. Asylum seekers apply for asylum to the Immigration and Nationality Directorate who then decide whether they should be allowed temporary admission to the country (while their claim is heard) or detained if their claim is manifestly unsound or if there is a strong chance that they might disappear into the community if allowed their freedom. Those given temporary admission are then referred to a NASS-funded reception assistant who ascertains whether they have any means of support. If they do not, they are then found temporary accommodation while the reception assistant helps them prepare a claim to NASS for support. NASS then decides within seven days whether the applicant is eligible for support,[27] and if this is the case, it then allocates them to accommodation in one of the cluster areas outside London and the south-east. Once bussed there, destitute asylum seekers are given free housing (including the cost of utilities) and benefits equivalent to 70 per cent of income support rates for adults and 100 per cent of income support rates for children. Only about £10 of this is paid in cash, with the remainder being offered in the form of vouchers that can be exchanged at shops participating in the scheme. Advice and assistance in the cluster areas are provided through one-stop centres created by local refugee councils. Having been temporarily settled, asylum seekers should expect to receive a decision on their claim for asylum within an average of two months, with a possibility of appeals in the subsequent four months. The full determination procedure should therefore be completed within a maximum of six months. If the asylum seeker is given refugee status or leave to remain they then have the right to live anywhere they wish and are not restricted to the cluster area to which they had originally been allocated.

Rather than replicate the errors of the Local Government Association dispersal scheme, the Act proposed that local organizations and authorities should come together into consortia which would be expected to provide the full range of services needed by asylum seekers, including 40 per cent of all housing. Each consortium would be given £100,000 per annum to organize, coordinate and administrate provision and promote positive media images of asylum seekers. Consortia are also expected to make provision for the long-term integration of those asylum seekers granted refugee status or exceptional leave to remain. This includes measures to help refugees find employment, provide them with language skills and ensure appropriate educational provision.

Thirteen cluster regions were eventually defined, and dispersal to these has been contracted out to consortia whose responsibility it is to provide all relevant reception services. Wales has two consortia. The Cardiff consortium signed its contract with the Home Office in March 2001, and the all-Wales consortium of the remaining twenty-one local authorities is about to sign its contract at the time of writing (early February 2002).

NASS also negotiates directly with other organizations for the provision of specific elements of support. Sixty per cent of all accommodation, for example, was expected to be volunteered directly either by local authorities, registered social landlords or the private sector. These organizations were to provide a range of appropriate accommodation as well as the necessary support package (for example, orientation, guidance on living skills and activities to prevent asylum seekers becoming isolated or bored).

Originally, the Wales cluster area was due to receive its first asylum seekers in April 2000, but delicate negotiations between central and local government and the desire to establish critical masses of asylum seekers in other parts of the UK led to delays in asylum seekers being sent to Wales, with the first only arriving in May 2001. By February 2002, the Cardiff consortium had received approximately 700 dispersed asylum seekers and the all-Wales consortium had yet to receive any asylum seekers. Private-sector providers had also been contracted to receive asylum seekers and as of early 2002 they had accommodated about 470, of which 200 were in Swansea, 200 were in Cardiff and 60–70 were in Wrexham. In addition, the Welsh Refugee Council has been contracted to provide emergency accommodation for those people making their asylum claim in Wales, and to date they have helped about 200 people.

Reactions in Wales

As yet there has been no comprehensive study of public attitudes to the arrival of asylum seekers in Wales under the dispersal programme, although Nissa Finney of the Migration Unit, University of Wales, Swansea, is currently undertaking such research. We can therefore only attempt to gauge the public response by an analysis of how the media has handled the issue, since this is both an important determinant of public attitudes and a reflection of such attitudes. Speers has already undertaken a study of how the media has reacted in her pamphlet *Welcome or Over Reaction? Refugees and Asylum Seekers in the Welsh Media*.[28]

Speers undertook an analysis of all articles concerning asylum seekers and refugees that were published in thirty-two different Welsh local newspapers between April and December 2000. She analysed the headlines that were posted above the articles, the language that was used within the articles, their key theme, their main sources and whether they used any photographic images to illustrate the text. Her overall conclusion was that 'the Welsh press covers the issue of asylum seekers without the hostility or hyperbole that can be seen in the UK-wide national media'[29] and that, in particular, 'unlike the national media, Welsh newspapers rarely use terms like "flood", "influx" or "wave" to describe the numbers of asylum seekers coming to Britain or Wales'.[30] She also praised certain Welsh politicians for adopting and disseminating a more positive attitude towards dispersal than their English counterparts and notes how the press and politicians had made a good deal of the warm Welsh welcome being offered to asylum seekers, and how this formed part of the tradition of Welsh tolerance.

Nevertheless, Speers did find much that could be criticized or improved, and she also identified an underlying negativity towards asylum seekers and their arrival in Wales. Many articles labelled asylum seekers as a 'burden', with the *Western Mail* on 4 November 2000, for example, writing of shouldering the burden of caring for asylum seekers. Almost half the articles analysed took as their main theme the national or local cost of dispersal, with 22 per cent mentioning that the arrival of asylum seekers was likely to have an adverse impact on local housing and education. Other articles carried the message that dispersal was being foisted on Wales to relieve pressure in the south-east of England. Speers also found that asylum seekers were being linked with crime and with the formation of ghettos, and that asylum seekers were being characterized as something to be feared. But one of the key findings was that the media was giving too little attention both to asylum seekers as people, and to their reasons for fleeing their home countries. Instead asylum seekers were being denied a voice and being reduced to numbers on a balance sheet:

> The most far-reaching conclusion of this report is the reduction of asylum seekers and refugees to either a financial cost or a statistic used to describe numbers arriving in the UK. The Welsh media rarely discuss why people seek refuge in Britain and instead coverage focuses on the costs of the dispersal process to their local community. In taking the human element out of the discussion about refugees and asylum seekers, it is easier to create a division between 'us', the valid citizens of Britain, and 'them' the asylum seekers 'using up' valuable government resources . . .[31]

Part of this process of dehumanizing asylum seekers involved not illustrating articles with images of asylum seekers, and seeking commentary on events and policies only from government officials, academics or other powerful figures, not from refugees or their community leaders. She recommended that this situation should be remedied and that we should hear more from asylum seekers themselves.

The lived experience of refugees and asylum seekers in Wales

Given that so little has been heard from asylum seekers in Wales, and that they have been invisible in media reporting, this last section of the chapter looks at the experiences of a small number of asylum seekers and refugees currently living in Wales. Sixteen respondents were located through the good offices of local refugee organizations and they were interviewed between autumn 2000 and spring 2001 for an average of ninety minutes each. In selecting the respondents I did not aim to gather a representative sample from which I could generalize. Rather, I wished to act as a conduit for as many voices as possible, each of which would have a different story to tell, based on different experiences. Obviously, limitations of space allow the presentation of only some of this material here, and two case studies have been selected which are in many ways typical of the others.

Case 1: Juan from Chile

Juan arrived in the UK in 1974 as part of the government's Chilean programme that brought 5,000 political prisoners and their families to the UK. They were accepted for settlement by the then Labour government which was opposed to the oppression of the Pinochet regime and which enjoyed the support in this of the trade union movement. Juan had been a student in 1973 in a provincial town, but had become involved in student politics and openly opposed the military coup that brought Pinochet to power by organizing a peaceful street demonstration. Fearing the worst, people such as he then took a very low profile and waited to see what reprisals the state would take. Juan described how nothing happened for three months and he was beginning to think they had been forgotten when the 'Caravan of Death' arrived in town. This comprised two helicopter loads of Special Forces troops, who descended on the town and shot twenty-four dissidents without trial to set an example. Juan was arrested and imprisoned and spent the next three and a half years in detention.

Whilst in prison he learned that the Pinochet regime wished to normalize its relations with the international community but that Chile's human rights record was standing in the way of this. To circumvent this difficulty, Pinochet was prepared to release many of his political prisoners provided they were settled elsewhere in the world. Juan benefited from this programme, but had no say over where he might be sent, and would have preferred to go to Canada or the USA. His name was put on the list for the UK without him knowing and when he was told that he would be leaving Chile for Britain he said: 'What! The UK. I didn't apply to the UK. I didn't know they were taking people!' But he accepted this since he thought he was only going into temporary exile and would be returning to Chile once Pinochet was deposed.

Juan arrived in Britain with refugee status and with all his papers in order. He was, however, struck by how 'harsh' the immigration procedure was, and also recounted the story of a female friend of his who was X-rayed on arrival whilst pregnant and then subsequently lost the child with leukaemia because of this. On first arriving in the UK Juan was struck by how cold and foggy it was in London, describing it as 'dark and miserable'. But, equally, he was familiar with the Beatles and they had created an image of Britain as a 'cool, free and anti-establishment' place. Because he was a 'quota' refugee he had immediate access to welfare benefits and was given a grant to study at university by the World University Service. It was this that had brought him to Wales. He describes this opportunity as 'incredibly generous', but went on to say 'I don't know of any case that actually people come deliberately [from Chile] because of the Welfare State – sincerely, honestly'. He went on to say that when visitors came from Chile to see him in the UK he would say 'Would you like to stay here? [and they would reply] "No, no, I'd like to go back to Chile" – because of the weather. Really people don't stand the British weather [laughter]'. He then commented that since the change in political complexion back in Chile, most of the original refugees have gone home: 'In [name of Welsh town] we used to be quite a vociferous community in the late 1970s and early 1980s, and now we are about three families left.'

Juan had been sponsored by a trade union based in Pontypridd and had been taken aback while he was still in prison in Chile by the Welsh names on the correspondence sent to him. He even thought these names might be some sort of code, as did his prison warders! He admits to having little knowledge of Wales before travelling here, noting that while Scotland and England had visibility overseas, Wales did not. He describes his early life as an exile as follows:

> we tended to live in a ghetto. So living in the UK was a very weird experience, because we spoke Spanish. But I remember we met in the

refectory – forty of us – Spanish. Spanish all day. In the evening – Spanish. In the night – Spanish. Everyday speaking Spanish. Our music, hooked to the radio, listening news, you know, producing leaflets about Chile or Latin America. Although we were in the UK, we were living in Chile. It's very weird.

But over time Juan has got used to living in the UK and when political conditions in Chile ameliorated, he returned 'home' only to find that he no longer wanted to live there. Instead, he came back to Wales, to settle for good. He even now claims to enjoy the weather (having been brought up in a desert area). He has a daughter, born in Wales, who is studying for a degree and his wife teaches English to newly arrived asylum seekers.

Case 2: Maria from Iran

Maria is a Kurd who formerly lived in Tehran, where she had been unemployed after graduating from university. She claimed this was because she was Kurdish. Her uncle had been imprisoned without charge and after two months the authorities said his wife could visit him. For three further months she visited the prison daily requesting access, only to be told each time that she would be allowed to see her husband the next day. Then in the third month she went as usual to the prison and was surprised to be allowed entry. However, her pleasure turned to shock when she was given her husband's belongings and told he had been shot. They were never allowed to recover the body.

Maria's father, a teacher by profession, was a member of the Kurdish Democratic Party and was found to be acquiring information about military activities against the Kurds through a contact in the army. He was tipped off that he was in great danger by one of his grateful students who was connected with the government. He had to flee Iran immediately, and two days later paid an agent recommended to him by another of his students to take him to Turkey. Three weeks later he was able to send for his wife and for Maria, who had in the mean time left Tehran to go into hiding. The same agent secured their journey to Turkey. In Istanbul they began to think of which country they would most like to settle in. They already had family who had recently fled to the UK and this became their first choice, too. They felt that they could not make an application for asylum in the UK through official channels in Turkey since this might trigger their repatriation (to certain death) or alert the Iranian authorities to their whereabouts. They therefore opted to find someone to facilitate their journey, and the agent they contacted initially only offered them Germany as a destination. They declined this offer and the agent returned three days later saying that he could arrange transportation to the UK so that they could claim asylum at the port of entry, but that this would cost £5,000 per head.

They arrived at Heathrow in 1998, and on arrival the agent – who had travelled with them – took their false passports and disappeared. Maria and her family were unable to speak English and knew nothing about Britain, its immigration system or welfare entitlements. Having taken ten days in London to complete their asylum claim, they travelled to Wales to join Maria's brother who already lived there. They had not realized that Wales was a distinct country with its own language and culture. However, they were very pleasantly surprised by Welsh people, who they thought to be much warmer and friendlier than Londoners. Maria describes being in Wales as 'very good'. However, she was very critical of how the immigration system worked. She feels sure that the family will eventually be given refugee status, but could not comprehend why they were being asked to provide written proof of their persecution in Iran. As she put it: 'When we ran we didn't take any papers. In my country they don't notify you that you are about to be arrested. They just take you to jail . . . [and] . . . you be there ten years.'

Maria had few illusions about welfare provision in the UK. She had expected to be taken to a refugee camp and held there for a lengthy period. Her family had been well off in Iran and had expected to transfer some of their assets to the UK after they arrived, but as soon as they left, the Iranian government seized all their assets and they were left penniless. As soon as she was able to work, Maria got a job in a pizza place, although this was well below her abilities as a graduate. She now works in the health service, helping others. Maria and her family are very appreciative of the sanctuary offered by the UK. She is astonished at the freedom of speech we enjoy, thrilled by how she can be herself rather than having to hide her feelings all the time, and enjoys choosing whether she has to wear a headscarf or not. Finally, Maria made the point that Kurdish refugees did not come to Britain to get work and become rich. They came simply because they were persecuted and not allowed to express their identity and opinions. As Maria put it: 'We are here because we just want to save our lives, you know. Nothing else. Not because we are interested to be in other country. We love our country . . . We love Kurdistan.'

Conclusion

The sea change in the world refugee system that occurred in the 1970s and 1980s converted Europe from being an interested by-stander to being an active participant. For the first time in many decades refugees were being generated in significant numbers within Europe and Europe also became a favoured destination for Third World refugees. As Europe moved nearer the epicentre of the refugee system, so too did the UK. Within Europe, Britain became one of the most popular destinations[32] and the numbers seeking asylum here grew very rapidly.

Prior to 1999 Wales had already accommodated refugees and asylum seekers in some numbers, for some time. Estimates from the 1990s suggest that Wales already hosted some 3,500 refugees before the dispersal programme got under way, and other research described how the Somalis already formed a viable and thriving community in Cardiff by the early 1990s. However, it was not really until 1999, and the Immigration and Asylum Act, that Wales became a truly significant element within a national settlement strategy for asylum seekers. After that Act, Wales became one of the cluster regions accepting dispersed asylum seekers awaiting decisions on their asylum claims.

As Wales becomes accustomed to its new role as a receiver of asylum seekers it needs to grapple with a number of issues with which it has little previous experience. First, it has to learn how to manage public attitudes in such a way that the indigenous population does not see the resettlement of asylum seekers as a zero-sum game in which one person's gain is automatically another's loss. Leadership will be an important element in this, as will responsible media coverage of the issue, but even more important will be changing public perceptions of immigration so that positive benefits are recognized as well as narrow xenophobic fears. There is clear evidence that the debate about legal labour migration to the UK has already embraced some of this new thinking,[33] but as yet there is no evidence that the debate about asylum seeking has shaken off its narrow, negative and reactive tone either in England or in Wales. Increasing street activity by the BNP in Wales also suggests that they, too, realize that public attitudes are in a state of flux and can be manipulated.

Secondly, while Wales is currently offering a temporary refuge for asylum seekers awaiting the outcome of their asylum claim, this will change. Either asylum seekers will engage in secondary migration to English cities after they receive refugee status or leave to remain, or they will put down roots in their new homes and settle permanently in Wales. Either of these scenarios requires active planning. If asylum seekers simply leave after six months, then the pattern of service provision needs to be attuned to a constant churning of new arrivals. If, on the other hand, asylum seekers in Wales become refugees in Wales then government and service providers need to give much greater thought to long-term issues of integration than has hitherto been the case (especially if Sully Hospital in Cardiff does become one of the eight new asylum seeker accommodation centres[34]). Dispersal simply sends asylum seekers to places where accommodation is freely available and relatively cheap. It does not guarantee that those places are also well suited to refugee integration. Wales needs to be looking to, and implementing, models of good practice in refugee integration now, such as those identified by the recent European Council on Refugees and Exiles Task Force on Integration.

Thirdly, central government needs to work much more energetically to challenge the cultures of ignorance, disbelief and denial that underpin so much thinking and inaction amongst service providers. Finally, we all need to remind ourselves and be continually reminded of two things. Namely that refugees and asylum seekers are not 'burdens', 'costs' or statistics but real people, many of whom have turned to the UK and to Wales to help them escape from persecution and oppression and enjoy the civil liberties associated with a free democracy. And while the indigenous electorate becomes increasingly disenchanted and apathetic about British politics and takes for granted freedom of thought, speech and action, we need to remember how much these freedoms mean to those who are denied them elsewhere in the world and the risks they are prepared to take to get to a country where they can experience them.

Notes

[1] This greeting to drivers entering Wales is found on road signs.

[2] P. Boyle, K. Halfacree and V. Robinson, *Exploring Contemporary Migration* (Harlow, 1998).

[3] See, for example, UNHCR, *The State of the World's Refugees* (Harmondsworth, 1993).

[4] UNHCR website, unhcr@org.ch (2001).

[5] A. Zolberg, 'The formation of new states as a refugee-generating process', *Annals of the American Academy of Political and Social Sciences*, 467 (1983), 24–38.

[6] V. Robinson, 'The refugee crisis: nature and response', in V. Robinson (ed.), *The International Refugee Crisis: British and Canadian Responses* (Basingstoke, 1992).

[7] A. Dowty, *Closed Borders: The Contemporary Assault on Freedom of Movement* (London, 1987).

[8] M. Cernea, 'Internal refugee flows and development-induced population displacement', *Journal of Refugee Studies*, 3 (1990), 320–39.

[9] See on the Vietnamese, V. Robinson, 'Up the creek without a paddle? Britain's boat people ten years on', *Geography*, 74 (1989), 332–8.

[10] Eurostat, *Asylum Seekers and Refugees: A Statistical Report* (Brussels, 1994).

[11] V. Robinson, 'The changing nature and European perceptions of Europe's refugee problem', *Geoforum*, 26/4 (1996), 411–27.

[12] J. Walvin, *Passage to Britain* (Harmondsworth, 1984).

[13] V. Robinson, 'The development of policies for the resettlement of quota refugees in the UK, 1945–91', in V. Robinson (ed.), *Migration and Public Policy* (New York, 1999).

[14] Eurobarometer, *Racism and Xenophobia in Europe* (Brussels, 1997).

[15] Readers' Digest, 'Are we a tolerant nation?', Readers' Digest website: ReadersDigest.co.uk/tolerant.htm/ (2001).

[16] J. Carey-Wood, K. Duke, V. Karn and T. Marshall, *The Settlement of Refugees in Britain* (London, 1995).

[17] V. Robinson, 'The importance of information in the resettlement of refugees in the UK', *Journal of Refugee Studies*, 11/2 (1998), 146–60.

[18] V. Robinson, *Refugees in Wales: An 'Invisible Minority'* (Migration Unit Research Paper 13, Swansea, 1997).

[19] V. Robinson and S. Hale, *The Geography of Vietnamese Secondary Migration in the UK* (Warwick, 1989).

[20] V. Robinson and C. Coleman, 'Lessons learned? A critical review of the UK government's programme to resettle Bosnian quota refugees', *International Migration Review*, 34 (2000), 1217–44.

[21] V. Robinson, *Refugees in Wales*.

[22] Save the Children, *The Somali Community in Cardiff* (Cardiff, 1994).

[23] Ibid., 5.

[24] V. Robinson, 'Cultures of ignorance, disbelief and denial: refugees in Wales', *Journal of Refugee Studies*, 12/1 (1999), 78–87.

[25] Ibid.

[26] V. Robinson, *A Review of the Literature on the Dispersal of Refugees and Asylum Seekers in the UK* (London, 2002).

[27] Audit Commission, *Another Country: Implementing Dispersal under the Immigration and Asylum Act 1999* (London, 2000).

[28] T. Speers, *Welcome or Over Reaction? Refugees and Asylum Seekers in the Welsh Media* (Cardiff, 2001).

[29] Ibid., 4.

[30] Ibid., 23.

[31] Ibid., 35.

[32] For a discussion of why, see V. Robinson and J. Segrott, *Understanding the Decision-Making of Asylum Seekers* (London, 2002).

[33] See S. Glover, C. Gott, A. Loizillon, J. Portes, R. Price, S. Spencer, V. Srinivasan and C. Willis, *Migration: An Economic and Social Analysis* (London, 2001) and V. Robinson, *Jewels in the Crown: The Contribution of Ethnic Minorities to Life in Post-War Britain* (London, 2001).

[34] Robinson and Segrott, *Understanding Decision-Making.*

12 Getting Involved: Civic and Political Life in Wales

PAUL CHANEY AND CHARLOTTE WILLIAMS

Introduction

Recent constitutional reform in the UK has been predicated on the idea that 'the democratic impulse needs to be strengthened by finding new ways to enable citizens to share in the decision-making that affects them'.[1] From the mid-1990s the shift from administrative to elective devolution prompted increasing debate on the nature of government in Wales. The 'big ideas' that underpinned constitutional reform were packaged in the buzzword 'inclusiveness'.[2] Yet for ethnic minorities in the country, government has always been about *ex*clusiveness and marginalization.[3] There have been no black MPs representing Welsh constituencies and even at a local government level just 1.4 per cent of local authority councillors are from black or ethnic minority backgrounds.[4] Away from the ballot box, just prior to devolution, none of the 452 appointees of the Secretary of State for Wales were 'non-white'.[5] This lack of elected black representatives contributed to the poor levels of communication and engagement between ethnic communities and government.

However, 'ethnic' marginalization from political life in Wales is about more than the number of elected black and Asian politicians. This follows because, in contrast to 'classical' definitions of 'political participation',[6] it is necessary to develop a broader perspective that includes civic activism and participation in community and voluntary organizations.[7] As a recent study has highlighted, a 'rigid delineation of the social and political arena' is inappropriate, for 'the political activities of ethnic minorities are often taking place at the boundaries of the political and social fields'.[8] Moreover, when compared to other social groups, members of these communities 'participate in politics differently'.[9] In this respect the findings presented here are a starting point for a fuller understanding of contemporary patterns of 'ethnic' political participation in Wales. Specific focus is now placed upon recent changes and engagement at the all-Wales level of government. The marginalization of ethnic minority voices from formal structures of governance both under the Welsh Office and during an earlier period make this an appropriate starting point. Where data exist, reference is made to wider civic structures and processes, yet it is acknowledged that subsequent work will be required to give a fuller understanding of the general ongoing renegotiation of the political culture of the civic and public sphere in Wales.[10] In particular, future research will need to look beyond the national tier of government and focus on voluntarism, activism and formal and informal participation of members of ethnic communities in civil society as well as other tiers of government.

Prior to 1999, very limited engagement took place between ethnic minorities and the Welsh Office. One black project officer recalls that,

> whenever there was an issue that related to the Black and ethnic minority communities before devolution, you would go to the Welsh Office and the Welsh Office would say: 'oh no that is not us, that is a Home Office issue'. You would then go to the Home Office and they would say, 'That is dealt by the Welsh Office'. It has been *abysmal*, absolutely *terrible* in the past.

After the 1997 general election the Secretary of State for Wales promised change. He 'pledged that ethnic and other minority issues should have a high profile in the National Assembly for Wales'.[11] Many doubted this, and few in Wales's ethnic communities were surprised when, subsequently, no black candidates were elected to the Assembly. As one black councillor put it: 'we knew this before the candidates ever went out for selection – unfortunately'. Three centuries of political marginalization were not to be undone by three years of inclusive rhetoric. However, leading politicians continued to make the case for a new relationship between ethnic groups and government. Just weeks after assuming office, the new First Minister stated that, 'The Assembly needs to address and relate to the aspirations and needs of Black and ethnic minority communities throughout Wales . . . I believe very strongly that we need to build the partnership with Black and ethnic minority groups.'[12]

If the public pronouncements of politicians are to be believed, then, devolution is about discontinuity with the past. Yet this is highly problematic; the new structures of governance are now in their third year but in respect of 'ethnic' participation they continue to present many questions. For example: how have ethnic minorities responded to the establishing of the National Assembly and rhetoric about the need to get increasingly involved in Welsh civic and political life? What is the nature of 'ethnic' involvement in the process of government in a 'devolved' Wales? How do the measures taken in the Assembly's first months measure up to the need to ensure effective participation from ethnic minority groups? In attempting answers to these questions this chapter draws upon a research project that has charted these developments from the outset.[13] The conclusions and the quotations in this discussion come from an extensive range of interviews with members and leaders of 'ethnic' groups, together with politicians and officials. This chapter is developed in three sections. It examines the black and ethnic minority response to the establishment of the Assembly, explores ethnic minority engagement with the Welsh legislature and relates the present findings to aspects of current academic debate and thinking.

The black and ethnic minority response to the 'establishment' of the Assembly

The response of members of 'ethnic' communities to the establishing of the Assembly reveals the barriers to overcoming past marginalization and the prospects for developing ongoing participation in government. It shows that at the time that the Assembly was established ethnic minority groups' expectations were rather narrowly focused on the symbolism of descriptive representation (that is, a situation whereby black Assembly Members represent black voters). The core aspiration appeared to be 'getting a voice' and beyond this there existed little coherent strategy. The use of both inclusive rhetoric in the pro-devolution campaign and positive action in respect of women candidates contributed to this situation.[14] When no black or Asian AMs were elected in the Assembly elections of May 1999 many were angry and despaired at the failure of 'inclusiveness' – or, as one interviewee called the rhetoric, 'empty words'. Asked about his feelings towards the new Assembly, a young black journalist spoke of his anger and concluded 'it's not inclusive at all and to date it's a real shocker'. At the other end of the age range, a black pensioner in Cardiff said it was 'a crying shame that the Assembly has no black representatives'.

Many were clear that this initial failure would have a lasting impact. A prospective Assembly candidate stated that,

> Trust is about building up some sort of respect, of being able to deliver a sort of hope. I think the Assembly itself will have to demonstrate that trust – rather than *us* trying to trust *them*. I think they will have to show their worth. I mean *why should* we believe them? I mean when the Labour Party had the opportunity to get a black and ethnic minority person [elected] – they didn't.

For other interviewees, it was the 'huge *mis*trust of politicians' that explained why few ethnic minority people voted in the first Assembly elections.

Opinions differed on the way forward. A Muslim leader asked of the Assembly, 'what will *it* do to include us in Wales?' Other interviewees anticipated a more proactive response. A project development worker said: 'we cannot really expect things to change unless *we*, as communities, come together and get involved in the political arena'. For another, future progress was to be achieved by 'encouraging the younger generation, to get involved in politics and then move forward that way'. Despite her initial despair a race equality worker was more sanguine about devolution, stating 'I really do believe that this is an opportunity, it is the first opportunity that we have had in Wales and we *have* to make a success of it'.

However, many of those interviewed spoke of ethnic communities' lack of preparation for the Assembly and the barriers to future engagement. One activist concluded that 'minority communities needed to acknowledge that they need to do their homework as a community and see ways of being more effective next time'. According to a lawyer, 'one of the things within the black community – you know – that we have to face is, the fact that the reality is, we have *no real infrastructure*'. A lack of lobbying skills was also identified as a problem. As a health specialist put it, 'the Welsh Office was seen as some ivory tower that wasn't welcoming to ethnic minorities . . . it wasn't a place we had access to'. Groups therefore had no direct experience of operating in an all-Wales policy-making arena. Yet, as one respondent said, 'obviously the skills and experience *do* matter in achieving effective participation'. The combination of these problems led a community worker to conclude: 'I'm more inclined to think that [we] need to be a bit more formal, a bit more effective, a bit more expert.'

National and cultural identity was a further barrier to participation and resulted in suspicion and ambivalence to the discourse of civic nationalism associated with the establishing of the Assembly. Whilst Ron Davies had asserted that the Assembly would give 'a clearer focus for the development of our Welsh sense of identity',[15] others remained sceptical. They felt that the new national Welsh legislature equated 'Welsh' with being white and, sometimes, Welsh-speaking. The point was made by a leading figure who saw issues of identity as the key to future engagement with the new institution – both for present and future generations. She stated that:

> Until the National Assembly states *who* its policies are for, including its adopted Welsh people – What I am trying to say is that – 'Welsh' is not simply through your genetic make-up. I mean my daughter was born in Wales and she is brown and she was born in [Swansea] and she identifies herself as *Welsh*. Are the people of Wales prepared to consider her as Welsh? I think that there is a lot of soul-searching and thinking that is necessary right now for the new Assembly . . . They need to say where are we going wrong, why is it that we are not getting a fair representation of people from the ethnic groups.

From an ethnic minority perspective, then, it was a disastrous start for the Assembly. Engagement with the devolution 'project' was frustrated through lack of political trust; the weakness of 'ethnic' networks and mobilizing structures; uncertainties and suspicions stemming from expressions of civic nationalism; a political skills deficit and failings by political parties in relation to descriptive representation. For the overwhelming majority the Assembly had set back rather than advanced race relations with government. This happened because devolution had promised change, but seemingly, it had delivered 'more of the same', thereby reducing trust in the political system and compromising future progress. After this unpromising start what has been the nature of 'ethnic' participation in the work of the Welsh Assembly?

A 'participatory democracy'?[16]

According to a senior civil servant, consultation with ethnic communities simply 'didn't use to take place in the Welsh Office'. Subsequent attempts to move away from this situation must be seen in the light of the blueprints provided by the National Assembly Advisory Group[17] and the Assembly's founding statute. The latter set out measures to achieve the promised 'participatory democracy' and much of what has happened in the Assembly's first years can be linked to its statutory duties.[18] Section 120 of the Government of Wales Act requires that 'the Assembly shall make appropriate arrangements with a view to securing that its functions are exercised with due regard to the principle that there should be equality of opportunity for all people.' This duty is unprecedented in a UK context. It is not found in the new legislatures in Belfast and Edinburgh, and nor does it apply to Westminster. The Assembly's Committee on Equality of Opportunity has the job of enforcing this equality duty. The legislature's Standing Orders state that the Committee should pay '*particular regard* to the need for the Assembly to avoid discrimination against any person on grounds of race, sex or disability'.[19] Overall, the equality duty is a development that means 'the people of Wales are the first in the UK to be given a series of positive rights to exercise and, if necessary, enforce through the courts in Wales'. In contrast to the European Convention on Human Rights (which has derogation provisions), 'the obligations under Section 120 stand unfettered, thereby making them of potentially greater significance to individuals in their dealings with agencies for which the Assembly is responsible'.[20] Thus devolution has simultaneously redefined the legal relationship between members of ethnic minority communities and government, and driven forward moves to foster 'ethnic' participation in government at an all-Wales level for the first time.

The legislature's strategy has been shaped by the size and geographical distribution of the ethnic population, as well as the way it is organized in civil society. The picture that emerges here is of a general weakness of pre-existing ethnic structures for policy-makers to engage with. Black voluntary sector activity in Wales is sparse. Black groups comprise just over 1 per cent of all voluntary groups.[21] The Wales Council for Voluntary Action's (WCVA) current *Directory of National Voluntary Organisations in Wales* lists forty-three groups under the heading 'ethnic'.[22] These include disabled people's groups (Association of Black Children with Disability – ABCD), health groups (Sickle Cell and Thalassaemia Association), faith organizations (Hindu Cultural Association), legal support (Joint Committee for Ethnic Minorities), the arts (Intercultural Community Arts), refugees and asylum seekers (Welsh Refugee Council) and women's groups (Pakistani Women's Association). In addition, there are local and community groups centred upon institutions like mosques, community centres and youth clubs. Local race equality councils and a limited number of 'umbrella' bodies'[23] also serve to link both individuals and membership organizations. Examples include the Minority Ethnic Women's Network (MEWN) and the Association of Muslim Professionals Wales with a membership of over 500 people.

In order to facilitate participation and overcome the weakness of the 'ethnic' organizational infrastructure, the Assembly has sponsored two networks in order to 'build capacity' in the consultative process.[24] The All Wales Ethnic Minority Association's (AWEMA)[25] aims are:

> To act as an effective vehicle for consultation, participation and communication between minority ethnic communities and the National Assembly for Wales. To continually examine ways in which minority ethnic citizens of Wales will be more actively involved in decisions that affect their quality of life and act to enhance the National Assembly. To examine effective ways of engaging minority communities to ensure that participation and partnership are used to enhance local, regional and national democracy in governance and accountability.[26]

The Association has 'two hundred professional members' and is structured around six subject committees that mirror and provide 'expert input' to the work of the Assembly policy-making committees.[27] Whilst it concentrates most of its energies on achieving horizontal (as opposed to vertical) structures of engagement in the policy process, it also pursues a community development approach. In the latter case the Association runs specific projects, with two development officers employed to increase voter registration in ethnic communities and address ethnic issues in primary health care. In respect of AWEMA's policy-scrutiny meetings, these are attended by up to thirty individuals drawn from a range of professional interests and organizations. The views of the Association are fed into the Assembly via position papers on specific issues, whilst the opportunity for a wider airing of views is given at quarterly meetings with officials and AMs. An important part of this network's development is its geographical expansion and regional committees based in Penmaenmawr, Carmarthen and Swansea. However, these developments have not been without criticism from some members of ethnic communities who have complained about what they see as the Association's 'gate keeper mentality'. Organizers have countered that membership of the Association 'is open to anybody'.

The Black Voluntary Sector Network Wales (BVSNW) has a composite membership of over 120 organizations and individuals and is part of the Assembly's statutory partnership with the voluntary sector.[28] The latter unique constitutional arrangement promotes participation in government by placing the legislature under a legal duty to consult voluntary organizations.[29] Details of this cross-sectoral partnership are formalized in the National Assembly Voluntary Sector Scheme. This states that 'the Assembly values volunteering as an important expression of citizenship and as an essential component of democracy . . . the goal is the creation of a civil society which offers equality of opportunity to all its members regardless of race [and] colour'.[30] The relationship between Black Voluntary Sector Network and the Assembly is set out in a formal agreement. This states that this partnership underpins

> a joint commitment to taking forward the race equality agenda at all levels; [it operates to] improve consultation and participation in policy and implementation; [and to] provide recognition of the role, contribution and needs of the [voluntary] Sector, [and will offer] capacity building, [and means of] developing infrastructure and sustainability.[31]

BVSNW promotes and facilitates activism and voluntary activity amongst members of the ethnic communities. It is a source of advice on funding, legal issues and administrative practices and from a low base, its membership has grown steadily during its short history. In terms of the Assembly's policy process, a senior civil servant has stated that 'the Black voluntary sector has a particular role . . . to bring together the views of the grassroots'.[32] This participation in government is via policy consultation exercises coordinated by the Network. These include round-table meetings for representatives of its member organizations and written policy response exercises. The BVSNW then feeds these views either directly back to the Assembly or via the voluntary sector's (somewhat labyrinthine) committee structures. The new participatory arrangements have also introduced bi-annual face-to-face meetings with Cabinet Ministers. These provide an opportunity for the views of the Network's members to be discussed with the Assembly's executive.[33] This is a significant development in that it gives the link between ethnic minority groups and the Assembly a formal (and legal) standing, as well as one that offers support and funding.

Within the new political and civic landscape these government-sponsored networks are significant in two respects. They appear, in contrast to leading democratic theory, to be potential instances where government has been instrumental in creating social capital.[34] As interviewees' comments acknowledge, they have encouraged new groups and individuals to, as one put it, come 'out of the woodwork . . . the word seems to have spread . . . because its gone beyond that old network now'. They have also effected systematic participation by ethnic minority communities across the breadth of government decision-making for the first time. Examining the substantive issues at the heart of this engagement lends a better understanding of this process of change. In short, it reveals the nature of the new involvement with the Assembly and what members of ethnic minority communities are saying when they participate in Welsh government.

The work of the Assembly's Economic Development Committee shows how ethnic minority participants have lobbied government to facilitate networking and co-working between the public, private and voluntary sectors. They have asked for policies to be changed to contain specific targets so that race equality policy outcomes can be measured. These early examples of lobbying also reveal keenness on the part of participants to extend co-working with the Welsh executive. Such conclusions are based on the participation of AWEMA and the Association of Muslim Professionals Wales. The latter set out its views on private-sector involvement in the programmes of the European Objective One Structural Fund Programme. In a position paper to the Assembly they called for less bureaucracy to be imposed on the private sector and emphasized the need for initiatives to promote clustering and networking in order to assist the growth of small and medium-sized enterprises (SMEs) in ethnic communities.[35]

AWEMA's response to the (draft) National Economic Development Strategy of the Welsh executive emphasized its desire for ongoing partnership with the legislature, and stated, 'we believe we can play a key role in helping the National Assembly, its agencies and its partners formulate its economic agenda and achieve the agreed objectives'. AWEMA's specific policy concerns included: the need for more statistical information and analysis of the economic problems of ethnic minority communities; the need to adequately highlight and understand the economic deprivation faced by them; and the need to secure effective monitoring and measurable race equality outcomes.

Away from economic development, the record of a meeting of AWEMA's Education and Lifelong Learning Committee shows the new participation in action. There was much dissatisfaction with the Assembly's new education strategy entitled 'The Learning Country'. The minutes record that 'there is only one paragraph on ethnic minorities and this is just a [passing] mention, it is a whole strategy for Wales, but there are no action plans, there are no proposals for positive actions'. It was proposed to ask the Assembly for a further month to allow AWEMA to develop a detailed response and lobby for changes to government of the National Assembly's education plans.[36]

Other examples of the new 'ethnic' participation and lobbying include regional meetings such as the Black Environment Network's response to the Assembly's Sustainable Development Roadshow,[37] and the co-opting of groups onto Assembly working parties and task groups. Examples of the latter include Race Equality First Cardiff's[38] membership of the Assembly's Education Working Party established in the wake of the Stephen Lawrence Inquiry,[39] and the Black Association of Women Step Out (a women's aid organization) and the Valleys Race Equality Council's involvement in the Assembly's National Housing Strategy.[40]

Interviewees have also given first-hand accounts of the quality of this new participation in government. Many referred to the relative accessibility of AMs in the new structures of governance. One manager with an umbrella body said, 'the main thing is that they're approachable; we *can* contact them'. Another added, 'rarely a month goes by without meetings at the Assembly . . . whereas I suppose [in the past] the chance of us going to Westminster was remote'. This level of contact with AMs is also evidenced by the growing number of organizations holding receptions and conferences, sometimes in the Assembly building itself, attended by AMs and ministers. However, similar satisfaction has not been evident in the timing of consultations with ethnic groups over the government of the National Assembly's policies. Many complained of short notice and unrealistic submission deadlines. This is a point acknowledged by the minister responsible, who stated that officials were 'increasingly accepting the need to engage with statutory and voluntary sector bodies at the outset of initiatives rather than playing catch-up at the end'.[41]

Interviewees were also concerned about the level of staffing and resources available to monitor, lobby and engage with the Assembly. One Cardiff-based project worker reflected the views of many, and stated, 'there's only two of us in the office, we think we cover things as best we can – but you just can't do everything, that's the bottom-line'. Several interviewees indicated ill ease when asked about the dual role that the new participatory structures required them to perform. In this respect, organizations found themselves at once acting for the Assembly as (Assembly-funded) coordinators of policy consultation exercises *and* operating as independent champions of members' interests as lobbyists of Welsh government. Others high-lighted both the complexity and inappropriateness of some of the new voluntary sector scheme structures. It was felt unhelpful that ethnic minorities were 'pigeon-holed' as one of twenty-one special interest networks, yet, in contrast to most other networks (that, for example, centred on environmental issues or the arts), 'ethnic' interests embraced the whole range of voluntary sector activities. A further concern was that consultees were frequently not updated after they had participated in the consultation process. They were therefore unaware of whether their comments had influenced matters until the finished policy documents emerged, at which point it was too late to respond to them.

With less than three years' experience of devolved governance, it is too early to determine the effectiveness of ethnic minority participation in the policy process in terms of actual policy outcomes. It is only now that significant numbers of policies are emerging from the Assembly and these have not had time to be fully implemented or evaluated (see Chapter 9).

Devolution has also resulted in major reform of the way government functions in order to end self-acknowledged 'institutional racism' at the National Assembly.[42] The aim here has been to increase the participation of ethnic communities in the process of government both as employees and as citizens.[43] The Equality Policy Unit, founded in response to the statutory equality duty, oversees the Assembly Civil Service's reforms aimed at increased ethnic minority participation in government. It has undertaken two equality audits of all fifty-seven divisions of the legislature's bureaucracy and is monitoring progress towards mainstreaming race equality in all areas of the Assembly's work. The unit is also coordinating mandatory equality awareness training which will be delivered to 3,500 staff, as well as specialist training provided for managers and personnel staff.[44]

In 1997–8, just 0.6 per cent of Welsh Office employees were from an ethnic minority background.[45] New measures to address this under-representation include: 'positive action in the career development of Black and minority ethnic staff'; the appointment of independent assessors to oversee and monitor these changes in human resource practices; circulating staff vacancies details to ethnic minority organizations; and a number of employment-related schemes, including work-shadowing, work-placements and secondments for ethnic minorities.[46] In addition, the Assembly convened a Recruitment Fair, which specifically encouraged applications from minority communities.[47] The Assembly bureaucracy has also initiated quarterly 'round-table' meetings with senior members of the black and minority ethnic communities in order to further these reforms and increase engagement in the policy process.[48]

Away from government there have also been party-political initiatives to encourage ethnic minorities to participate in political life in Wales. One local party chair reflected 'we need to get more black and ethnic groups involved at the outset'. Some party managers have realized this and have approached the director of one of the racial equality bodies, requesting help in getting greater numbers of black and ethnic people involved as party members. He noted, 'in fairness, some of them individually have been very proactive, people from both Plaid Cymru, the Liberal Democrats and recently one or two individuals from the Labour Party . . . but we have had absolutely no interest from the Tories . . . none whatsoever'.

Discussion

The findings presented in this chapter suggest that, following centuries of marginalization in the political decision-making process, to the overwhelming majority of people from an ethnic minority background the arrival of the Assembly retarded rather than advanced race relations with government. Initial suspicions and ambivalence to the discourse of civic nationalism associated with the establishing of the Assembly were followed by disillusionment owing to the lack of black Assembly Members. According to theoretical notions of 'deliberative democracy',[49] better government can only be realized by 'collective decision-making with the participation of *all* who will be affected by the decision'.[50] Yet, after all the inclusive rhetoric of the 'Yes' referendum campaign, the political parties failed in this respect and the absence of black or Asian AMs had a major and detrimental impact on the already low levels of trust towards formal politics prevailing in Wales's ethnic communities. Contemporary research has shown that 'political trust will allow the multicultural democracy to function properly'.[51] It is something that operates to 'link ordinary citizens to the institutions that are intended to represent them thereby enhancing both the legitimacy and effectiveness of democratic government'.[52] In addition, it shapes the propensity of individuals to participate in 'political or society-oriented associations'.[53] Thus on a number of levels the first Assembly elections were a major setback to the stated aim of 'a participatory democracy in which there is the greatest possible involvement of citizens'.[54]

One of the most significant developments following devolution is the shift from a mode of government whereby race equality and 'ethnic' participation operated in a *laissez-faire* system dependent upon political will of elected representatives to a situation where the Assembly has a legal duty to deliver race equality outcomes and 'ethnic' participation. The major challenges facing the Assembly in fulfilling this statutory duty go far beyond rebuilding trust. Little is known about the pattern of ethnic mobilization in Wales, or indeed prevailing levels of social capital.[55] Anecdotal evidence and geographical realities suggest that there are comparatively fragile links between different ethnic communities across the country. This is symptomatic of the relative weakness of a 'Welsh' civil society and the absence of a strong and indigenous Welsh policy lobby.[56]

Marginalized from political decision-making, ethnic minorities in Wales have effectively been denied the lobbying skills, political role models and experience of participating in government. These factors led to a general unpreparedness for devolution amongst ethnic groups. Put in terms of the theoretical literature on social movements, ethnic minority communities therefore lacked the mobilizing structures and cultural framings necessary to maximize the political opportunities presented by modernizing reforms of government.[57]

In order to respond to these realities, the Assembly has adopted a managerialist or 'neo-corporatist' strategy to facilitate 'ethnic' participation in the policy process.[58] The ethnic minority consultative networks that the new legislature has developed may be the beginnings of a potentially comprehensive and systematic process of engagement that addresses many of the earlier barriers to 'ethnic' participation. But the theoretical literature also highlights dangers associated with the 'dilemma between a top-down approach or a bottom-up approach' to 'ethnic' participation whereby 'they can come together in a positive way or clash'.[59] In the latter case, this can lead to consensualism, assimilation and the suppression of diverse views.[60]

In contrast to the theories of associative democracy that led to constitutional reform and the creation of the Assembly, the present evidence shows that, as yet, there is limited demand from the majority of black and Asian citizens to engage with the new legislature and participate in its work.[61] As a result, a 'service-oriented' rather than 'citizen-oriented' mode of participation is currently operating.[62] At the moment 'ethnic' involvement in the process of government is mostly limited to comparatively small numbers of people giving specialist input to policy consultation exercises initiated by the new legislature. As the Welsh Assembly's own *Equality Report* notes, ethnic 'consultation [is now occurring] on a regular basis *but with limited groups*'.[63] The major challenge for the Assembly and ethnic communities is to increase the numbers that participate in the process of government. Barriers to this include low levels of understanding both about the legislature's work programme and its powers.[64] These stem from poor communications, weak media and the opaqueness and excessive complexity of the current constitutional settlement.[65] Further problems come from a lack of political trust, the weakness of 'ethnic' networks and mobilizing structures, uncertainties and suspicions stemming from the perception of devolution as an exclusive and nationalist project, a political skills deficit and failings by political parties in relation to descriptive representation.

Notwithstanding these formidable barriers and setbacks, the first years of 'devolved' governance have seen unprecedented political commitment and positive measures to achieving of 'ethnic' participation in the process of government. This is a major move away from the closed doors of the Welsh Office.[66] However, the goal of a 'participatory democracy' that secures the effective engagement of ethnic minority groups will require much further action both inside and outwith the Assembly. It can only be achieved by the renegotiation of the political culture of the entire public sphere in Wales in a way that exhibits multiple social, cultural, economic and political modes of 'ethnic' incorporation.[67] Specifically, it will need increased mobilization, activism, lobbying skills among black and ethnic minority groups. It will also depend upon continued political efforts and determination to building an open, responsive and multicultural system of governance.

Notes

[1] T. Blair, *The Third Way – New Politics for the New Century* (London, 1998), 15.

[2] P. Chaney and R. Fevre, 'Ron Davies and the cult of "inclusiveness": devolution and participation in Wales', *Contemporary Wales*, 14 (2001), 131–46.

[3] C. Williams, 'Race and racism: some reflections on the Welsh context', *Contemporary Wales*, 8 (1995), 113–33.

[4] A. Brown, A. Jones and F. Mackay, *The 'Representativeness' of Councillors* (York, 1999), 5.

[5] D. Hanson, *Unelected, Unaccountable and Untenable: A Study of Appointments to Public Bodies in Wales* (Cardiff, 1995), 4.

[6] For example, S. Verba and N. Nie, *Participation in America: Political Democracy and Social Equality* (Chicago, 1972), 2, define it as a concern with the selection and influencing of politicians.

[7] J. N. Edwards and A. Both, *Social Participation in Urban Society* (Cambridge, 1973).

[8] H. Bousetta, 'Extending democracy: participation, consultation and representation of ethnic minority people in public life – a report on the Bristol experience', paper presented to University of Bristol Centre for the Study of Ethnicity and Citizenship, Department of Sociology, 'Participation and representation of black and other ethnic minority people in public life', Conference, 12 and 13 October 2000, 18.

[9] Ibid.

[10] Research is currently being undertaken in ESRC project R000239410, 'Social capital and the participation of marginalised groups in government', Ralph Fevre and Paul Chaney (Social Sciences, Cardiff University), and Charlotte Williams and Sandra Betts (Sociology and Social Policy, Bangor University).

[11] R. Davies, 'Shaping the vision', *Red Kite* (June 1995), 14–17.

[12] Alun Michael in a speech at the launch of AWEMA, Pierhead Building, Cardiff, 24 July 1999.

[13] 'The effectiveness of "inclusive" government: a study of the participation and representation of minority groups in the first two years of the National Assembly for Wales', Ralph Fevre and Paul Chaney (Social Sciences, Cardiff University), Charlotte Williams, Sandra Betts and John Borland (Sociology and Social Policy, Bangor University). Funded by the University of Wales Board of Celtic Studies.

[14] P. Chaney and R. Fevre, 'Is there a demand for descriptive representation? Evidence from the UK's devolution programme', *Political Studies*, 50 (2002), 897–915.

[15] R. Davies, 'Shaping the vision', 14

[16] National Assembly Advisory Group, 'National Assembly Advisory Group Recommendations' (Cardiff, 1998), 6, paras 1.09, 1.10. Also P. Hain, *A Welsh Third Way?* (London, 1999), 14.

[17] Established in December 1997, NAAG advised the Secretary of State on the form and functioning of the future Assembly. Membership included a wide range of fields, including the four main political parties in Wales, the Yes and No (referendum) campaigns, business, local government, trade unions, equal opportunities and the voluntary sector. Cf. NAAG, 'Recommendations'.

[18] D. Lambert, 'The Government of Wales Act: an act for laws to be ministered in Wales in like form as it is in this realm?', *Cambrian Law Review*, 30 (1999), 60–71.

[19] National Assembly for Wales, Standing Orders (2000), 14.1.

[20] L. Clements and P. Thomas, 'Human rights and the Welsh Assembly', *Planet*, 43 (1999), 7–11.

[21] Wales Council for Voluntary Action, *Wales Voluntary Sector Almanac 1999: Key Facts and Figures* (Caerphilly, 1999), 5.

[22] Wales Council for Voluntary Action, *Directory of National Voluntary Organisations in Wales* (Caerphilly, 2000), 15.

[23] That is, linking individual membership organizations or branches.

[24] National Assembly for Wales, *Second Annual Report on Equality of Opportunity* (Cardiff, 2000), 9.

[25] Originally known as the 'The All Wales Black and Ethnic Minority *National Assembly* Consultative and Participatory Association'.

[26] *AWEMA Times* (2 November 2001), 2.

[27] Ibid. Two further committees covering 'sport and mother tongue and the Welsh language' are planned. See also 'What we are looking for is expertise from the communities within subject areas', Naz Malik, speech to 'Right To Vote Conference', Cardiff, October 2001.

[28] P. Chaney and R. Fevre, 'Inclusive governance and "minority" groups: the role of the third sector in Wales', *Voluntas: An International Journal of Third Sector Research*, 12/2 (2001), 131–56.

[29] Cf. Government of Wales Act, Section 114(4)(c). 'The Scheme shall specify how the Assembly proposes to consult relevant voluntary organisations'.

[30] National Assembly for Wales, *Voluntary Sector Scheme* (2000), ch. 2, para. 2.7.

[31] Papers of the Voluntary Sector Partnership Council, *Black Voluntary Sector Network Wales* (2001), 2.

[32] C. Willie, speech to Black Voluntary Sector Network Wales conference, Cardiff, 6 October 2000.

[33] Assembly Government Cabinet Papers CAB (00–01) 48, *National Assembly For Wales Cabinet: Working with the Voluntary Sector*, Paper by the Minister for Health and Social Services (August 2001), 1.

[34] R. Putnam, with R. Leonardi and R. Y. Nanettti, *Making Democracy Work* (Princeton, NJ, 1993).

[35] National Assembly Economic Development Committee. Minutes, 3 November 1999, item 4.

[36] AWEMA Education and Lifelong Learning Committee. Minutes, 11 October 2001, p. 3, item 6.

[37] NAW, 'Policy and structural mechanisms for the enhancement of ethnic inclusion', paper for the Wales National Assembly by the Black Environmental Network, reproduced in the *Papers of the North Wales Regional Committee, Friday, 11 February 2000* (Cardiff, 2000).

[38] A Race Equality Council.

[39] NAW, Committee on Equality of Opportunity Papers, 3 February 2000, *The Stephen Lawrence Report* (Cardiff, 2000).

[40] NAW, *National Housing Strategy Task Group 4 – Ensuring Decent Housing for All – Meeting the Requirements of Vulnerable Households: Final Report to the National Assembly for Wales* (Cardiff, 2000).

[41] E. Hart, *The Official Record*, 5 July 2000, Plenary Debate on the Annual Report on Equal Opportunity Arrangements.

[42] Cf. 'Lifting every voice: a report and action programme to address institutional racism at the National Assembly for Wales', a report by Roger Mckenzie on behalf of the Public and Commercial Services Union. March 2001.

[43] Cf. Government of Wales Act 1998, section 48, and the Race Relations Amendment Act 2001.

[44] National Assembly for Wales (2001), Equality Training and Raising Awareness Strategy (ETAARS).

[45] Welsh Office, 1999: ch. 2, table 2.02: The Democratic Process: Key Targets and Performance.

[46] J. Shortridge, Minutes of NAW debate on *Second Annual Equality of Opportunity Report* (2001), 9.

[47] It achieved 'the induction of 16 such staff into the Assembly', *Second Annual Equality of Opportunity Report*, 11.

[48] Ibid., 7.

[49] Cf. J. Bohman and W. Rehg (eds), *Deliberative Democracy: Essays on Reason and Politics* (Cambridge, MA, 1996); A. Gutmann and D. Thompson, *Democracy and Disagreement* (Cambridge, MA, 1996); J. Elster, *Deliberative Democracy* (Cambridge, 1998).

[50] J. Elster, *Deliberative Democracy*, 8.

[51] Cf. M. Fennema and J. Tillie, 'Voluntary associations, social capital and interest mediation: forging the link', paper presented to the ECPR Joint Sessions of Workshops, Copenhagen, 14–19 April 2000, 5.

[52] W. Mishler and R. Rose, 'What are the origins of political trust? Testing institutional and cultural theories in post-Communist societies', *Comparative Political Studies*, 34/1 (2001), 30–62, 30.

[53] M. Hooghe and D. Stolle, 'Voluntary associations, social capital and interest mediation: forging the link', ECPR Workshop 13, Copenhagen, 2000.

[54] P. Hain, *A Welsh Third Way?* (London, 1999), 14.

[55] Variously described as the resources, assets and advantages individuals acquire as participants in a social or community setting (J. Coleman, 'Social capital and the creation of human capital', *American Journal of Sociology*, 94 (1998), S95–S120). Or the 'stocks of social trust, norms, and networks that people can draw upon to solve common problems' (R. Putnam, with R. Leonardi and R. Y. Nanettti, *Making Democracy Work* (Princeton, 1994).

[56] Cf. R. Wyn Jones and B. Lewis, 'The Wales Labour Party and Welsh civil society: aspects of the constitutional debate in Wales', paper presented to PSA Annual Conference, University of Keele, 7–9 April 1998 and G. Day, D. Dunkerley and A. Thompson, 'Evaluating the "New Politics": civil society and the National Assembly for Wales', *Public Policy and Administration*, 15/2 (2000), 25–37.

[57] Cf. D. McAdam, J. McCarthy and M. Zald (eds), *Comparative Perspectives on Social Movements* (Cambridge, 1996).

[58] Cf. J. Mansbridge, 'A deliberative perspective on neo-corporatism', *Politics and Society*, 20/4 (1992), 493–505, F. L. Wilson, 'Neo-corporatism and the rise of new social movements', in R. J. Dalton and M. Kuechler (eds), *Challenging the Political Order: New Social and Political Movements in Western Democracies* (Cambridge, 1990).

[59] M. Martinielo, R. Penninx and S. Vertovec, 'Multicultural Policies and Modes of Citizenship in European Cities Working Paper 4', UNESCO/MPMC Workshop in Zeist, March 2000.

[60] Cf. P. Weinreich, 'Social exclusion and multiple identities', *Soundings*, 9 (1998), 139–44. C. Mouffe, 'The radical centre: a politics without an adversary', *Soundings*, 9 (1998), 11–23; S. Vertovec, 'Minority associations, networks and public policies: reassessing relationships', *Journal of Ethnic and Migration Studies*, 25/1 (1999), 21–42.

[61] P. Hirst, *Associative Democracy: New Forms of Economic and Social Governance* (Cambridge, 1994).

[62] Cf. A. Kearns, 'Active citizenship and local governance: political and geographical dimensions', *Political Geography*, 14/2 (1995), 155–75.

[63] Papers of the Assembly Equality Committee, 9 May 2001, *Equality Maturity Profile*, 2nd Equality Audit, appendix A3, 33.

[64] C. Betts, 'Assembly urged to impress public with popular policies', *Western Mail* (2 August 2001).

[65] A. Sherlock, 'Born free, but everywhere in chains? A legal analysis of the first year of the National Assembly for Wales', *Cambrian Law Review*, 31 (2000), 61–72.

66 C. Williams and P. Chaney, 'Inclusive government for excluded groups: ethnic minorities', in P. Chaney, T. Hall and A. Pithouse (eds), *New Governance: New Democracy?* (Cardiff, 2001).

67 Cf. S. Vertovec, 'Multiculturism, culturism and public incorporation', *Ethnic and Racial Studies*, 19/1 (1996), 49–69.

13 Claiming the National: Nation, National Identity and Ethnic Minorities

CHARLOTTE WILLIAMS

A central and contested idea of this volume has been the notion of tolerance. Several chapters have tussled with the mismatch between the myth of tolerance and the realities of the lived experience of minorities in Wales. Yet this so-called 'myth' has a perennial and almost immutable status in the national imagining both on the part of majorities and minorities in Wales. It is not uncommon to be welcomed to Wales by an Asian taxi driver at Cardiff station and to be assured of the warm, friendly and tolerant nature of the Welsh. In a recent discussion of race and Wales, one commentator somewhat naively laid the responsibility for racism in Wales at the door of BNP infiltration and/or liberal, middle-class English in-migrants, whilst describing the indigenous culture as characterized by 'its spirited survival, its longevity, its rootedness, its emphasis on community over rampant individualism, its creativity, its spirituality, its less strident but very present, nonetheless – *pluralism and tolerance*'.[1] At dinner parties all over Wales should the conversation turn on the ugly spectre of racism the subject is quickly dispensed by reference to the well-integrated rainbow city of Cardiff, comfortably switched to what is seen as the real issue of Welsh racism, English/Welsh animosities, and then dismissed because nobody wants to talk about 'the language issue' anyway. Such confused and befuddled thinking about race and the reluctance or inability to debate seriously what are central issues to the development of Welsh identities because of complacency or fear can only hamper progressive attempts to realize the potential of Wales as a multicultural society.

Wales is a divided nation. It is also a diverse nation. The two are not synonymous. Long-standing cleavages between north and south, east and west, urban/rural, Welsh-speaking/English-speaking, indigenous/in-migrant, working class/'taffia' are cleavages that mark the experiences of minority ethnic communities as well as the majority population. This differentiation inevitably raises a number of questions about Welsh nationhood and identity. What is it that binds us other than the border of Offa's Dyke? On what basis do we invest in Wales as a nation-state? How is nation discussed and realized? What are the dominant conceptions of Welshness? And on what basis do minority ethnic communities claim any sense of belonging and ownership to the nation? Post-devolution Wales brings some of these questions into sharp focus. The ways in which they are debated and addressed will tell the story of how multiculturalism is fashioned in the new Wales. One of the clear implications of devolution is the opportunity to rework discourses of race and ethnicity, to reconfigure discourses of nation and national identity and to re-imagine Wales in deliberate and conscious ways rather than as a product of drift or uncontested 'common sense'.

This is evidently an ambition of the new Assembly in Wales. Ron Davies, the recognized architect of the National Assembly for Wales, declared:

> Once the Assembly is established it must reflect the diversity and plurality of Welsh social, political and cultural life. By doing that we will have a greater status for the Assembly as a national institution; we can give a clearer focus for the development of our Welsh sense of identity.[2]

In 1999 Paul Murphy, the then secretary of state for Wales, spoke of:

> a new sense of citizenship – where the Bangladeshi community in Swansea and the Somali community in Cardiff have the same stake in our new democratic Wales as it has for me, the great grandson of Irish immigrants . . . who crossed the Irish sea 130 years ago, looking for a better life in Wales.[3]

Political speeches are currently littered with the terminology of inclusiveness – pluralism, multiculturalism and tolerance.[4] What they are not littered with is any acknowledgement of the tensions and tangles that aspects of Welsh social and political life pose for the achievement of racial equality and the establishment of new Welsh identities. Whilst institutionalized politics provides an important forum for these debates (see Chapter 12), it is not the only forum worthy of inspection – politics also has wider public discursive elements. This chapter aims to explore some of these central debates as they impact on and are shaped by Wales's minority population.

'Race thinking' in Wales

As might be expected, devolution has had a notable impact on the complexities of Welsh identity. The achievement of a measure of self-governance by a small but highly self-conscious nation was bound to carry more symbolic significance in terms of Welsh identity than the disruptions of constitutional reform itself. One noticeable shift has been from a situation where the Welsh were more likely to be identified as an ethnic minority in the wider UK framework, more specifically in relation to English dominance, to a situation that is witnessing the emergence of the English as a politicized ethnic minority within Wales. The English are by far the biggest ethnic grouping in Wales and sustained and significant levels of in-migration mean they command considerable political attention. English monoglot speakers form 80 per cent of the Welsh population, about 19 per cent of whom were born in England.[5] English/Welsh conflict surfaces regularly on the political agenda, notably in debates about the 2001 census categories when the identification 'Welsh' was denied. The arguments that ensued expressed strong sentiments of ethnic affiliation and identity not only for the Welsh but con-comitantly for the English. The ongoing debates about English colonization and transformation of the socio-linguistic nature of rural Wales serve to heat up the boundaries of the English/Welsh axis to the extent that this divide has more recently come to be viewed as 'racialized'. The police forces in Wales now include English/Welsh animosities as part of racially motivated crime statistics. One measure of the exacerbation of this conflict is evidence from the Commission for Racial Equality (CRE) and race equality councils in Wales indicating they have received a sudden and unexpected increase in the number of discrimination claims by those who regard themselves as of English origin. Speaking of his work with Swansea Bay Race Equality Council a worker reported:

> for the first time some quarter of the cases that I've been dealing with are to do with English people living in Wales, who have chosen to live here,

and they perceive that people are discriminating against them because they are English.[6]

It is now not unusual to hear heads of these organizations and commissioners for race equality in Wales speaking out on the subject of Welsh/English conflict. However, by and large they are seen to provide an inadequate response to the issue. Simon Brooks has argued:

> They do not, as it were, comprehend the fears of the main ethno-linguistic group that they serve, namely the Welsh-speaking Welsh, and they don't show a lot of zeal for changing their attitude either. In London a suitable term has been given to an attitude of this type: 'institutional racism'. And, yes that is a suitable term for the conduct of the CRE in Wales too: institutional racism against the Welsh-speaking Welsh.[7]

In response to this issue radical Welsh-language organizations such as Cymuned have advocated restrictions on the freedom of movement and settlement of English speakers and compulsory bilingualism in schools. Commenting on this proposal, the Lib Dem AM Peter Black said: 'You are trying to create ghettos which exclude people who have not been born and bred in the area. When councils in London tried to introduce these policies they were told this was racist.'[8] This is just one example of a new confidence in asserting anti-English sentiments. The reporter Beca Brown openly and repeatedly used inflammatory language – some might say the language of incitement – characterizing the Welsh/English relation-ship as based on 'hate'[9] and Seimon Glyn, chair of the housing committee in Gwynedd, met with opprobrium from his own party, Plaid Cymru, when he used racist terminology to voice concerns over in-migration. Defending his position Seimon Glyn said: 'When we dare to raise the issue we are immediately branded as thugs, racists and bigots.'[10] Others have suggested the Welsh media have used the Seimon Glyn debacle to discredit Plaid Cymru and seen 'the tactic of calling Seimon Glyn "racist" as a great political tactic by opponents of the Welsh-language to undermine the moral case of Welsh language campaigners'.[11] Dafydd Iwan commented: 'it is about time that we in Wales mature politically and understand the reality of the prevailing situation and deal with it in a sensible and practical way, and get rid of this nonsense about "racism" in this context – once and for all.'[12] These debates clearly indicate that the 'race problem' in Wales is not prescribed simply in terms of colour, as is the case elsewhere in the UK, but significantly on the front of the generalized 'other' as English or English-speaking.

The interface of the so-called 'language issue' with race issues has an uncomfortable history and continues to receive reluctant, albeit increased attention. I have argued elsewhere[13] that the language issue has operated to deflect attention away from issues of race on the political agenda that in turn serves to foster the myth 'there is no problem here'. A recent and very public tussle over the constitution of the newly established North Wales Race Equality Network (NWREN) is illustrative of the tendency to deflect issues of colour racism. Cefn, an organization primarily aimed at scrutinizing language discrimination, challenged the right of NWREN to use the term 'race equality' exclusively in relation to black and ethnic minorities, presumably as this label held capital in relation to its application to language issues. This in turn was interpreted as both a denial of the territorial significance of colour racism in north Wales by members of NWREN and an attempt to colonize the debate on race by linguistic minorities to the exclusion of other minorities in the north. This interface is indeed complex and far-reaching in its implications and an important factor for Welsh governance to acknowledge and address. It is a debate that not only makes more visible aspects of the nature of Welsh racism but one that resonates with competing claims over Welsh identity.

A number of factors contribute to confusion over the issues. Prior to the Welsh Language Act 1993 and the establishment of the Welsh Language Board, the main mechanism for settling disputes of language discrimination was the Race Relations Act 1976. Indeed this continues to be the main mechanism for the settlement of disputes where 'national origin' is the established point of discrimination. This piece of legislation was always found wanting in relation to the satisfaction of claims, not least because it was seen to be fuzzy over the fundamental issue of whether the Welsh were indeed a race or not,[14] an issue that was often interpreted as a denial of a separate identity. This institutional mechanism in itself must be responsible for contributing to the construction of the language debate within racialized terminology. In the absence of any other discourse, this became the way to view the issue and offered the terms with which to discuss it. Alongside this, there is considerable evidence, both historically and in contemporary Wales, to suggest that in the popular imagining the oppression of the Welsh was and is paralleled with the plight of the black man.[15] This parallel is used as a type of short-hand concept for depicting the exploitation of the Welsh by the English not simply in economic terms[16] but also in the negative perceptions of the Welsh by the English as 'dark strangers'. Note, in this vein, controversy over the description of the Welsh as 'dark ugly trolls'[17] and in 2001 the outcry over the BBC broadcaster Ann Robinson commenting that the Welsh are 'useless'. Again this serves to invite the use of racist and necessarily emotive terminology. It is well known that the nationalist organization Cymdeithas yr Iaith Cymraeg frequently used the term 'white settlers' to describe English incomers, explicitly evoking racist categories in which the Welsh white majority are aligned with the 'black' oppressed. The legacy of these tendencies is that valid concerns over threats to the vibrancy of small Welsh communities in terms of protecting a minoritized culture and language have been overlaid with all the imagery, fears, threats and terminology of racism in the way that the problem is both perceived and described. In turn the idea of 'the Welsh' and 'the Welsh community' are constructed as fixed and immutable entities both culturally and linguistically and in the antipathy towards *the other* – the English are also constructed as a monolithic block. Arguably, within this bilinear construction of 'us' and 'them', there is no place to locate black and ethnic minorities. They become neither English, nor Welsh – just an inconvenient complexity to the debate. Seimon Glyn may have taken pause if his comments had been construed as keeping non-Welsh-speaking Asian families out of Welsh villages, but the white-faced Englishman is easily derogated as a 'race' apart.

The incomer debates have a number of spin-offs for any discussion of race and national identity in Wales. First, they present a homogeneous and static picture of the Welsh community. It can be argued that communities in Wales, and indeed in rural Wales, are much more internally diverse than is purported and sustained in these arguments[18] and that they are subject to wider forces of economic development, globalization and Europeanization in changing their demographic profile. They cannot and will not stand still in the ways we may wish in order to preserve linguistic enclaves – other mechanisms will be needed to counter the impacts on linguistic integrity of migrations in and out. The movement of labour, considerable youth out-migration, the dispersal of asylum seekers and other 'push and pull' factors of geographical mobility will necessarily affect Welsh communities. Secondly, this discourse has a tendency not only to present an idea of Welsh national identity in fixed and static ways but also to contribute to widely internalized ideas about 'proper' Welsh identities and cast other claims as somehow spoiled or lacking.[19] Too often the word Welsh is used synonymously to denote Welsh speaker, both in popular and political parlance, leaving the non-Welsh-speaking Welsh with 'not', 'lost' or 'apologized' identities. Ideas of 'Welsh Wales' that have been academically demarcated on the basis of empirical evidence[20] feed into everyday ideas about who belongs and who does not belong, who can settle and who cannot. The bipolar nature of the incomer debates serves to deny the complexity and variety of Welsh identities. Thirdly, it could be argued that the 'tolerance' thesis has not yet been fully tested. Most of Wales has not been characterized by the mass immigration of minorities from the Commonwealth as is the case in several English cities. A more visible and immediate touchstone of the tolerance idea is the English/Welsh divide and perhaps in the near future the settlement of asylum seekers and refugees (see Chapter 11).

This type of thinking forms a key context to debates on race. This discourse has also produced a curious territorial containment of the *types* of 'race' debate. The 'colour race problem' has a geographical locale in the south of Wales, with much of 'white' Wales distancing themselves from the issue, and similarly the 'language race problem' is seen as something to do with the north and with rural areas. These imaginings are sometimes disturbed, for example, by the activities of the BNP in rural Wales and for example by the gains made by Plaid Cymru in by-elections in the south – but they are nevertheless tenacious and provide the specific locales of race wars in Wales.

A major implication of these demarcations, both imagined and real, is that what may be in danger of being created is a bicultural, rather than a multicultural Wales, in which on one side of a simple two-sided coin there is little or no attempt to acknowledge and accommodate significant diversity. When key resources such as housing, jobs, services and even whole territorial areas are ring-fenced around language communities the problem of integration is magnified and what are produced are parallel but never overlapping communities, not a plural and multicultural society.[21] For some minority families this may mean that they continue to live in rural areas but never become part of the life of the place and never achieve any sense of belonging.

Identities and nationhood

Theorists of nationalism have hotly debated the relationship of racism to nationalism. For Nairn,[22] writing in the context of British politics, racism is a derivative of nationalism. He argues that the post-war resurgence of racism was possible because of the lack of any major mobilizing myth of nationalism in a post-imperial Britain. Thus the politics of Britain became racialized in the post-war period in tandem with economic decline and 'black' immigration. Other writers develop this thesis, arguing that racism is embedded in British nationalist ideology.[23] By contrast, Anderson frees up any axiomatic relationship between the two ideologies, suggesting both race and nation as imagined communities: 'on the whole racism and anti-Semitism manifest themselves, not across national boundaries, but within them'.[24] For Anderson, nationalism and racism are not synonymous and can be articulated as distinct discourses. Whilst there are obviously points of theoretical disagreement, writers such as Anthias and Yuval-Davis[25] have suggested more broadly that most ethnicities of hegemonic national collectivities contain *elements* of racist exclusion within their symbolic orders, and that particular boundaries become *racialized*. Since the early 1990s, writers such as Paul Gilroy, Stuart Hall and Tariq Modood have not only contributed to making public and political the relationship between Britishness and racism but have significantly challenged dominant notions of Britishness and British identity, giving evidence of new and emerging black British identities.[26] Few attempts, however, have been made to theorize these issues at the level of the Celtic nations – to ask to what extent Welsh/Scottish/Irish nationalism contains racist and exclusionary elements.[27]

Post-devolution, these issues are receiving much more urgent attention. In relation to Wales some discussion is offered by Chaney and Fevre, who have begun an analysis of the extent to which Welsh nationalism can meet the challenge of 'inclusive' politics. Focusing on Plaid Cymru – the Party of Wales, the principal nationalist political party, the authors chart a journey from 'espousing an *ex*clusive to purportedly *in*clusive nationalist ideology' – that is, from overtly ethnic nationalism to the promotion of civic nationalism. They conclude:

> Our findings revealed that those in the marginalised groups generally acknowledge the *bona fide* attempt by the principal nationalist party in Wales to achieve a constructive form of engagement. However, despite encouraging signs, our analysis shows that Plaid Cymru has a long way to go in its attempts to fully reconcile itself to the concept of inclusiveness.[28]

The study suggests that Plaid's ostensible transformation is the work of a small caucus of modernizers and that the traditional core supporters 'were dragging their heels and even engaging in a rearguard action'.[29] Shifts in party-political orientations can only, however, have limited impact in terms of changes in national identity.

In the Williams and Chaney study of ethnic participation and the National Assembly,[30] issues of national identity were raised almost incidentally and suggest an ambivalent and uneasy relationship of minority communities to the majority Welsh society. Respondents grappled with identification with an institution that apparently had little meaning or relevance for them. The demand for a NAW, associated as it was with ethno-cultural nationalism, may well have provided its *raison d'être*, but basing Welsh governance on an exclusively ethnic criteria would be bound to alienate the ethnic minority constituency. The sense of disenfranchisement conveyed by interviewees was frequently linked to their loose affiliation to definitions of Welshness and Welsh society. For both minority and majority communities the dominant conceptions of Welshness conformed to the formula 'Welsh equals white' and at times 'Welsh equals Welsh-speaking'.[31] On the other hand, this study also revealed responses containing strong expressions of attachment to things Welsh and to Welsh identity especially evoked by reference to long settlement in the Cardiff area.

Commenting on the perspectives of Scottish devolution from the minority viewpoint, Grant finds a much more unequivocally positive connotation with the word 'Scottish':

> In conversation with an Indian family recently, the older members of whom had come to Scotland thirty years ago, it was clear that their hopes for devolution were purely practical and not based on any notions of

identity. They did not need devolution to feel Scottish. Indeed, it was not helpful to them to have Scottishness which they defined as 'just being accepted here and feeling you are contributing' redefined through old domestic grievances and an outdated victim status.[32]

Some anecdotal evidence from the strategy Operation Black Vote in Wales indicates people not turning out to the polls because they do not consider themselves to have the right to do so in Welsh society. The overall picture is clearly one of ambivalence. It could be argued, however, that one of the key differences between Wales and Scotland is the relatively weak affiliation to 'Welshness' articulated in the population as a whole by contrast with stronger national identification in Scotland.[33]

The imposition of objective, institutionally contrived identities is all too frequently out of step with subjectively experienced localized identity formation.[34] Less attention has been paid in political theory to the realm of what can be called 'banal' interactions – borrowing from Billig's term 'banal nationalism'.[35] Billig's analysis is significant because he shifts attention from the traditional focus of political theory to a consideration of how ideas of nation and the language of nationhood are reproduced at the level of routine social practices – how we in our everyday lives construct inclusions and exclusions, how we speak about and experience belonging and how we communicate our perceptions of who belongs and who does not. Billig's banal nationalism provides an interesting theoretical framework from which to pursue the interface of race and nationalism at the level of specific localities and communities. To what extent does, for example, Wales and Welshness remain an abstraction to those who identify as Butetown black? To what extent are specific territorial areas of Wales seen as multicultural such that ethnic minorities in 'white' Wales remain and are contained as 'outsiders' to be tolerated? What types of identifications with Welshness and Wales do minorities seek and/or attain?

A glimpse of the complexities of these issues comes from a small handful of studies. Scourfield et al.'s (2001) study of children in the Valleys found a variety of responses to questions of Welsh identity. Although most of the children in their study saw themselves as different from other Valleys children, they offered a variety of identity affiliations, some based on religion (Muslim), some based on other nationalities (Pakistani) and amongst their dual heritage respondents' identifications with Welsh Valleys culture were at times strongly expressed, at other times not. The study concludes that: 'Identity is not especially problematic for any one type of family. What is potentially problematic for any of these children is growing up in such an overwhelmingly white environment, with substantially limited access to alternative sources of cultural affirmation.'[36] At the other end of the age spectrum, in the BBC publication *Voices of Wales* (1999), a Rhondda man expresses strong Welsh identifications and a sense of belonging:

> I'm a boy from Maerdy in the Rhondda, that's who I am. The fact is my father was a West Indian and my mother came from Cardiff. That doesn't matter at all here in the Rhondda because I'm Alfie Lawes of Maerdy, that's how they know me. My colour doesn't matter one iota . . . I was brought up in the mountains and when I die I'll be buried beneath the mountains and that's it.[37]

It seems that ethnic minority affiliation to Welsh nationhood is mediated by a number of factors. Migrant communities are neither homogeneous nor static; indeed, the demographic profile of Wales's black and ethnic minority population reveals considerable diversity not only in terms of ethnicity but also length of settlement, migration pattern, age, socio-economic status and so on. In addition, minority communities mobilize their ethnic identification in complex patterns, referencing country of origin, country of settlement, country of onward settlement as well as cultural distinctiveness.[38] It is conceivable that the identifications of second- and third-generation black Welsh will be quite different from those who have more recently migrated for work from English cities. It is also apparent that gender and age mediate identity quite significantly. It is also the case that new points of identification are emerging. Writing about the Scottish situation, Grant has argued:

> The truth is that in terms of a redefining of Scottish identity, devolution has missed the boat. Already young Scots, glued to the Internet and digital television, think in global rather than national terms. They identify not by haggis but by haircut . . . Few of them read the *Scots* magazine, idolise Sean Connery or listen to Holyrood debates . . . young Scots are happier defining themselves individually through contemporary consumer fads than through anything traditionally defined as Scottish.[39]

These influences are no less felt on second- and third-generation minority ethnic youth in Wales, by now experienced cross-cultural navigators. The expansion and strength of black British identity is also a key contextualizing influence despite negative connotation with the idea of Britishness.[40]

These studies indicate that it is not useful to speak about simple identification but of multiple identifications across a number of axes. Neither is it reasonable to talk of *the* Welsh identity in either aspirational or empirical terms. More useful is the concept of Welsh identities. As Day and Suggett have suggested:

> the question we ought to address is not that of the real 'nation' or national identity which lies behind concepts employed in political life, but that of the formation, articulation and propagation of the concepts themselves. Nationalist ideas, myths and definitions have to be deconstructed. This means that we need to treat 'Wales' as it has figured in successive, rival discourses, and consider the question 'How many Wales?' or 'How many ways of being Welsh?'[41]

Such pluralistic conceptions of nation are yet to appear.

Wales and multiculturalism

Nations and nationalisms necessarily seek homogenizing norms, symbols and identifications. They also vary considerably in the ways in which they seek to engage with diversity and the facts of multiculturalism and in terms of their operational principles of inclusion and exclusion. Aspects of multiculturalism and nation-building have been extensively theorized.[42] The Parekh Report reviews the key models and opts for the notion of 'a community of communities' which it claims combines liberal and pluralistic approaches.[43] This notion, now adopted by CRE Cymru, offers a thin rhetorical mask that glosses over both the difficulties of the notion of *community*, both normatively and experientially, and the fact that different groups have very unequal resources – economically, socially, politically and demographically. It must be possible within such a 'community of communities' to remain tame and marginal exotica rather than equal citizens. In terms of the public sphere there is still a considerable way to go ensuring rights and representation for minorities. On the positive side, in the post-devolution Wales there is evidence of attempts to build the infrastructure for promoting inclusiveness and some of the immediate impacts of constitutional change are the galvanizing effect it has had on mobilization of the minority voice and the proximity it has brought to those in power through the new structures of governance. However, trends suggest these new structures of governance may be contributing to the maintenance of a safe and acquiescent minority population, carefully contained within rigidly defined and essentialist categories and tokenistically co-opted at the margins of the true centres of power. The Welsh political class now numbers 109 counting MPs, AMs and MEPs, and over 600 if you include public appointments to the 143 public bodies. In 1999 just 1 per cent were from the minority ethnic population.[44]

At the level of civil society it is still the case in Wales that significant challenges to the myth of integration and social cohesion are yet to be seen. Whilst Welsh black sporting achievement is widely celebrated and the spectre of Shirley Bassey draped in the Welsh flag at the Millennium celebrations may provide comfort for some, all too few symbols, images and rituals of nation reflect cultural diversity. What images there are tend to be stereotypical or sensationalist. Studies of associational life in Wales are as yet thin on the ground, but comment and speculation suggest that in many respects Wales is still a very closed society comprising a small number of elite networks with overlapping membership. There is also some suggestion that minority networks stretch way beyond the Welsh borders in ways that confound any notion of Welsh civil society. Despite long settlement and a high degree of intermarriage as compared with other areas of Britain, there is no commensurate degree of economic integration for ethnic minorities in Wales, nor sound evidence of the claimed high degree of social integration, particularly at the levels where it counts. Cardiff may boast its multicultural community as an example of harmonious relations, but public politeness is no substitute for racial equality; tolerance no substitute for true multiculturalism.

The opportunities provided by devolution are, nevertheless, immense. There are opportunities to transform the debate on race beyond the colour divide, to change 'race thinking' and engage in the sophisticated debates around the emergence of new ethnicities both within the context of Wales and across Europe. There are opportunities to challenge the myths of Welshness and to identify and disengage those symbols and meanings of national pride from narrow ethnic absolutism to points of relevance for a wider and engaged civil society. And there are opportunities to bolster an infrastructure that gives people from black and ethnic minority communities a visible, legitimate and influential public presence.

Notes

[1] M. Parker, 'Loaded dice: incomers and racial attitudes', *Planet*, 148 (2001), 11.

[2] R. Davies, 'Shaping the vision', *Red Kite* (June 1995), 17.

[3] Speech by Rt. Hon. Paul Murphy MP, Secretary of State for Wales, Bournemouth, 29 September 1999.

[4] C. Williams and P. Chaney, 'Inclusive government for excluded groups: ethnic minorities', in P. Chaney, T. Hall and A. Pithouse (eds), *New Governance, New Democracy?* (Cardiff, 2001).

[5] 1991 census.

[6] B. Powys, 'Y Cymru Hiliol', *Barn*, 459 (2001), 20.

[7] S. Brookes, 'Colofn fisol y golygydd', *Barn*, 457 (2001), 9.

[8] Tom Bodden, 'Your plan for Welsh language will split our nation in two', *Daily Post* (8 November 2001).

[9] B. Brown, 'Dwi ddim isho dod o Birmingham', *Barn*, 459 (2001), 25.

[10] Seimon Glyn, 'Our way of life is dying . . . that's why I had to speak out', *Daily Post* (19 January 2001).

[11] S. G. Jobbins, 'Drefus Cymru a'r Wlad Newydd', *Barn*, 467 (2001), 36–9.

[12] D. Iwan, 'Tai, iaith a saeson', *Barn*, 459, (2001), 28.

[13] C. Williams, ' "Race" and racism: some reflections on the Welsh context', *Contemporary Wales*, 8 (1995), 113–31.

[14] See amongst others Richard Townsend-Smith for a discussion of case law in *Wales Law Journal*.

[15] C. Williams, ' "Race" and racism'.

[16] M. Hechter, *Internal Colonialism: The Celtic Fringe in British National Development 1536–1966* (London, 1975).

[17] *Western Mail* (2 January 1998).

[18] G. Day, 'A community of communities? Similarity and difference in Welsh rural community studies', *Economic and Social Review,* 3 (July 1998), 233–57.

[19] R. Fevre and A. Thompson (eds), *Nation, Identity and Social Theory: Perspectives from Wales* (Cardiff, 1999).

[20] D. Balsom, 'The three Wales model', in J. Osmond (ed.), *The National Question Again* (Llandysul, 1985).

[21] D. Denny, J. Borland and R. Fevre, 'Racism, nationalism and conflict in Wales', *Contemporary Wales*, 4 (1991), 150–65.

[22] T. Nairn, *The Break Up of Britain: Crisis and Neo-Colonialism* (London, 1977).

[23] Cf. P. Gilroy, *There ain't No Black in the Union Jack* (London, 1987).

[24] B. Anderson, *Imagined Communities: Reflections on the Origins and Spread of Nationalism* (London, 1983), 136.

[25] F. Anthias and N. Yuval-Davis, *Racialised Boundaries* (London, 1993).

[26] T. Modood and P. Werbrier (eds), *Debating Cultural Hybridity: Multicultural Identities and the Politics of Anti-racism* (London, 1997); S. Hall, 'Attitude and aspiration: reflections on Black Britain in the nineties', *New Formations*, 33 (Spring 1998); P. Gilroy, *There ain't No Black*.

[27] See D. Denny, J. Borland and R. Fevre, 'Racism, nationalism and conflict in Wales', C. Williams, 'Passports to Wales? Race, nation and identity', in R. Fevre and A. Thompson (eds), *Nation, Identity and Social Theory*; R. Miles and A. Dunlop, 'The racialisation of politics in Britain: why Scotland is different', *Patterns of Prejudice*, 20/1 (1986), 22–3; P. Hainsworth, 'Politics, racism and ethnicity in Northern Ireland', in P. Hainsworth (ed.), *Divided Society: Ethnic Minorities and Racism in Northern Ireland* (London, 1998).

[28] P. Chaney and R. Fevre, 'Welsh nationalism and the challenge of "inclusive" politics', *Research in Social Movements, Conflict and Change*, 23 (2001), 227–54, 247.

[29] Ibid., 248.

[30] C. Williams and P. Chaney, 'Inclusive government for excluded groups'.

[31] Ibid., 89.

[32] K. Grant, 'The dull consensus of Scottish identity', *Soundings*, 18 (2001), 146–53, 150.

[33] C. Williams and P. Chaney, 'Devolution and identities: the experience of ethnic minorities in Wales', *Soundings*, 18 (2001), 169–83.

[34] See, for example, G. Day and A. Thompson, 'Situating Welshness: "local" experience and national identity', in R. Fevre and A. Thompson, *Nation, Identity and Social Theory*, on how local experience of national identities diverge from public and political identifications.

[35] M. Billig, *Banal Nationalism* (London, 1995).

[36] J. Scourfield, H. Beynon, J. Evans and W. Shah, 'The experience of black and minority ethnic children living in the south Wales valleys', unpublished report, Cardiff School of Social Sciences, 2001, 31.

[37] *Voices of Wales* (BBC Publications, 1999), 65.

[38] T. Modood, 'Ethnicity and political mobilisation in Britain', paper presented to the ethnicity and social mobility in the US and UK conference, 30 March–1 April 2000.

[39] K. Grant, 'Dull consensus', 149.

[40] B. Parekh, *The Parekh Report: The Future of Multi-Ethnic Britain* (London, 2000).

[41] G. Day and R. Suggett, 'Conceptions of Wales and Welshness: aspects of nationalism in nineteenth century Wales', in G. Rees, J. Bujra, P. Littlewood, H. Newby and T. L. Rees (eds), *Political Action and Social Identity* (London, 1985), 96.

[42] W. Kymlicka, *Multi-Cultural Citizenship: A Liberal Theory of Minority Rights* (London, 1995).

[43] B. Parekh, *Future of Multi-Ethnic Britain*.

[44] National Assembly for Wales, Report on Public Appointments submitted to the National Assembly Equality Committee, 25 October 2000.

Index